PENGUIN BOOKS

Andrew Marr was born in Glasgow in 1959. He studied English at the University of Cambridge and has since enjoyed a long career in political journalism, working for the *Scotsman*, the *Independent*, the *Daily Express* and the *Observer*. From 2000 to 2005 he was the BBC's Political Editor. He has written and presented TV documentaries on history, science and politics, and presents the weekly *Andrew Marr Show* on Sunday mornings on BBC1 and *Start the Week* on Radio 4. He lives in London with his family.

ANDREW MARR

THE BATTLE FOR SCOTLAND

PENGUIN BOOKS

PENGUIN BOOKS

Published by the Penguin Group
Penguin Books Ltd, 80 Strand, London wc2r orl, England
Penguin Group (USA) Inc., 375 Hudson Street, New York, New York 10014, USA
Penguin Group (Canada), 90 Eglinton Avenue East, Suite 700, Toronto, Ontario, Canada m4p 2y3
(a division of Pearson Penguin Canada Inc.)
Penguin Ireland, 25 St Stephen's Green, Dublin 2, Ireland (a division of Penguin Books Ltd)
Penguin Group (Australia), 707 Collins Street, Melbourne, Victoria 3008, Australia
(a division of Pearson Australia Group Pty Ltd)
Penguin Books India Pvt Ltd, 11 Community Centre, Panchsheel Park, New Delhi – 110 017, India
Penguin Group (NZ), 67 Apollo Drive, Rosedale, Auckland 0632, New Zealand
(a division of Pearson New Zealand Ltd)
Penguin Books (South Africa) (Pty) Ltd, Block D, Rosebank Office Park,
181 Jan Smuts Avenue, Parktown North, Gauteng 2193, South Africa

Penguin Books Ltd, Registered Offices: 80 Strand, London wc2r orl, England

www.penguin.com

First published in Penguin Books 1992
Reprinted with a new Afterword 1995
Reissued with a new Introduction in Penguin Books 2013
001

For their kind permission to reproduce copyright material the author and publishers
acknowledge the following with gratitude:

isbn: 978-0-241-96793-5

www.greenpenguin.co.uk

MIX
Paper from
responsible sources
FSC™ C018179

Penguin Books is committed to a sustainable
future for our business, our readers and our planet.
This book is made from Forest Stewardship
Council™ certified paper.

To Jackie

We brushed the dirt off, held it to the light.
The obverse showed us Scotland, and the head
of a red deer; the antler-glint had fled
but the fine cut could still be felt. All right:
we turned it over, read easily *One Pound*,
but then the shock of Latin, like a gloss,
Respublica Scotorum, sent across
such ages as we guessed but never found . . .

Edwin Morgan, *Sonnets from Scotland*, 1984

Contents

Introduction to the 2013 Edition

I am a Scot by upbringing, education and sentiment, who lives in England, or rather in London, which is not quite the same thing. Whenever London Scots get together and talk about independence, there is a general assumption that the people back home will never actually vote for it; the opinion polls have been quite strongly in favour of the Union, and the general assumption that a vote for the SNP in Holyrood is simply the latest wheeze to put pressure on London for financial favours is blandly repeated in bars and television studios. 'They willnae.' During the very late spring of 2013, as I have started to pay more attention, I have become less certain: next September, they micht. If Scotland votes to leave the UK, it would certainly be an enormous shock. It would go against the opinion polling predictions, the settled predictions of the London party leaders and the betting companies.

But whether it happens or not, I have become increasingly frustrated by the lack of understanding of the Scottish impulse to self-government and some kind of independence. People talk as if it is a new thing, conjured out of nowhere, by a political magician called Alex Salmond – more *Game of Thrones* than ordinary modern politics. This shows profound ignorance; a blind spot to an aspect of the British story that has been with us since Edwardian times, at the very least. When I first wrote this book, I was a much younger man and very ardent for a Scottish parliament. Not every judgement in it stands up well in retrospect – though I think most do. But above all, it tells a story that, ahead of 18 September 2014, deserves to be better known, now more than ever.

Does Scottish Independence Really Matter?

Life would go on, wouldn't it? There would be no riots, no violence. Ordinary families would carry on, shopping, squabbling, worshipping, and collecting pensions and benefits. For Scots, who would remain inside the sterling zone, using notes produced by the Bank of Scotland and RBS, and who already watch devolved news programmes and read home-produced newspapers about their own political scandals, life might carry on feeling surprisingly the same.

And yet, should the Scots vote for independence happen, they will shake the rest of Britain rather more than we are generally told. The remaining UK (RUK?) would have less punch inside Europe and in international terms, quite possibly losing her seat on the UN Security Council. The fleet of nuclear submarines on which Britain's claim to world-power status rests would be decommissioned and dismantled: the SNP has made it crystal clear that they want closure of the Faslane nuclear base, and the Ministry of Defence is equally clear that building a new nuclear facility in the south of England would be prohibitively expensive.

The disappearance of more than fifty Scottish MPs would have a dramatic effect on the balance of power between Tories and the left-leaning parties of England; a Scotland-less UK election in 2010 would have given David Cameron a clear majority. This, of course, might rebalance itself over time. The change to the status of national politicians in Westminster may not seem to matter very much to daily life. Yet, from the evening weather map to arrangements for post, taxes, the armed forces, and the prevalent politics of England, the whole of post-independence Britain would feel different. An international border 400 miles north of London and about eighty miles south of Edinburgh would sunder businesses. Individuals, including me, would have to choose which passport to carry. Scottish negotiations with Brussels over issues such as fishing rights, open borders and petroleum rights would have to be watched with some anxiety from London. This would be quite a big deal.

No one can be sure, of course, about which way Scotland will vote: there has never been a referendum like this – the two on devolution were smaller beer, and with less at stake. But this will be the closest

Scotland has come since the Act of Union in 1707 and the disappearance of the original parliament then to reclaiming her independence. Even the Jacobite rebellion of 1745, while it originated in Scotland, was a religious and dynastic crusade, not a nationalist one. What follows is my attempt to investigate why this vote could be closer than most people have so far assumed. I am not taking either a Unionist or a nationalist position, but simply trying to explain the history of 'the Scottish case' and where we are now.

By and large politics works best when people feel a sense of ownership over their democracy, and have to take responsibility for the money their government spends. In 1992, when this book was first published, I was writing after the long dominance of Margaret Thatcher, with little idea of how Tony Blair would change the British political landscape, for good or ill. New Labour, pursuing some policies which followed on from Thatcherism (crucially, City deregulation, the withdrawal of the state from industrial strategy, and staunch support for the United States in the Middle East), was still young and untested.

In Scotland a genteel, moderate form of old Labour was majestically and somewhat complacently enthroned. It seemed like a craggy sandstone fortress against which the SNP broke in foamy waves, falling back time and time again. That is, until the tower suddenly, dramatically, collapsed in 2011. Long-time critics of devolution such as the former MP Tam Dalyell, who warned about the 'break-up of Britain' during the 1970s, have the right to say: 'I told you so.'

Are Scots Different?

At the heart of the story, there is a paradox which has not gone away. The more distinctive and nationalist Scottish public opinion seems to be, the more it turns out to be affected by what happens in London, rather than anywhere in Scotland. The narrative of the rise of Scottish nationalist agitation and sentiment is a home-made tale – of poets, mass movements and unusual individuals, including borderline terrorists, challenging the preconceptions of the British state at Westminster. Yet the way Scotland actually votes seems to depend, rather embarrassingly, on exactly what is going on down in the House of Commons.

Why did Scotland get her parliament eventually? Yes, because so many Scots voted for it; between 1979, when around 2.3 million Scots (51 per cent of the total voting) said yes to a Scottish parliament, and 1997, in the wake of the new Labour victory, when around 2.77 million Scots (around 73 per cent) voted for a new parliament, there had clearly been a substantial shift in allegiance. But again, why? Very roughly, half a million people seemed to have changed their minds. They had done so because of what had been going on at Westminster. A long-standing distaste for Thatcherite politics, more pronounced in Scotland than in England, was, quite clearly, the dominant political happening of the intervening years. This was a shift not based on emotional nationalism, waving the sole tyre, but on a preference for mildly left-wing and pro-welfare social-democratic politics. The SNP may not be the Socialist republican party it once seemed to be, but its programme is still well to the left of any other major parliamentary party in the UK.

Too Many Deaths?

It was possible to exploit this hostility to a British prime minister in a new way because Labour had won its historic 1997 general election promising to legislate for a second Home Rule referendum. Why did that happen? Because of the actions of another British prime minister, not enormously popular in Scotland. Many Scots may disdain Tony Blair for all sorts of reasons, but they have to accept that it was his decision to honour a promise made by his deceased Scottish predecessor John Smith that led directly to the new parliament at Holyrood. To call Tony Blair the prime mover behind the rise of Alex Salmond's SNP is to be equally offensive to both sides; and yet there is truth in it, too.

But this is also a story of the unexpected, in which chance plays an important part. We don't often think of death as a factor in the course of democratic politics, but this story was dominated by a series of early, sudden deaths, removing three of the dominant figures of the Scottish Labour establishment. (This is not *entirely* coincidental: Scotland has had the worst adult mortality rates in Western Europe since the 1970s.) First, on the morning of 12 May 1994, Smith, the then party leader, had a massive heart attack in his London flat, and died. There was widespread shock and public mourning, but not everybody thought Smith a political genius.

Very shortly before his death, I happened to have been in company in a Scottish pub with Tony Blair. He believed that John Smith, for all his moral integrity and popularity, never understood the English south and was therefore likely to be a failure in the forthcoming general election. I recall him bitterly bemoaning Labour's condition, and wondering about whether he, Tony Blair, had made the right decision to enter politics at all and perhaps should have stayed as a lawyer. Yet, remarkably soon after that conversation, the young Blair was the party leader and Prime Minister in waiting, after another Scot who felt he was entitled to the job, Gordon Brown, had reluctantly stood aside. So perhaps, when it came to devolution, Tony Blair felt that he owed Smith a debt of honour; certainly, Scottish Home Rule was never something he cared about much himself or, it might be said, really understood in an emotional way.

Six years later, Scotland lost the man credited as the father of her new parliament. Smith's best friend in politics, Donald Dewar, slipped in the streets of Edinburgh and suffered a brain haemorrhage which killed him. By then, he had led the Labour campaign for a yes vote, had overseen the opening ceremony – the legislation began resonantly, 'There shall be a Scottish parliament . . .' – and had become Scotland's first First Minister. A dry, dyspeptic and aggressively anti-nationalist intellectual from Glasgow, Dewar seemed the ultimate safe pair of hands and had been all but canonized in the media, a fate which made him squirm. His death left a huge gap.

Next, in August 2005, the most radical and peppery of leading Scottish Labour politicians, Robin Cook, who had led Labour opposition to the Iraq war, and could well have emerged in Edinburgh as the SNP's most formidable opponent, collapsed while walking down a mountain. He fell eight feet on a remote hillside and died of heart disease, despite the arrival of a helicopter ambulance.

Labour, of course, had other talented figures. But there was nobody at that time of really high stature and esteem who would choose to vacate Westminster to pursue a political career in Edinburgh. Later, when pro-Unionist parties complained that the exuberant personality of Alex Salmond too much dominated the Scottish battlefield, they should have blamed fate and their own lack of ambition. Too many of the leading Unionists in cocked hats on horses had been picked off before the fight really started, and too few others volunteered to take their place.

Caledonia Today

So what kind of country was this Scotland that was to be fought over now? Proud, certainly, and quick to take offence, even today. If you listen to Alex Salmond's speeches and interviews, in which he rarely lets an opportunity slip to praise the English people and promise good neighbourly relations, you would assume that the ancient and almost racist Anglophobia of earlier periods in nationalist politics had mercifully declined in modern Scotland. If you watched some of the pro- independence videos available on the Internet, which tend to feature blood-spattered medieval helmets and, in the middle distance, crowds of kilted men running with broadswords and screaming, you might be less sure.

Like so much of England, Scotland has a large number of immigrant communities and prides herself on being tolerant and open. (There is even a Sikh tartan, though there have been deeply unpleasant racist attacks in Glasgow.) The dominant modern political mood in Scotland could be described as northern-European welfarist and in favour of a strong state – Scotland has a larger proportion of her economy and housing stock in the public sector. This puts her more in line with Scandinavian countries, Iceland and Canada (latitude is an underestimated political influence).

Inside this political culture, the biggest recent event has been the collapse of Labour as the dominant Scottish party, and the parallel growth of the SNP. Labour only really rose to dominance in the 1960s, when the Conservative Unionists took the brunt of Scottish hostility to Margaret Thatcher. Then, in a parallel movement, like a foursome reel, it was Labour's turn. Political positions taken in Islington and Millbank by the Thames had a huge pact on how people voted in Dumbarton and on the banks of the Forth. Tony Blair, despite his Scottish name, was never much appreciated, or perhaps understood by, what he described as 'Middle Scotland'. There, opposition to new

Labour reforms, a greater social conservatism and, in particular, hostility to the Iraq war made his government steadily less popular. To put it brutally, radical Blairism trashed the Scottish Labour brand almost as effectively as Margaret Thatcher had trashed the Scottish Tory one.

There were plenty of warning signs that New Labour would not work north of the Border in the same way as it did to the south. Different people, different customs. As early as 1998, the SNP had a three-point lead over New Labour, then at the height of its power in England. Later, according to polls by Mori, as the Iraq war began some 38 per cent of British voters were against it; in Scotland the figure was nearer 65 per cent. Labour in Scotland then suffered because of its new-found discipline: Scottish Labour leaders and the party in general were generally loyal to their leader. This left an opening for the SNP to present itself as the mainstream party of opposition to 'illegal wars' and in favour of traditional Scottish social-democratic values. Alex Salmond's political rhetoric in 2013 still harks back to the Iraq war with telling regularity.

A New Parliament

The official opening of the first Scottish parliament for 300 years, on 31 July 2009, was emphatically a British state location. With the Queen, arriving by carriage and surrounded by clattering, scarlet-tunicked Life Guards from London, at the centre of proceedings, along with Westminster-style heralds, and the presentation of a new mace, it seemed clear that this was another example of the British constitution evolving through continuity. Despite the huge crowds, bagpipers and a solemn procession of sober-suited Scottish politicians, the message was that ultimately power remained where it always had been. There were dissonant voices: a major march against the tuition fees policy which had made Labour particularly unpopular was led by the Scottish Socialist Party, while Alex Salmond warned that this was not the end of the journey. But it seemed, overall, a reassuringly traditional rather than a challenging event – pageant-swaddled patriotic evolution, not raw, separatist revolution. The loudest cheers were still reserved for the angular, reassuring, figure of Donald Dewar.

Yet the new parliament being celebrated was very different from any institution seen in the UK before. It had almost been designed as a criticism of the ancient Imperial Parliament. Westminster runs on two houses, and a strong system of party whips who can see everyone voting in person. Its representation is based upon a single, first-past-the-post voting system. The British Parliament has no right to appoint a prime minister or government – that is reserved for the monarch. It is, in short, a complex series of compromises made over hundreds of years.

The Edinburgh parliament, designed from scratch, is elected on a proportional voting system, divided between first-past-the-post constituency members and others based on a regional party list, to smooth out disparities in support. This has led to Green, Scottish Socialist and independent MSPs gaining seats alongside the bigger parties. Second, without any revising or upper chamber, it allows much more power to parliamentary committees. Third, it consciously distances itself from Westminster rituals: voting on key measures takes place each day at the same time and is mostly done electronically, with the members of the Scottish parliament sitting in their seats. Unlike the House of Commons, the Scottish parliament directly votes for the First Minister.

Anyone accustomed to Westminster who then goes to visit a session of the Scottish parliament will above all be struck by the difference in atmosphere. The Scottish parliamentarians sit in a pizza-like wedge, allegedly to promote consensus, and in an airy, light room. MSPs tend to clap rather than shout, though they are capable of just as much and a defying abuse when the mood takes them. In policy terms, the most controversial measures the new parliament legislated for have been free tuition for Scottish students, plus a much more generous health and care system for pensioners, including free prescriptions.

To English politicians, this seemed a classic case of Scotland irresponsibly spending without making the tough choices to raise money: the Scottish parliament had been given powers to vary the rate of income tax by up to three pence in the pound, but declined to use them. In 2009 the Calman Commission, set up in Scotland to investigate the financial and organizational implications of Home Rule, pointed out the absurdity of parliament being unable to raise its own taxes in a serious way. (Today, many pro-devolution opponents of national separation favour 'Devo Max' or a continuation of the current arrangements but with parliament able to raise most of its own revenue.)

Wee Stushies in Paradise

Constitutionally, however, what followed for the first few years was undramatic. The new parliament met in the old Assembly Rooms of the Church of Scotland, overlooked not by some socialist or nationalist hero but by the grim figure of John Knox. Indeed, this was entirely appropriate as temporary accommodation, while the new building was being argued about and erected; the Kirk had been the nearest thing Scotland had to a national voice during the centuries without parliament. After Donald Dewar's death, his right-hand man in Scotland, Henry McLeish, succeeded as First Minister. After embarrassing details of attacks on colleagues emerged, followed by a minor scandal over the rental of his constituency offices, he resigned quite quickly, to be followed by Jack McConnell, a man he had just defeated for the top job. Later, McConnell's successor, Wendy Alexander, was forced out as Labour leader after a small row over expenses, surviving for just a few months in the job. Small ripples in a small pond, this demonstrated that Scottish politicians were no more angelic than the Westminster variety.

The saga of the new Scottish parliamentary building was rather more serious. Like most people, I had assumed that any new Scottish parliament would be based in the rather traditional and unpretentious Greek-style Old Royal High School building sitting at the foot of Edinburgh's Calton Hill. This was where pro-devolution protesters had traditionally gathered. Instead, members of the Scottish parliament voted for a much more radical structure, designed by Enric Miralles, a Catalan architect who died while it was being built. Rising from the site of an old brewery opposite the Palace of Holyroodhouse, and surrounded by the dramatic hillscape of Arthur's Seat, an extinct volcano, the new building was consciously intended to be a radical break from other parliaments – open, modernistic and shaped to mimic upturned fishing boats. It is genuinely inspiring to some; others find it makes them squirm with anger and embarrassment.

What is not inspiring is the fact that it took more than ten times as much money to build as was budgeted for, and arrived two years late, not opening for business until the autumn of 2004. A long enquiry into what went wrong and who was to blame followed, but the biggest casualty was the blithe assumption that Scottish politics would be automatically more efficient – a Brave New World compared to the much mocked failures, petty and otherwise, of Westminster.

After the departure of Henry McLeish, Jack McConnell, a more robust figure, continued the early Labour hegemony. His most notable achievements as First Minister included Scotland's smoking ban – controversial at the time, but which has saved many lives – and an energetic attempt to lure more people to come and live in the country. Again, there was no sense of a political earthquake having taken place. McConnell at any rate failed to capture the national imagination and, despite implementing modest reforms, Labour narrowly lost out to the Scottish Nationalists during the 2007 election. This was quite a shock at the time, though much worse was to follow. Under Alex Salmond, the Scottish Nationalists were able to form their first minority coalition government with the Scottish Green Party.

Enter the Ringmaster

That was a political risk by the SNP leader, and at this point we must turn directly to the enigmatic, provocative and (to some) highly charismatic figure of Alex Salmond himself. Once a wiry, leftist dissident who worked as a highly effective oil economist at the Royal Bank, he always enjoyed provocation: he used to keep a bust of Lenin on the mantelpiece of his stately New Town office. The left-wing republican fire may have disappeared, but underneath his favoured dark-blue business suits and conservative ties, he remains a radical and tactically ruthless figure. He wooed the media baron Rupert Murdoch and won the support of the *Scottish Sun*. Scottish journalists found him 'good for copy' and have followed him as the best story they are likely to see in their working lives.

Like other leaders who began on the Left, Salmond's historic achievement was to move to the centre, bringing others with him, and thereby changing the dynamics of Scottish politics. He lost some friends but he managed to reconcile many formerly hard-line Nationalists who had wanted nothing to do with devolution, to a programme of what might be called Fabian nationalism, moving stealthily and in stages towards ultimate independence.

This check on his natural impulsiveness had been slowly learned. He had first emerged as leader in 1990, replacing the rather grey, gloomy figure of Gordon Wilson, and led the SNP through some bleak years when it failed to make any kind of breakthrough. This period of leadership saw a bitter falling out with his old ally, the rumbustious and outspoken Jim Sillars, as Salmond ditched some of his previous leftism and was portrayed by Sillars as a slippery turncoat, no true nationalist at all. Small parties, like small villages, tend to enjoy particularly vicious personal feuds. The Scottish Labour Party has boasted some vendettas, but the SNP has generally been able to trump them.

Salmond next pursued his career at Westminster, where he led the Scottish Nationalist MPs and made a name for himself in London as one of the most outspoken and relentless critics of Tony Blair and his foreign wars. His enemies, even then, thought him a dangerous demagogue, but he had a cheerful, rubbery self-confidence which many Scots, watching at home, adored. Dissident Labour left-wing MPs also admired him as a cocky provocateur. Self-abasement has never been his thing.

By the time he returned in 2004 to stand as SNP leader for a second time – something he had virtually ruled out before – Salmond was head and shoulders above any rival as the country's best-known nationalist. Taking office in Scotland at the head of a minority administration, which seemed to be unlikely to do much or last for long, was a characteristic gamble by the horse-racing addict. And, in truth, that first SNP-led administration was pretty dull. With hindsight, the most important thing was that Salmond was able to make himself a symbol of cheekily unrelenting opposition to the Blair–Brown government as it entered its least popular phase in power at Westminster. His reward was the election landslide of 2011, winning sixty-nine seats to Labour's forty-seven, with the Scottish Liberal Democrats crashing down to just five MSPs.

This changed everything. From now on, for the first time, the Scottish Nationalists had real power north of the Border and a mandate for their long-standing aim of independence. If Salmond is able to achieve this final step, his policy of softly-softly will be triumphantly vindicated and he will emerge as one of the most significant leaders of any small country in Europe. Before any of this, of course, there has to be another referendum. Salmond has got his way on the preferred timing of it – 2014 is an anniversary of Scotland's famous victory over the English at the Battle of Bannockburn in 1314 – and over the expansion of the electorate, extending the vote to sixteen- and seventeen-year-olds, who are (marginally) more in favour of independence than their elders.

On the question to be asked – 'Should Scotland be an independent country?' – the British Prime Minister won a small victory against a more loaded alternative, but overall there was a sense that Salmond had outmanoeuvred David Cameron over the details of the poll. Today Salmond continues to dominate Scottish politics, though Unionist campaigners believe he is seen as sufficiently untrustworthy, too 'flash', to make voters flinch at the last moment.

So What's This Really About?

If we trust the opinion polls, there is still a clear and consistent majority against independence in Scotland. Only around a third of Scottish voters seem in favour. Yet Labour was doing quite well in the polls before being smashed in that 2011 Scottish election, and nobody can be entirely sure of what will happen next. Salmond is a canny gambler, as we have seen, and is still enjoying what looks like a spectacular run of good fortune. He may, or may not, have a cunning plan: he works as much by bold opportunism as by strategy.

In choosing the former Chancellor, Alistair Darling, as a leader of the 'Better Together' pro-UK campaign, Labour has found somebody about as unlike Salmond as it is possible to be in public life: a naturally cautious, dry wit and a somewhat pessimistic figure, with a rare reputation for cool economic management, won during the banking crisis. This promises to be, among other things, a contest about which of the two is the favoured caricature of modern Scottishness: the bouncy and demagogic upstart rebel or the furrow-browed man of authority; or as Scots will understand it, Wee Eck or Pa Broon.

The biggest single question is over the condition and the future of the Scottish economy. Unionists portray it as weak, and likely to collapse after independence under the weight of much higher taxation, and a flight of capital. For nationalists, Scotland is a huge potential growth area, which has been under-invested in – a rainy Eldorado, brimming with new energy resources, forests and clean water. Both of these exaggerated prospectuses should be taken with a handful of salt. Not just in Britain, but all around the Western world, we have recently seen enough economic shocks to make us cautious about grand financial extrapolations.

But in many ways this goes to the heart of the case for independence: how independent can any country, apart from the largest, be from the huge and fast-moving global forces of twenty-first-century capitalism? If Scotland's future is to be compared to that of Greece, Cyprus, Ireland or Iceland, then the 'What's the point?' question becomes hard to evade. The SNP, rightly and naturally, cites the example of small countries such as Norway, Sweden and Denmark; though the original 'arc of prosperity' included both Ireland and Iceland, now ravaged by the banking crisis.

By most measures, Scotland remains more dependent on the public sector than the UK generally – 23 per cent of Scottish jobs are public sector jobs, for instance, as against 20 per cent in the UK generally. In hard economic times, with countries across Europe implementing public spending cuts, and without a big personal tax base, this is clearly a potential worry. Scotland's most famous and politically contentious economic resource is of course North Sea oil and gas, which as early as the late 1960s inspired the SNP's first really successful campaign, 'It's Scotland's Oil.' Today, Scotland remains Europe's largest producer of petroleum, and the SNP case for independence still leans heavily on the assumption that a decade or more of high oil revenues, based on new discoveries and new technologies, could be better used by a Scottish parliament to provide for the long-term health of the Scottish economy.

This depends on many unknowables: the ease of recovery of new reserves; world energy prices at a time when shale gas and renewables are changing the game; and the exact negotiation about the seabed boundary following the break-up of the UK. It also assumes that this bonanza would be used for significant long-term investment, not for mitigating the politically critical pain of public spending austerity. It has all become an argument hopelessly entangled in politics: nationalists tend to an ebullient optimism about oil reserves and prices, almost as a matter of faith, while Unionists are constitutionally depressive and head-shaking about them, more or less for the same reason.

The other great additional strength of the Scottish economy, whisky aside, had been the financial services industry, mostly based in Edinburgh. Scotland retains formidable investment trust and life assurance companies, but was devastated by the collapse of the Royal Bank of Scotland and almost as serious failures in HBOS – the merger between the Halifax building society and the Bank of Scotland. The sudden collapse of RBS in 2008 was a familiar example of the arrogant and over-extended world of global banking at the time: RBS had grown by leaps and bounds from a cautious local institution to become one of the world's largest financial institutions, when it took one leap too far and paid too much to take over a Dutch bank, ABN Amro. Under its autocratic and arrogant boss, Sir Fred Goodwin, RBS eventually cost the British taxpayer £45 billion, with many billions more in guarantees and loans, and was largely nationalized; in 2009, RBS made corporate history with a £24 billion loss, the biggest in Britain ever. It is now 82 per cent owned by the British taxpayer. Sir Fred became Britain's public enemy number one and was stripped of his knighthood.

Meanwhile, over at HBOS, once another highly traditional and conservative Scottish bank, which by a helter-skelter pursuit of short-term profit and commercial speculations boosted the pay of its senior managers while betraying its investors and staff, a second major collapse occurred in 2008. Its former chief executive, Sir James Crosby, later admitted to MPs that 'management incompetence' was to blame; campaigners branded the once-impeccable Bank of Scotland 'the worst bank in the world'. Similar errors of a similar magnitude had been made by banks in many other places, including the United States and across Europe; but Edinburgh had something special to lose. For a long time, it had retained the reputation of a particularly sober, hard-headed and shrewd financial culture, and indeed liked to contrast itself to the freewheeling and greedy City of London. Many in Scotland pointed out that if this was a failure of regulation, regulation was still run by Westminster, not in Scotland. Yet the damage to Scotland's prized financial reputation was terrible and spread widely; Alex Salmond himself, who had once worked for RBS, and championed Sir Fred, was obliged to apologize and admit that, with hindsight, 'I'd do things differently.' Before the credit crunch and banking collapse of 2008, one of the most potent SNP lines had been that independent

Scotland would have joined Ireland, Iceland and Scandinavia in an 'arc of prosperity'. With Ireland effectively bust, Iceland suffering its own financial crisis and in the wake of RBS, this became a sound-bite to forget.

Yet the Scottish economy, down, was not out: Scotland retains some impressive manufacturing output and the vestiges of the once-overpraised 'Silicon Glen', as well as important whisky, tourism and forestry sectors. Launching a Scottish government paper on the future of the Scottish economy in May 2013, Salmond said: 'Despite our strong economic foundations and excellent global reputation Scotland, with Westminster in control of our economy, is not reaching our potential as a nation.' His government paper said that if Scotland's geographical share of oil and gas was included, Scottish GDP per head would be 118 per cent of the UK average; outside oil, more traditional sectors such as the food and drink industry, tourism and life sciences were also big contributors to Scottish prosperity.

Indeed, despite the collapse of heavy industry, Scottish unemployment is only marginally higher than that of the UK as a whole, and Scottish wealth per head compares favourably with most parts of England, outside London and the south-east. Yet Scotland, with a relatively sparse population spread over a large area and a very poor history of health, seems fated to require larger quantities of public spending than England: with 8.4 per cent of the UK population, Scotland takes 9.3 per cent of public spending. Since Scottish pensioners and students, among others, get a more generous deal from the state, this is resented by many English politicians and voters, who would like to impose a serious financial penalty if Scotland voted for full independence.

We should not get too hung up about percentages: economic statistics are the daily media pegs on which baggier, more colourful questions of belonging, values and the nature of political power hang. Let's start with belonging. The nationalist case has, on the face of it, changed enormously: no more *Braveheart* dissing of the English, but instead an optimistic, inclusive and open vision of a fairer and more self-confident Scotland. As I argued before, you don't have to scratch very deeply to find darker, emotional resentment of the English. On the streets of Edinburgh in May 2013, there was a classic miniature confrontation which goes to the roots of one of the problems of nationalist politics.

Nigel Farage, the leader of UKIP, was barracked and abused by Scottish nationalist protesters outside a pub. Presumably referring to his hostility to mass immigration, they chanted 'Nazi, Nazi' at him. One of the banners of the Radical Independence group invited Mr Farage to stick his Union Jack up his bottom (they used another word) and return with all due speed to England. He responded by calling them 'fascist swine' who were extremely anti-English, adding that there were parts of the independence movement 'that are deeply, deeply unpleasant. Everybody knows it, but nobody dare say it.' Alex Salmond then weighed in against Mr Farage, calling his politics 'obnoxious' and, perhaps fairly enough, pointing out that there was a difference between a student protest and the Dreyfus trial.

Though one should not make too much of a single small fracas, it was hard not to notice two rival nationalisms each resorting to Second World War terminology to abuse the other. Though UKIP is not formally a nationalist party, it certainly flies the flag for England. So this was degenerating into: 'My nationalism is better [e.g. less nationalist] than your nationalism.' Or, alternatively: '*We* are Patriots, hooray! But *they* are nationalists, hiss!'

In one important area, however, the modern Scottish nationalists have taken the old argument on: 'Scottish' now simply means anyone living in Scotland, of whatever background. In terms of the right to vote in the referendum, it does not include people who are Scottish by blood but live in England or elsewhere – like me. My family had virtually no non-Scottish members going back for four or five generations, with the single exception, so far as I know, of a French academic. But I left Scotland to work in London thirty years ago, married an English-woman, and my children are more English than Scottish, if I'm honest. In gatherings of London Scots, there is much grumbling about the fact that none of us has the right to vote on the future of our country. Personally, I would find having to choose between a Scottish and a British passport agonizing – my own past and cultural baggage versus my current family. However, I infinitely prefer a notion of Scottishness which downplays heredity, with its emphasis on 'breeding' and racial purity. Much better an identity based on geography, which classes a first-generation Croatian immigrant in Perth as Scottish but does not class me or Sir Alex Ferguson as Scottish, than a 'blood and soil' belief in race and the superiority of certain strains of DNA.

Yet once you pull away at that thread, much more follows. One might suspect that refusing a vote to Scots living in England simply removes from the electoral equation an anti-nationalist segment of Scots. But once you deny Scottishness as a blood or race issue, you have to confront the question of whether the Scottish people as such are in any sense special. Do the Battle of Bannockburn, the Declaration of Arbroath or the Edinburgh Enlightenment have any significance at all in modern Scotland, or or any place in modern politics?

It's very hard to imagine the SNP without its patriotic history; but if blood doesn't matter, why should anyone living in Scotland now feel any particular pride in the behaviour of long-dead armies or philosophers? Scots have always been history-soaked, and the old stories of resistance against the larger and better-armed English have a closeness that few outside Scotland perhaps understand. The impression given by modern nationalism is that immigrant outsiders, if they have the right 'attitude', can be quickly marinated in it and therefore teach themselves to be Scottish, even down to the prickliness. The trouble is that that itself is an exclusive rather than an inclusive notion of identity: it requires much more of the incomer than, for instance, Britishness does.

What about the broader question of values? This seems likely to be the main ground on which the referendum will be contested. In essence, are the English and the Scots so politically different that they are better governing themselves separately than together? Unionist politicians, like Labour's Douglas Alexander, naturally emphasize the shared social-democratic heritage. In a speech in 2013, he spoke about his own emotional enthusiasm for the Olympics in London the previous year: 'Like many I was unsure what to expect and found myself, somewhat to my surprise, cheering along . . . the 2012 Games showcased the very best of our country and gave us the opportunity to celebrate what unites us: perhaps again to our surprise we found afresh that we in these islands are a pluralistic and outward-looking family of nations, confident and capable when working together towards a common endeavour.' He used this as a contrast to the SNP view that 'Whatever the words on the ballot paper, it will be a choice between a "social contract" Scotland or a welfare-obliterating Westminster.'

Certainly, that is going it some; but it is hard to deny that there is a large slice of the English electorate which has become profoundly hostile to the European project, and would prefer tax cuts and deep spending cuts to an extension of welfare rights; and that this is not nearly as popular a view in the more left-wing Scottish political environment. There is a serious danger of each side unfairly caricaturing the other: Scots libelling the English as selfish, short-term xenophobes, while the English smear the modern Scots as hypocritical welfare junkies, sucking on the teat of English prosperity. Are voters in Liverpool, Manchester or central London really so different from those in Glasgow and Edinburgh?

The evidence is patchy but does point to interesting differences of emphasis. A YouGov opinion poll for the *Sunday Times* carried out in November 2012 found that just 17 per cent of Scots polled favoured tax cuts for the rich and for business, against 30 per cent of Londoners and 26 per cent of people polled in the rest of the south of England. (But note that even in the richest parts of the UK, this is still a minority view.) On the question of an EU referendum, 62 per cent of southern Englanders wanted one; but then again 47 per cent of Scots did too. There are real differences and the SNP is not cooking up evidence from nothing; yet perhaps the differences are not quite as large as is generally assumed.

The problem leftish Unionists have, however, is that the country is perhaps just halfway through a long and grim period of austerity and paying off debt, which will make London seem even less sympathetic politically to Scots. Labour politicians are saying to the Scottish electorate, in effect: 'Just be patient, we'll be back before too long; and then normal social-democratic business will resume as before.' Maybe, but it really depends, doesn't it, on the surrounding political landscape.

Not just in the UK, but across the West, there have been decades of relative economic failure, which became critical at the time of the credit crunch – our decline which still hangs over governments in Europe and North America. The political consequence has been widespread cynicism about politics generally, and in particular the ability of the state to alter life for the better. Scottish public opinion seems not much different from that found anywhere else in this regard.

An Oasis – or a Blur?

The most significant political strength of Alex Salmond's SNP is its exuberant optimism about the ability of national government to change society. Here is the opening paragraph from the case for independence on the SNP's current website:

Sweden has its enhanced parental rights, including generous maternity and paternity leave; Norway its £300 billion Pension Fund from oil; and Denmark has been able to lead the world in onshore wind technology. And what do they have in common? They are all small independent states. Independence will allow us to take decisions in Scotland that will improve the lives of families, communities and individuals across our country. With independence . . . we can work together to make Scotland a more ambitious and dynamic country.

This is an exhilarating but profoundly unfashionable view of politics. By the dollar and the euro, by Amazon, Google and Microsoft, in which culture is exported globally and where the fast fortunes of the super-rich manage to float above mere national territories, how much actual, usable power does a modestly sized traditional nation have? We live in an age when politics as a potent force, as distinct from the market, has been in headlong retreat.

Isn't it interesting that a nationalist programme which assumes just the opposite, that traditional political power matters more than anything else, is getting a hearing at all? The danger from the Unionist point of view is precisely that exhilaration. Perhaps, by playing the fear card – asking whether an independent Scotland could afford to pay proper pensions, and harping on the size of its share of the UK national debt – Unionists are making a mistake.

It's not that these things don't matter. They do, very much. So do the terms of trade under which an independent Scotland would have to reapply to the current EU. Ditto, the costs and penalties of maintaining sterling, but without control of monetary policy, which would continue to be run by the Bank of England. Big risks, which are obviously worth arguing about. Yet if the SNP is playing the optimism or 'hope' card, it should not be underestimated: hope very often trumps fear. And, in the end, if politicians aren't persuading voters that they can change at least their corner of the world, why would anyone vote for them?

So the real question, given all the undoubted risks of independence – and accepting that there are risks in staying inside the Union too – is whether a separate Scottish state can make enough difference to ordinary life to justify the gamble. So far we have heard surprisingly little about exactly how an independent Scotland would differ from a Scotland inside the UK, run by a more congenial centre-left government. Where is the distinctive tax system? Scotland, which used to be known around the world for the brilliance of its education, is these days pretty average: where is the ambitious programme of school and university reform, designed to make Scotland one of the toughest, gold-standard systems in the world? Where is the industrial policy which shows how to fund a system of incentives that could lure major companies to Scotland, without bankrupting the government?

Can we envisage a society in which the values of the Church of Scotland, and the scant Scottish Catholic Church, have a stronger role, as clerics protest against the secular and liberal agenda set by metropolitan London? Would Scots-English be promoted as the national language, with Gaelic being aggressively revived, as Irish and Welsh have been? Would this be a pacifist country? In short, where is the foreground of the vision, alongside the blur of purple hills and blue seas in the distance? Meanwhile, the SNP champions the vision of a Scotland proud of its National Health Service, its welfare state and its environmental energy policy – all of which arrived thanks to the work of Labour politicians and Liberal Democrats during the twentieth century.

The people who would be most radically affected by independence are the political and media elite, which is perhaps why they are so obsessed by constitutional change. For journalists and ambitious politicians working in Edinburgh, independence would be Christmas and a lottery payout gift-wrapped together. For Westminster politicians, it would be a big bump down. This book attempts to explain the deep sources of Scottish national feeling and the political drive for Home Rule and independence which have created the current uncertainty. We may be about to see a new country – indeed, two new countries – emerging on these islands. Half a lifetime ago, I sat down to write this book as a work of history. It has become current affairs.

In the Beginning:
In the End

Let us start at the sunset of an Empire, with a long-haired Englishman, in a baggy suit, in the House of Commons, one May night in 1912.

Herbert Henry Asquith was inclined to be convivial. After dinner he would stumble and slur, to the embarrassment of his colleagues. But the Prime Minister was on song that night, swiping aside interruptions, stamping derisively on the arguments of rival statesmen and forging through the hubbub to his conclusion. He had a vision of what was wrong with Britain and he wanted to share it: 'We start . . . from a congested centre. We start from a Union . . . which has this peculiarity: that while for common purposes all its constituent members can deliberate and act together, none of them is at liberty to deal with those matters which are specially appropriate and necessary for itself without the common consent of all.' This might, indeed should, provoke a shiver of recognition in the 1990s. Asquith was explaining his notion of 'Home Rule all round' during the second reading of the Government of Ireland Bill, shortly to be followed by a Home Rule measure for Scotland.

We do not know whether Asquith would have got his federalist blueprint right. We may doubt it – he was certainly careless of Ulster. But he was at least wrestling honestly with one of the recurring dilemmas of constitutional politics: how to preserve small national identities within larger structures. This is not merely a recurring dilemma; it is an important one. People's souls are nourished by the specific, the traditional and even the quirky – 'These are my songs, this is my dialect, that is my architecture.' Across much of Europe this may often mean 'This is my small country.' But the same people gazing with wet eyes and a lump in the throat will also require the greater security and wealth that tend to come inside larger organizations, whether empires or federations or

1

the European Community. Such people are backward-looking romantics – and modern and businesslike too. Perhaps most of us are.

So although it was part of a lost world, a long-ago Edwardian Britain that was shortly to be destroyed in Flanders, the Asquithian Parliament was engaged in an argument that we could pick up and continue today, almost without taking breath. Asquith's Parliament too was greatly worried by the centralization of power and had heated arguments about federalism. The power-swollen centre in question was the British Imperial Parliament at Westminster, not the European Commission at Brussels. But the disagreement was essentially about what we, in our barbarous tongue, would call subsidiarity. Like all constitutional arguments, it was about who should do what, where. Although it had been provoked by the long and violent struggle for Ireland, it was not necessarily a nationalist argument. Asquith's great predecessor, Gladstone, said in Cardiff in 1887: 'It is the recognition of the distinctive qualities and the separate parts of great countries and empires which constitutes the true basis of union, and to attempt to centralize them by destroying those local peculiarities is the shallowest philosophy and the worst of all political blunders.' By the time Asquith had taken the torch from Gladstone the British Empire was already in decline. And Westminster's long failure to concede Irish home rule ended in rebellion, war and independence.

Scotland's Home Rule Bill agitation of the same period also failed – the relevant Bill disappeared as the Imperial Parliament turned itself to war measures in 1914. Between Asquith's day and our own there has been a persistent and widespread demand in Scotland for home rule and a smaller but louder agitation for full independence. Only from the mid-1950s to the mid-1960s was it really quiescent. But Scotland never rebelled. There has been virtually no violence and relatively few outbreaks of mass protest – merely a sullenness, an emptiness, at the centre of Scottish public life. And this is natural. In modern times Scotland has never been an oppressed nation as Ireland was. The constitutional strains caused by its incorporation into the British Parliament were therefore less painful in the last and current century. But the lack of a separate Scottish democracy was felt in Asquith's day, and had the First World War not intervened, it would probably have been answered inside a remodelled, federal Britain, including a parliament sitting in Edinburgh. Since then eighty years have passed. And in Scotland, though rarely in England, the argument has gone on.

This book is about the argument – about one northern European nation battling to create a political and constitutional settlement that would make it feel secure and content with its place in the world. That battle, which has been one of words and votes, continues but will not necessarily conclude with the achievement of self-government. Scotland may become reintegrated into the British Union. It may be that Scots eventually decide to articulate their nationhood on a purely cultural and sporting level and turn from the search for political solutions. They have not turned away yet, but politics has not served Scotland particularly well, and this book records more frustrations than solutions. Whisky and pocket volumes of Burns and Wembley tickets are portable and convenient commodities and may seem respectable substitutes. Nor is it any part of my intention to suggest that politics is all-important: in a democracy it is rightly considered more boring and trivial than families, friendships, good books, high mountains and sniffing the first crisp morning air of autumn. But abdicating from the political would not, for Scotland or anywhere else, be a simple or cost-free decision. It would be the rejection of a whole world of social and intellectual choice that most societies find they need. It was well said of old Eastern Europe that 'Under Communism, the minorities dance.' An absence of self-government can imply a retreat into folksiness, provincialism and immaturity. This is a danger Scotland always faces; and some of the extremism and silliness recorded later in this book derives, I believe, from the lack of a complete and rounded political culture.

Scotland's political history is a specific story, which inevitably draws out and insists on one small country's different way of doing this or its different tradition in that. But the dilemmas Scottish politicans have faced – what priority to give the national versus the ideological, when to embrace one's rival and when to kick him in the face, how to protest and negotiate from a position of extreme weakness – are ones that have been experienced far further afield and will be again. The Scots are a thoughtful, option-weighing people, and their continuous assessment of the risks and opportunities of nationalism ought to have a resonance for others – above all for

3

the inhabitants of a continent that includes Croats as well as Germans, Catalonians as well as Spaniards, Walloons as well as Frenchmen. Readers following the growth of Scottish Nationalism, or the story of the Constitutional Convention, might like occasionally to squint and imagine that this is the story of Anywhereland, a small country struggling inside the European Federation fifty years hence. Certainly, nationalism of various malign and benign varieties is re-emerging in Europe; one of the big questions of the next generation may be whether English nationalism, for instance, reawakens in a bad temper or a good one.

So the specific story will have some general lessons. But the more obvious and immediate purpose of this book is to record the specific, an important, colourful story that is too little known or understood even among modern politicians. In historical political writing Scotland tends to fall between Westminster-hypnotized biographers, who record Scottish affairs in the odd footnote or (if the nation is particularly blessed that month) a subsidiary clause, and the Scottish academic historians who pursue particular themes for the enlightenment of small audiences. There have been some good, though now rather old, accounts of Scottish nationalism and some serious research on the Labour Party too. But only 'Patronage and Principle', the 'essay, with some judgements speculative' by the Tory historian Michael Fry, has attempted to cover the whole field. It is an erudite and academic work, particularly good on Victorian Scotland, which I have mostly ignored, but it is inevitably now a few years out of date.

This present book, I should stress, is a reporter's notebook, not an historian's grand narrative. Having worked for years as a Westminster reporter, I have tried to stick the London-parliamentary and the Scottish-political halves of the story back together again.

It is also a Home Ruler's book, which is to say only that I hold to self-determination, a principle regarded as a benign commonplace when applied beyond Britain but as vicious heresy when applied within the island. I have tried to understand the distinction but have so far failed to do so. Perhaps the answer is that Home Rule, however logical, comes up against the emotional conservatism of British nationalism. This is to twist the conventional distinction between Scottish nationalism (reactionary, emotional) and British-

4

ness (forward-looking, logical) the other way round. Well, why not? We have heard as much gilt-edged historical guff from some British Unionists as from the hairiest of Scottish Nationalists. Margaret Thatcher was inclined to harp on the need to preserve the heritage of the Empire and of two world-war victories. I am not a nationalist of either the Scottish or the British variety. Like many, maybe most, of my fellow countryfolk, I am a patriotic Scot and a legal Briton and an unpatriotic European. I have tried to keep the main narrative distanced from the occasional eruptions of polemic. But having failed, from time to time, to observe reporterly dryness, I conclude this introduction with a short advertisement for the other side. In February 1992 an economic forecaster and Labour supporter called James Murphy wrote an impassioned attack on what he described as an intellectual betrayal and corruption of Scottish society. Published by the *Herald* newspaper in Glasgow, it was headed 'J'accuse' and included the words: 'I accuse Scottish intellectuals . . . of spinelessly abandoning their obligation to speak truth to their society. Of warping our history, of cruelly deceiving the unemployed and the homeless, the lost and the lonely, by offering them a single, all-weather explanation for their plight: England.' I hope that I have avoided this; were there a single explanation for Scottish problems (and there is not), it would be Scotland. Still, readers who detect spasms of emotional nationalism can at any stage leaf back to here and nod angrily with Mr Murphy.

Where, finally, will this 'battle for Scotland' take us? Time to quote Asquith again, though not perhaps at the full flood of his eloquence: 'I am afraid we must wait and see.'

1

The Dreams of a Small Country

Scottish nationhood . . . is supported by a culture reaching back over centuries and bearing European comparison in depth and quality.

A Claim of Right for Scotland, July 1988

We Scots need [the English] because otherwise we would have slaughtered each other in a kind of ghastly turned-inwards energy, which is after all the history of Scotland, pre-unification.

Norman Stone, historian, *Sunday Times*, February 1992

What makes a nation? First, the accidents of geography and migration, the curve of a river, the angle of a promontory, the zig-zag of a crumbling line of mountains. Had the big island off the north coast of Europe been a few hundred miles shorter (or rather flatter), there would, perhaps, have been no Scotland. But the Scots are defined by having cold salt water on three sides and the English on the fourth – sometimes, they feel, the less hospitable one.

Next, after the challenges of geography, answered by the ancient movement of peoples, comes history. Had Scottish independence been killed off in medieval times by ironclad southerners on lumbering horses (as, at times, it seemed it would be), Scottish nationhood would not have happened either: by now London's northern territories would have exhibited merely regional variations. Instead the development of institutions – courts, universities, religious systems – produced a place recognizable as a nation. The 'why' is a philosophical matter best left to philosophical historians: accumulated accidents of personality or the historical dialectic? Take your pick. But no one can doubt that Scottish nationhood is a matter of popular will: the belief transmitted through generations that this folk, this land, is distinct of itself and not a continuation of a neighbouring people. Fundamentally Scotland is a nation because it believes itself to be one.

Central to that belief is history: Scotland the nation exists because of the way its people understand their own past. But there is more: Scotland is an insecure nation, and we know this because Scots argue about the meaning of that history and have been curiously eager to swallow historical libels about that past. In a happy, well-adjusted nation history is no more politically contentious, for most people, than the study of geography or particle physics. In Scotland, there is too little neutral history. I do not mean by that to libel the eminent professional historians who have been opening up Scottish history and popularizing it. I mean that Scotland is so interested in unravelling its own 'Scotlandness' that the neutral facts these historians recover, order and drill are then pounced upon and squeezed for contemporary political messages.

The 'Whig' interpretation of the Scottish Enlightenment of the eighteenth century is a good example. It taught that this great flowering of Scottish thought was part of a smooth, upward curve of modernization caused by the union of backward Scotland with forward England. From small to big; from peripheral to central; from darkling superstition to clear Enlightenment. Onward and upward and outward. Since the 1960s this traditional view has been shredded by many historians – left-wingers, Tories, nationalists and sceptics who are simply part of the worldwide reaction against moralizing, story-telling history. Because it affects Scotland's self-image, this academic debate about the eighteenth century has leaked into politics through paperbacks and pamphlets and television programmes and newspaper articles.

The day will never come when Bannockburn or the events of 1707 matter more in Scottish politics than the funding of the Health Service or the best kinds of examination for 16-year-olds. (I hope not, anyway.) But the shadow of Scottish history falls across public life and politics in a way that it does not, for instance, in England. Societies named after Scottish historical thinkers like Fletcher of Saltoun, John Mair and John Wheatley and after events like the radical rising of 1820 keep popping up in nationalist and left-wing circles. In the Commons Scottish MPs lard their constitutional speeches with historical examples and even, on occasion, row about things like the precise status of the Scottish parliament of the 1690s. The historical itch is not confined to the left or the Nationalists: in the late 1980s the then Scottish Secretary, Malcolm Rifkind, tried to relieve the beleaguered Scottish Tories with an erudite and satisfying scratch at their Jacobite origins.

So, to understand what is happening now in Scottish politics, it helps to know a bit of the history and to be aware of how it is used. That is what this chapter is for. Sometimes politicians rubbish this notion: 'We are interested in the future of Scotland, not the past.' Hooey. Mere marsh gas and night soil: nationalists are nationalists because of history; socialists take a quiet pride in the specialness of Scottish socialism because of its history; the Scottish Liberals are struggling to reclaim their historical inheritance; and even the Scottish Tories, the least historically obsessed of the parties, have had their lecture from Mr Rifkind. The politicians' words and their wars are drenched in history. Since I am not an historian, I have chosen only four things to discuss briefly as an introduction to the political narrative that follows. First, the medieval independence battle, which is Scotland's national epic. Second, its union with England, which was either its Fall from Eden or its escape into the real world, depending on how you look at it. Third, its Highland myth and 'national dress', which are its disgraceful bits. And, fourth, its national Church, which is still as near as the old girl has to a soul. Without some of this, the 'What came before?', I cannot begin to make sense of the here and the now.

Myths of Medieval Scotland

Scotland existed as a state of some kind for nearly 700 years. Propaganda surrounded it as early as any records exist. And for very good reasons. King Duncan I (later murdered by that good king Macbeth and his pious wife Gruoch) was the first to rule over most of Scotland when he came to the throne in 1034. But what was 'Scotland'? A mere century before Duncan 'Scotia', or Scotland, had referred to what we now call Ireland. Duncan's Scotland was barely a nation, divided between Angles, Scots from Ireland, Norsemen, Picts and Welsh-speaking Britons. Different parts had different laws. This 'Scotland' was poised somewhere between a tiny multicultural empire and a rather grand tribal federation. Some historians date Scotland from even earlier, the reign of Kenneth MacAlpin, who became the first joint king of the Scots and the Picts in 843. To us it hardly matters. But to the kings of medieval Scotland and their historian-propagandists it mattered a lot. The legitimacy of the new nation was challenged from very early on. The English invasions that nearly snuffed out Scotland were justified by the argument that Scotland was a mere vassal state whose kings owed feudal homage to the English crown. According to the medieval view of sovereignty Scottish nationhood depended on divinely inspired Scottish monarchy. There is some evidence that the Scots never quite went along with this divine right of kings business – the Scottish kings never touched for scrofula, the 'king's evil', as the rest did. But, by and large, the status of the nation was the status of its ruler; so the antiquity and independence of the monarchy was essential to establishing the nation's legal independence.

The English claimed superiority on various grounds, but a key one was the myth that Britain had been founded by the expatriate Trojan warrior Brutus. His eldest son, Locrinus, inherited England, but Scotland fell merely to his youngest son, Albanactus. Hence the Scots owed fealty to the English. To modern ears this may seem a hilariously irrelevant excuse for marching large armies north against smaller ones. But there is no doubt that in the medieval world, just as in this century, excuses mattered to rulers – to the Popes, among others – and were used to justify their actions. As late as 1542 Henry VIII of England was using the whole Brutus nonsense to justify attacking Scotland.

Scottish historian-propagandists had to demonstrate that their country had not been founded by the Trojan Brutus but was even older. Eventually it was decided that Scotland had been founded by a Greek prince (Greeks beat Trojans, remember), Gedyl-Glays, who married Scota, the daughter of Pharaoh. After Moses had defeated Pharaoh in the Red Sea Gedyl-Glays and Scota went to Spain and then to Ireland. From there, carrying the Stone of Destiny (which today sits in Westminster Abbey and is considered by romantic Scottish Nationalists to be an essential symbol of the nation), the pair came to Scotland. And, being love-struck, procreated. (All true Scots are thus the descendants of a Greek hard man and an Egyptian immigrant.) To link these lovers from biblical times with the medieval Scottish monarchs who really did exist lists of mostly spurious

Pictish and Scottish kings were then created. A 'Chronicle of the Picts and Scots', in existence by 1259, took the story from around 200 BC and a certain Pictish King Cruthin to AD 750. Since some of the earliest settlers in Scotland and Ireland probably set off by sea from the Mediterranean and bounced northwards past Spain up the west coast of Europe, there may even have been some folk memory behind these propagandistic legends of the Scots' origins.

At any rate, such propaganda-history was an essential part of the early Scottish kingdom's belief in itself. Any historically conscious modern Scot knows of the Declaration of Arbroath, the patriotic address by Scottish barons in 1320 that was sent to the pro-English Pope to persuade him of the legitimacy of King Robert the Bruce following the independence wars. It contains the rousing words 'For so long as an hundred remain alive we are minded never a whit to bow beneath the yoke of English dominion. It is not for glory, riches or honours that we fight: it is for liberty alone, the liberty that no good man relinquishes but with his life.' For Scots those words, translated from medieval Latin, have a resonance similar to William Shakespeare's speech of Henry V before Agincourt for the English.

The Declaration also contains the promise that, despite his martial successes, King Robert would be deposed by his people if he compromised their independence. He was 'King of Scots', not King of Scotland, already a limited monarch of a people, not lord and owner of a land. In medieval constitutional thought this was a radical claim – and is cited today by Nationalists and Home Rulers as evidence of the modernity of early Scottish thought. Up to a point: the Declaration bases its historical claim on the statement that the Scots came from Greater Scythia, via the Pillars of Hercules, to Spain, 'and thence coming, 1200 years after the setting forth of the people of Israel, they won for themselves by victory after victory, and travail upon travail, the abodes in the west ... Within their realm have reigned one hundred and thirteen kings of native royal stock, never an alien on the throne.'

This first myth of Scotland was given more detailed shape by an Aberdeen priest, John of Fordun, who travelled across Scotland and to the 'out isles' seeking material for his 'Scotichronicon', which he started writing in 1384. Some thirty-five years later Andrew

Wynton, the Augustinian prior of St Serf's on Loch Leven in Fife, wrote a massive world history that was based on French, Silesian, Spanish, English and Scottish sources. He began with the Creation and ended with the Scottish wars of independence, with no gaps in between. (Its first printed edition was completed by a French ancestor of the current author for the Scottish Texts Society and sits, in six ancient yellow paper tomes, in my house. It is very boring.) By then Scotland's self-image was clear and confident. The myth of the founding of Scotland continued to be elaborated by Scots like Boece and Buchanan, and challenged by revisionists, through the 1500s. As late as 1648 rosy-faced Scottish monarchs from hundreds of years BC were being painted in serried ranks in the Palace of Holyroodhouse, and the antiquity of the peripatetic Scottish people, the lost tribe in the north, was still cited by anti-Union pamphleteers in the first years of the eighteenth century. The current enthusiasm for reclaiming Scottish history has seen a huge translation and publication of Walter Bower's fifteenth-century Latin 'Scotichronicon' by St Andrews University. Musty fare for old moles only? Not entirely; it includes modern-sounding arguments about 'independence in Europe' (under the Pope, however, not the Commission).

The propaganda-history that mattered to early Scots may have mattered little through modern Scottish history. But the military achievements of the medieval leaders – above all, the independence wars led by William Wallace and Robert the Bruce – have mattered, and still do, as a symbol of Scottish resistance. There are countless examples, many of them subversive. In the years since the Union, tens of thousands of Scots have made political or personal pilgrimages to Bannockburn. In the early part of the nineteenth century Scottish radicals used Robert Burns's patriotic 'Scots wha hae' (harking back to Wallace and Bruce) as a battle-song; it was thought so dangerous, according to one historian, that Paisley magistrates considered making it an offence even to tap out the tune on a drum. In the 1920s Labour Party supporters gathered for rallies at Elderslie, Wallace's birthplace. In the 1930s the Scottish communists carried placards of Bruce and Wallace alongside Marx when they marched against unemployment. At a more naïve level tens of thousands of Scottish children (including this author) have gulped their way through Sir Walter Scott's Victorian accounts of the Scottish wars in *Tales of a Grandfather*.

Think too of the hoarse waves of 'Flower of Scotland' that billow across Murrayfield rugby stadium in Edinburgh. If a Scot knows only one historical date, it will probably be 1314. The Bruce story is Scotland's national epic; the first of the great Scottish poets, John Barbour, who was probably born in the year of the Declaration of Arbroath, wrote his long verse narrative 'The Brus' in 1376. If a future Scottish government funded a national video company, its first film would probably be called *Bruce I: The Terminator*. And this is all quite natural. A country's defining moments tend to come when it survives threatened extinction. The independence wars, opened by the rural guerrilla William Wallace with the support of the Scottish Catholic Church, really were critical to Scotland's existence. Professor Donald Watt, overseeing the publication of the 'Scotichronicon', mentioned above, speculated that had Bannockburn gone the other way, today's Scots would have been like the Welsh. The country would have disappeared into vassalage in the early 1300s had it not been led by a military genius. Scotland's 1314 was, in that sense, like Britain's 1940.

The very simplicity of the Bruce story makes it potent propaganda. But what was medieval 'nationalism'? Many Scottish nobles of the time held lands in England and had a mixed sense of identity. Bruce changed sides a bit before becoming the hero-king. As for most of the rest. it is impossible to analyse the nationalist feeling of the ordinary people, to pick over its nuances and discuss its quality. Unlike their shoes and cutlery, their unwritten thoughts cannot be excavated. The 1320 declaration was a sophisticated act of international diplomacy by the aristocracy and Church leadership. It proves nothing about why the lost, dumb-to-history schiltroms of Scottish spear-carriers were fighting at Bannockburn. Fear of the (feudal) boss? Because of horror stories about the bairn-mutilating English? In the hope of gaining an old-age pension by looting the jewelled crab-shells of dead knights? All we can guess is that it had little to do with contemporary arguments about the nation-state. Although anti-English resistance involved many common people and small lairds, medieval Scotland was not a democracy, or democratic in any sense. It never had the oppressive legal structure of extreme feudalism, as practised on the Continent, but the essential fact of its political system is well captured in part of an Italian sonnet by the Roman scoundrel Belli, thus translated by the fine twentieth-century Edinburgh poet Robert Garioch:

> Yince on a time there wes a King, wha sat
> Scrievin this edict in his palace-haa
> Til a' his fowk: Vassals, I tell ye flat
> That I am I, and you are bugger-a.

The Scottish kings possessed, necessarily, a limited sovereignty – a sovereignty hedged about by Highland rebellion, Lowland baronial power, relative poverty and English military intervention. But they wanted absolute power, even if they never quite got it. Indeed, the history of Scottish kinghood struggling to assert itself explains the fanatical belief of the later Stuart monarchs in the doctrine of Divine Right – an extreme expression of personal sovereignty that brought England, as well as Scotland, to civil war and revolution. As we will see when we discuss the Scottish Church, advanced ideas about the limits of power did become current in Scottish ecclesiastical circles in the sixteenth century. But there is a misty gulf between arguments about their relative positions among clerical intellectuals, barons and the monarchy and the beliefs of the vast majority of the people of Scotland. To link contemporary belief in popular sovereignty and even democratic values with the epic independence wars may be good nationalist propaganda. But it is, at best, doubtful history.

Myths About the Union

The history that falsely pictures Scotland as a coherent, united and democratic nation during its anti-English wars of independence is patriotic propaganda. But the history of Scotland, the nation-state, is often used for anti-nationalist purposes in just as ahistorical a way: old Scotland was backward, bloody and racked by more or less perpetual civil war. Among Unionist MPs arguing in the House of Commons or in books, English historians, Scottish historians, journalists and novelists, the view of Scotland's independent history as a bloody, squalid farce has often been the consensus. In recent years this consensus has been challenged by a new generation of Scottish historians, but they remain in the minority. The first point to make is, of course, that much of the bleak picture of pre-Union Scotland is accurate. There was plenting of hewing, stabbing and poisoning, not to say fast-sickening, slow-starving and long-despairing. Clans behaved clannishly in the Highlands, and Lowland barons revolted. Renegade Scots were often to be found in English armies. Scottish kings were murdered or imprisoned, sometimes by their revolting children. Edinburgh stank. It rained.

And so what? English or French medieval history was hardly a soft-focus Arcadia. There was the odd civil war, the more than occasional royal murder, the pox, burnings of witches, plagues. Germany was crazy-paved into warring fragments. Poles and Spaniards starved too. Yet other European countries do not use their early history masochistically. How often does one see a Hamburger shaking his head and slowly demonstrating that the Hundred Years War proved Germans were incapable of self-government? Yet Scots have used, and still do use, the far-back history of their country as evidence of a continuing national—psychological malfunction. A terse but representative sample of this genre of self-flagellatory historiography is quoted by the modern Scottish novelist William McIlvanney in his account of Scotland's disastrous World Cup foray to Argentina in 1978. At the end of the match with Iran a big Aberdonian with a Scottish saltire, who had been leading the singing, touched his arm and whispered through his tears, 'We'll never do anythin' richt, will we?' Historians of pre- and post-Union Scotland have put it less pithily, but their underlying theme has been identical.

Wars, rebellions and, in particular, the terrible years of famine and stagnation in the late 1600s are used as proof positive that Scottish independence was, and is, hopeless. How strange, particularly since historians have often based their views on descriptions by English travellers or reformers with an interest in blackening the old. The English historian Lord Dacre (of Hitler's diaries fame) has attacked the backwardness and 'faction' of seventeenth-century Scotland and used it as an argument for the modern Union. But he would not dream of discussing the competence of today's English Parliament by reference to the English Civil War or the economic policies of the Ranters.

Civilization is a process, not an event. Pre-Union Scottish history is an almost meaningless precedent for modern politics. Scotland then was a society always threatened by a far larger power. For generation after generation it was invaded, had its kings kidnapped or ransomed and lost its ruling class in battle. In just two weeks in September 1544 an English force destroyed seven monasteries, sixteen castles and towers, five market towns and 243 villages. The year before that Edinburgh and its surrounding towns and palaces had been utterly destroyed by English attacks. Small wonder that the Scottish kings devoted so vast an amount of their meagre resources to war – Scotland's best late medieval monarch, James IV, spent about 10 per cent of his income on salaries for the crew of a single warship, the *Great Michael*. Even so, he died horribly (fighting on with one hand hanging off by its skin and skewered with bundles of arrows) at the Battle of Flodden. Most of the Scottish ruling class and much of the country's fighting manhood perished there too. Among those who fought were, rather pathetically, James's sons' tutor and his secretary, who had been given the task of firing the Scottish cannon.

The Scottish crown was often close to being toppled by English intrigue or simple bad luck. In an age when virtually every European society saw protracted disputes between the local power of barons and the central power of monarchies, it is hardly surprising that Scottish lords engaged in periodic bouts of civil war. The historian Jenny Wormald has shown that 'If relations between crown and nobility are considered in comparative terms, then it appears that the Scottish monarchy got off very lightly.' Yet at the same time, Scotland saw universities endowed and fine abbeys and castles built. It produced three very fine poets – William Dunbar, Robert Henryson and Gavin Douglas – and scholars with a European-wide reputation. If there was plenty to be ashamed of, there was something to be proud of too. But not too proud: Scotland's centuries as a nation-state are held by some of today's patriots to be a glittering, heroic period and by some Unionists to be a shameful and best-forgotten time of darkness. Each puerile misuse of the history of Scotland's statehood tells us only that something is wrong with the current stateless nation.

The potency of the attack on pre-Union Scotland is that the union of the parliaments was followed, after a time lag, by rising Scottish prosperity and the great Enlightenment. Scots have long argued about its cause and the Union's effect. Broadly speaking, Nationalist propagandists have concentrated on the questionable events surrounding the Union of 1707 itself, while Unionist propagandists have skated over them to claim the achievements of the following century as the result of wise statesmanship by the Unionists. The omniscient Whigs, the liberal upper-class rulers of later times, saw the Union as simply an expression of Progress, an unqualified Good. Their views are often echoed by today's Conservative and Labour Unionists.

But they never had it all their own way. Robert Burns, the nineteenth-century radicals and Home Rulers, modern Nationalists, all have portrayed 1707 as Scotland at her worst, a shameful capitulation by the ruling classes. Independence was sold by 'a parcel of [aristocratic] rogues' for English gold. It is no surprise that the intellectual elder statesman of the Scottish National Party (SNP), Paul C. Scott, is today studying Fletcher of Saltoun, the Scottish parliamentarian who opposed the Union. Fletcher was also the subject of a pamphlet from the Scottish Home Rule Association in the 1880s. Now he has his own Nationalist society and an annual lecture. On the other side, anti-devolution MPs regularly attacked Fletcher's reputation during House of Commons debates in the 1970s, noting that he had advocated slavery for impoverished Scots. (He did, but as a form of welfare system.) The same MPs derided the pre-Union Scottish parliament; in one 1975 debate Labour's Robin Cook noted that it had barely 2,000 electors, had met only two days a year until twenty years before the Union and, in its dying days, had passed an Act for 'the serfdom of salt-panners'.

The Union was a defining moment for Scotland, and the chill shadow of its politics falls across most politically aware Scots today. Some of the Union arguments seem unimportant now. Who cares which competing litter of slack-jawed dumplings had the greater claim to a crown? Most of the assorted Stuarts or Hanoverians would be candidates for community-care orders if they pitched up at Leith harbour today. The religious schism that underpinned their pretensions is also, thankfully, a forgotten question. Yet behind the apparent archaism of the early 1700s was an explosive brew of alarmist economics, fervent nationalism and constitutional debate that is strikingly relevant in the 1990s. Malcolm Rifkind, the

Conservative politician, is fond of analysing the history of Scottish nationalism as a perpetual battle between Scotland's aspirations and Scotland's interests, in which its interests tend to win over its aspirations. The Union of 1707 supports his thesis, though, even through fat years, Scotland's aspirations continue to make it squirm.

The years just before the Union saw unusually severe famine and the catastrophic imperial adventure known as the Darien scheme. This was an ambitious project intended to open up American and Pacific trade routes by establishing a Scottish colony straddling Panama. Huge sums were raised to finance this by a Scottish entrepreneur who had earlier helped found the Bank of England. But Spanish hostility, English indifference and, above all, the plaguey climate of Panama turned it into a disaster, both human and financial. Scotland was unlucky but was also simply too poor to compete at a time of imperial expansion and this was an important part of the backdrop to Union. Scottish exasperation provoked at first hostility to England – English mariners were hanged before a jeering Edinburgh mob after rumours that they had attacked one of the few vessels of the short-lived Scottish African Company. Later it led to virtual surrender. Scotland's military weakness was also important; the sound track of the parliamentary debates on Union in London and Edinburgh should include the distant booming of Marlborough's continental armies routing Scotland's old ally, France. As one Scottish observer put it in 1702, the main aim of the unified court was 'to shut up Scotland, as a Backdoor for invasions upon them from France or elsewhere'. Even so, the first attempt to get an agreed parliamentary Union in that year ran into the ground, significantly, over arguments about Scottish access to the Indian and African trades.

Long debates, at times furious, occupied the Scottish parliament on and off for the next few years. As one pro-Union knight put it: 'We were often in the form of the Polish diet with our swords in our hands, or, at least, our hands on our swords.' The anti-Unionists were divided between Jacobites, or Cavaliers, and the anti-Jacobites, known as the Country, or Patriotic, Party. Fletcher was associated with the second group. His speeches were published at the time and have been a staple of Scottish Nationalist history ever since. Their potency derives from Fletcher's seeming modernity. He strongly believed in the need for a limited, constitutional state, bitterly attacking the 'slavish principles' of court rule. His twelve principles of limitations on royal power over the Scottish parliament went so far as to lead his enemies to argue that their publication as a 'Claim of Right' was a blueprint for a Scottish republic. Even more striking, however, was his clear analysis of the distribution of power. The English parliamentarians and courtiers had demanded an incorporating, perpetual Union (a takeover), but many Scots still hoped for a federal British state. So far as can be discovered, majority Scottish opinion was in favour of what we would call devolution or Home Rule. Fletcher's argument for a federal Britain echoes modern debates about regional policy and the 'overheated south-east'. Comparing London with 'the head of a ricketty child', he pointed out that the remoter parts of England also suffered economic damage from its dominance and suggested economic development across Britain, centred on a series of regional capitals. He concluded: 'That London should draw the riches and government of the three kingdoms to the south-east corner of this island, is in some degree as unnatural, as for one city to possess the riches and government of the world.'

Fletcher's high reputation and the undoubted bribery of Scottish parliamentarians by the Unionists have tended to obscure the fact that the pro-Union Scots had some good and honest arguments too. At times they found their English allies at their wits' end with the Scottish parliament. Fletcher himself quotes an English lord: 'What a pother is here about an union with Scotland, of which all the advantage we shall have, will be no more than what a man gets by marrying a beggar, a louse for her portion.' The pro-Unionist Earl of Seafield (his title a reward for supporting the royal case) told the Scottish parliament that his fundamental reasons for 'conjoining with England' were, first, that this would help secure the Protestant religion; second, that 'England has trade and other advantages to give us' (including a payment to cover the losses of the Darien scheme); third, 'England has freedome and liberty and that the joyning with it was the best way to secure that to us'; and fourth, 'I saw no other method for secureing our peace, the two kingdomes being in the same island.' Barring the Protestantism, Seafield's arguments are not dissimilar to the Unionist case as it has been presented ever since.

Still there is no doubt that the majority of Scots were fiercely against the form of union their parliamentarians voted for eventually – an incorporating, perpetual union, not a federal one. As we shall see when we discuss the Kirk, that form of union tried to fuse two separate constitutional traditions in a way that has caused problems since. In a famous judgment in 1953 Lord Cooper, a senior Scottish judge, argued that the principle of unlimited parliamentary sovereignty was a distinctively English one, which had no counterpart in Scottish law:

Considering that the Union legislation extinguished the Parliaments of England and Scotland and replaced them by a new Parliament, I have difficulty in seeing why it should have been supposed that the new Parliament of Great Britain must inherit all the peculiar characteristics of the English Parliament but none of the Scottish Parliament, as if all that happened in 1707 was that Scottish representatives were admitted to the Parliament of England. That is not what was done.

Legally, Lord Cooper, sir, no. In practice, yes. For most purposes, the 'union' was really a takeover: the Scots arrived at the English Parliament as a permanent and small minority. In view of current arguments about the right number of Scottish MPs at Westminster it is worth bearing in mind that this too was a real problem for the negotiators in 1706–7. The proposals ranged from using Scottish land tax as a basis (which would have given Scotland only thirteen MPs out of 533) to using population, which would have produced eighty-five MPs. Eventually, the compromise was forty-five.

None of this was lost on Scottish opinion at the time. After the details were published in Edinburgh an anti-Unionist Jacobite, Lockhart of Carnwarth, described the mob's attack on the house of one of the men who had agreed the treaty: they 'threw Stones at his Windows, broke open his Doors and search'd his House for him, but he having narrowly made his Escape, prevented his being torn in a Thousand Pieces. From thence the Mob, which was encreas'd to a great Number, went thro' the Streets, threatning Destruction to all the Promoters of the Union, and continu'd for four or five hours in this Temper.'

Lockhart wryly commented that the pro-Union courtiers had until then affected not to believe the people were against it, but the rioting had made it 'evident that the Union was cramm'd down Scotland's throat'. Nor was this merely the slanted account of a staunch Nationalist. Daniel Defoe, writing as an English agent from Edinburgh, recounted: 'I heard a Great Noise and looking Out Saw a Terrible Multitude Come up the High Street with a Drum at the head of Them shouting and swearing and Cryeing Out all Scotland would stand together, No Union, No Union, English Dogs and the like.' Nor again was it only the Edinburgh mob. There were riots in Glasgow too, and in the final stages of the parliamentary debate anti-Union petitions and addresses started to flood in from across Scotland: first from Forfarshire, then Stirling and Dumbarton, then Linlithgow, Dunkeld, Fife, Glasgow, Kirkcudbright, Lanark, Berwick, Dunblane, Lochmaben, Peterhead . . . on and on and on. Eventually about ninety protests arrived – so many that one earl suggested they ought to be used for making kites.

And in the first years after the Union the fears of the Scots (which had been paralleled by scenes of joy in England when the Union was agreed) seemed to be borne out. Fletcher had warned about the flood of Scottish money that would go south to London and the effect of free trade on Scottish manufacturing. Defoe, writing twenty years after the Union on a return visit to Scotland, concurred. His testimony is particularly interesting because he was a convinced but honest Unionist. Most of his countrymen who visited Scotland to write about it had (knowing their audience back home) stressed the poverty and dirt. But Defoe tried to dig beneath the unappetizing surface. He found that Glasgow was doing well with the tobacco trade opened up by Scottish access to Virginia and New England, but elsewhere the Union seemed little more popular than it had been when first concluded. Travelling north from the capital, Defoe noted, 'We did not find so kind a reception among the common people of Angus . . . we found it was because we were English men . . . it was on account of the Union, which they almost universally exclaimed against, though sometimes against all manner of just reasoning.' And in the Highlands Defoe and his English party found it 'much for our convenience to make the common people believe we were French'. There were good reasons for Scottish popular dismay at the Union's effects. Defoe noted the decayed palaces, undercut and struggling cloth manufacturers and the stagnant ports that showed its early impact. He listened to local complaints and shared with his hosts a romanticized vision of a richer, pre-Union Scotland:

Then it was the sea-port towns had a trade, their court was magnificent, their nobility built fine houses and palaces which were richly furnished within and without ... whereas, now their Court is gone, their nobility and gentry spend their time, and consequently their estates [i.e. rental income] in England; the Union opens the door to all English manufacturers and suppresses their own.

What Defoe was seeing was a classic example of a small, protected economy suffering the first blasts of exposure to a wider market. Freer trade would bring its rewards in time. In the next two centuries the Scottish economy did benefit strongly from the bigger market created by the Union and the English colonies. In those rougher times the English could (and would) have excluded Scottish goods and consigned the country to economic stagnation for generations. Defoe made an earnest, if amateurish, attempt to assess the Scottish balance of trade and believed it strong but found old Scottish industries succumbing to the lower prices of cheap English imports. Nevertheless ultimately some of those apparently dying industries – like the Border textile industry or the fish curing of the east coast – would thrive.

The common view is that the Scottish economy was boosted by the importation of English men and English methods. Yet after the Union, and with the huge exception of the English soldiers who helped to crush the Jacobite rebellion of 1745, London rule did not weigh heavily on Scotland. Indeed, Scotland seemed to get on remarkably well with hardly any politics at all. Most of the agricultural improvers were Scots; the Scottish Convention of Royal Burghs helped modern-ize the linen and fishing industries; Scots law, the universities and the Scots Kirk were left mostly untouched (not entirely, as we shall see). Economically, the Union was a two-way street: the Scots undoubtedly lost a rich chunk of the ruling classes who, had they stayed home, might have developed the country more quickly. But the trading advantages of the English colonies were of huge importance to Glasgow. Scots had found their nation and capital too weak for the imperialist project and joined the English as junior partners in theirs.

The arguments surrounding the Treaty itself are continued when Scots and English discuss Scotland's eighteenth-century explosion of cultural self-confidence. After many in the Lowlands had united with the English crown to destroy Jacobitism in the first half of the century there was something of a 'North Briton' cult. Scots whose minds made them famous throughout Europe took elocution lessons to get rid of their accents. The Highlanders were absorbed into British regiments, though far from painlessly. Some of the most talented Scots, like the medical Hunter brothers, the novelist Tobias Smollett and the great biographer and diarist James Boswell, looked to London. The eighteenth century saw extraordinary achievements in Scottish agriculture and industry, in philosophy and the arts and in the sciences and architecture. As the century progressed, so Scots seemed to lose touch with their pre-Union history. In a famous passage in his 1814 novel *Waverley* Sir Walter Scott said the increased wealth and expanded commerce of Scotland 'have since united to render the present people of Scotland a class of beings as different from their grandfathers as the existing English are from those of Queen Elizabeth's time'. Recently the Scottish writers Craig Beveridge and Ronald Turnbull have shown how these developments have been presented as an almost miraculous release from pre-Union poverty and superstition – a dawn following Scotland's dark ages. Indeed, the tone of awed amazement that many historians have used to describe the effects of the Union is paralleled only by the 1930s Marxist propagandists who described the Russian revolution as the miraculous remaking of that country.

In the grown-up world things are messier. A revisionist wave of Scottish historians has shown that the great Enlightenment was rooted in pre-Union Scotland. The Kirk, then led by its Moderate party, had helped produce both the education and the spirit of debate that nurtured the great philosophers, social scientists, historians and doctors. Edinburgh at the height of its intellectual ascendancy has been described as a city having a perpetual conversation with itself. The readiness to argue things out from first principles, which became a staple of the Scottish universities' compulsory philosophy courses, can be credited to the Kirk's emphasis on reading, following arguments in sermons and close analysis of texts. Presbyterianism may have been a dark, forbidding religion, but it was also a thinking, even cerebral, creed. It was the Kirk-influenced universities that started producing philosophers and sociologists by the 1740s, before the Englightenment proper took hold. Great intellectual movements do not spring, ready-formed, from the minds of men and women; they require stimulus, even the stimulus of opposition. The calm rationalism of that extraordinary man David Hume or the prejudice-demolishing prose of Adam Smith owe a great deal to the religion they were brought up in and reacted against. Clear northern light shines through them.

The intellectual tradition that the Enlightenment carried forward involved many English thinkers, but it was dependent on the sensationalist philosophers of France, like Condillac, and the spirit of inquiry brought back by Scots from the Dutch universities too. Throughout the period Scots had been scurrying back and forth to northern Europe (just as they had done pre-Union) to study and to lecture. In the days of poor coach travel on rutted tracks the Netherlands could seem nearer than London. The great Enlightenment sociologists like the lords Monboddo and Kames had emerged from a Scottish-European legal tradition, not an English one.

If Scotland was remote in religion, travelling time and intellectual tradition, her post-Union political management was equally distant from London. Until the Napoleonic wars, indeed, English ways and Westminster administration had only a limited impact. A series of Scottish managers of parliamentary business, from the Argyll family after the '45 rebellion to Lord Bute and then the extraordinary Henry Dundas, Lord Melville (who has been described by Michael Fry, the conservative historian, as the father of the Tory party in Scotland), acted as the conduits of patronage. Beyond their immediate circle, the Kirk, the universities and the legal profession – the biggest professional group by far – continued by and large to rule themselves.

This is not to suggest that the Union had no beneficial effects in the century following its creation. The defeat of the Jacobites removed any threat of military invasion from the Scots for the first time in their history. Energies could be directed elsewhere, into the arts and sciences. Freed from political pressure or court intrigue, the universities and polite societies could flourish. The growth of relatively affluent middle-class groups in Edinburgh (and, again, the disappearance of the military threat that kept the city huddled round its castle) enabled the New Town to be built and settled. The first generations of Scots went to India and Canada, and some of them made, and brought back, fortunes. Agricultural improvers did learn from Englishmen; the mingling of the Scottish and English ruling classes in London certainly increased the flow of ideas and brought useful innovations into Scotland. To deny that the eighteenth-century Scottish Enlightenment was a miraculous creation of the Union is not to deny that eighteenth-century Scots learned a lot from the English. Less of Johnson without Boswell, but a lesser Boswell without Johnson.

The underlying argument about the Union and the eighteenth century is unanswerable: no one can know what Scotland would have been like without it. Perhaps the Highlands would have been populous and Gaelic today; perhaps Edinburgh's New Town would have remained unbuilt; perhaps Scots would have had another courageous defeat to lament – the Battle of Longforgan of 1787? All we should note is that the great Scots of the eighteenth century did not think that they had sprung, godlike, from the new Union; they were children and grandchildren too. By the end of the century Scots were almost as divided about their identity as they are now. Scottish regiments were prominent in the fight against Napoleon, yet when pro-French revolutionary enthusiasm was sweeping parts of Britain the Scottish Jacobins sang anti-English songs. In Paris the Scottish revolutionary Thomas Muir of Huntershill (who had been transported to Botany Bay, escaped to North America, been captured by Indians and then reached Europe again on a Spanish ship after being wounded in a sea battle with British vessels) was vainly urging the French to support a Scottish rising aimed at creating a revolutionary Scottish republic. No doubt some of his Glasgow neighbours called themselves North Britons and fought for Wellington.

By the beginning of the nineteenth century rival traditions of Scottish nationalism, which had been evident during the parliamentary debates on the Union in Edinburgh in the early 1700s, were still twitching. The Whiggish nationalism of the Union debates had been replaced by an evangelizing Whig Unionism – partly to ensure that the corrupt Tory patronage of men like Dundas was replaced. A nationalist tradition was passed down to radicals – groups like the

United Scotsmen and the rebel democrats of 1820 – and for the rest of the century radical reformers would occasionally harp back to the injustice of the Union. Their brand of dissident nationalism eventually reappeared in mainstream politics through the radical faction of the Gladstonian Liberal Party and the Crofters' Party and then broke cover again in modern times (as we will see) among the socialist Home Rulers. A unified, coherent tradition of thought? Not really – but a thread, sometimes hidden, sometimes clear, that can be traced.

Savages on Shortbread Tins

The other big nationalist tradition, Jacobite nationalism, was also seen in the last Scottish parliament but was destroyed as a live threat forty years later at Culloden. Remarkably soon, however, the sentimental shell of Jacobitism was being used as the centrepiece of a Highland cult. This 'Celtification' of Scotland developed into a rival kind of Scottish patriotism – far more widespread, and far less threatening, than the radical nationalist tradition. Sir Walter Scott was not the originator of this Celtification – it was, for instance, the spirit behind the tragicomic episode of James Macpherson's fraudulent 'Ossian' poems, supposedly composed by a Gaelic Homer, which fooled Napoleon, Goethe and much of civilized Europe but did not fool that sly old tortoise Samuel Johnson. Nor was Scott its most extreme proponent; he was followed by much sillier men and women. But still Scott links pre-Union and Jacobite Scotland with its Victorian caricature like no other man. As a youth he was peripherally involved in genuine, raucously anti-Unionist Jacobitism. Later, as a middle-class Lowlander, he could feel spasms of his old nationalism erupt; in the 'Malachi Malagrowther letters' he attacked London measures that threatened to destroy the Scottish note-based banking system.

Yet, despite his deep and complex understanding of his country's history, Scott turned his early Jacobite rebelliousness into a gooey pastiche first of itself and then of all Scotland. Like a Caledonian Tussaud of the imagination, he resculpted the disturbing truth into a jolly, brightly painted waxwork and then led both people and monarchs past it, selling his books like tickets at the door. Lowland

Scotland was never waxed: it was still too vigorously alive and self-aware to be so falsified and too close to Scott's everyday life for him to be able to sentimentalize it. His waxwork of Scotland therefore wore tartan and stood in a glen. Scott's promotion of the Highland cult enabled him to reconcile conservative loyalty to the fat Unionist lecher George IV with moist-eyed Scottish nationalism.

Scott was not alone; various Highland societies, Celtic clubs and what-not had been formed to promote, in safely ornamental form, the Gaelic society that had been broken at Culloden by Butcher Cumberland and was even then being destroyed in the Clearances by landlords who preferred the profits of sheep-farming. Some of the Celtic romantics were chiefs who had actually fought at the infamous battle. The climax of this bifocal approach to Scottish history was George's theatrical visit to Edinburgh in 1822, when the gross monarch was draped in Highland regalia (kilt and pink tights) and welcomed with a massive and largely spurious tartan pageant masterminded by Scott. Jacobite airs were played and Highland chiefs fawned. The historian John Prebble has written an absorbing and angry account of this 'King's Jaunt', and a revolting event it was. It is astonishing to recall that within the lifetime of people who remembered the Jacobite rebellion and its bloody aftermath a Georgian king was participating in the play-acting of another 'Jacobite' court in Edinburgh. Lowland Scottish observers were disgusted and angry that Scott had made out his country to consist of the Highlands – and some Highland observers felt humiliated too. Everyone has heard of Marx's saw about history repeating itself, first as tragedy, then as farce. But rarely has the farce been as farcical, or arrived as quickly on the heels of tragedy, as Scott's Celtification of Scotland.

Yet the 'jaunt' of 1822 was in its way as much a defining moment for Scotland as Culloden or the Union. After it, the tartan cult grew until ordinary Scots succumbed to it almost unquestioningly. Scotland moved from nation-state to spectacle, an *ersatz* land and race, grounded in deceit. The fashion for historical play-acting has never ended, as anyone who has seen the Honourable Company of Archers frolicking around Edinburgh after the Queen can testify. The debris from this tartan cult still clutters almost every corner shop and half the public houses in the land. Hostile analysis of it, unsurprisingly, has become one of the most powerful and wide-spread themes in contemporary Scottish culture: from the left-wing theatre company 7:84's popular touring show in 1973, *The Cheviot, the Stag, and the Black, Black Oil*, to films and exhibitions like Murray Grigor's *Scotch Myths* in 1980 and books like Prebble's *King's Jaunt* in 1988 or Peter Womack's *Improvement and Romance* of 1990. Indeed, the deconstruction of the tartan cult is in danger of itself becoming a cult.

The importance of tartanism was twofold. First, it helped to draw the teeth of Scottish nationalism during the heyday of the Empire (letting Scots go forth and enrich themselves as an exotic but familiar British tribe). Second, it nearly succeeded in smoothing away the great internal fault line in Scottish culture – the Highland line, which has been compared in its importance to the Mason–Dixon line dividing the United States. Scotland had been two countries throughout its entire independent history and beyond. In the lowlands the descendants of Scots, Picts, Angles, Scandinavians and Norman invaders gradually became homogenized into a coherent culture, speaking a language they themselves referred to as English but that we would now call Scots. Its southern borders were liquid, at times pouring deep into Northumberland, until finally fixed in the middle of the thirteenth century. But to the north the Highlands stayed a different world, a Gaelic-speaking clan country with its own oral history, legends, law, economy and ways of fighting. The Lowland kings spent hundreds of years trying to bring the Highlands and Islands under their control, fighting the Lords of the Isles and the Norwegian crown as well as local rebellions.

When Robert the Bruce was fighting the English (with the help of Highland allies, not subjects), the jagged territory now known as Scotland was still customarily divided into districts called Galloway, Lothian and Scotland; 'Scotland' meant the Highlands. Orkney and Shetland became part of the Scottish kingdom only in 1472, and the Highlands were still regarded as lawless, dangerous badlands in the late 1500s. The cultural division of Scotland has never quite ended. In the Lowlands the Highlanders were at times thought of much as white settler Americans regarded the Sioux or (coming closer to home) the English regarded the Irish Catholics – as treacherous, incomprehensible savages. (Indeed, the caricature Highlander and caricature Irishman of Victorian middle-class humour was virtually interchangable – the same character with a slight transliteration of accent and a few squiggles of costume adjustment.) Around 1600 the Lowland poet Montgomerie fantasized about God creating a Highlander out of a lump of horseshit. When God asked the Highlander what he would do first, he answers, in Montgomerie's poem: 'I will doun to the Lowland, Lord, and thair steill a kow.' In fact, Gaelic culture was deep and sophisticated; Gaelic music had a complexity that Bach would have loved; Gaelic medicine was developed through contacts with European medical schools; and Gaelic poetry developed a verbal and syntactical richness that compares with Renaissance English. The Gaels regarded the southern Scots as cold, materialist and ignoble. But since they lost the military struggle, and since the southerners could not understand Gaelic, their views had little impact on the culture of modern Scotland. Anti-Highland or 'teuchter' jokes told by Glasgow comedians such as Billy Connolly focus on naïvety, not criminality, but the anti-Gaelic prejudice survives.

All this was exported to England soon after the Union, but in the eighteenth century, a time when the English were becoming fascinated by other cultures, the Highlands were also visited by travellers trying to deduce universal truths from their more primitive stage of development – Johnson's and Boswell's tour is perhaps the best-known example. Forty years or so before they set off from Edinburgh Daniel Defoe said of the continuing mystery of the Highlands: 'Our geographers seem almost as much at a loss in the description of this north part of Scotland, as the Romans were to conquer it; and they are obliged to fill it up with hills and mountains, as they do the inner part of Africa, with lions and elephants, for want of knowing what else to place there.'

The Highlands were being slowly opened up to the quizzical but not necessarily hostile gaze of the outside world before the 1745–6 rising, and visitors continued to write about the region interestingly afterwards. But the destruction of Highland military power, and then the Clearances (undertaken by Whiggish Scottish landlords who thought of themselves as liberal reformers), did allow a kind of suffocating cultural takeover to occur that otherwise might not have happened.

At Culloden in 1746 many of the troops on the 'English' side were Lowland Scots or Campbells. All proper Scots derive a bleak, masochistic satisfaction from the contemplation of Butcher Cumberland and his Redcoat savagery. But at the time much of Lowland Scotland was delighted that, at last, the lawless badlands beyond the Highland Line were being purged. There was little sympathy in the neat burghs and far-off Lowland villages for the feckless, irreligious Erse-speaking clans. By some their extirpation was seen as a positive liberation, a leap towards modernity, brought about by the Union with England. It was only afterwards, when clan power had been broken, that the cult could infect the Lowlands. The twists in attitude can be seen by looking at what became the symbol of Scottishness, tartan.

When 'Bonnie Prince Charlie' arrived with his army most Lowland Scots regarded tartan as an alien and even threatening costume; when he arrived in Edinburgh solid citizens draped themselves in tartan as a precaution, not as a mark of pride. After Culloden tartan was banned as part of a more general attempt to wipe out Gaelic culture. The first Highland societies of the early 1800s, however, tried to promote Gaelic songs and the wearing of the now unbanned tartan – though by then most Gaels had (literally) lost the habit. Tartan, which had derived from a centuries-old fashion for striped and checked cloth and had only finally emerged in its full-blown, clan-by-clan distinctiveness around the end of the seventeenth century, was then further codified by the Victorians with inventive but unhistorical precision (so that even today MacThises and McThats proudly wear 'their' tartan, part-created by a sharp London or Lowland salesmen in the nineteenth century!). New tartans were devised for the Highland regiments, and the kilt (a late, Lowland version of the full drapery actually worn by Highlanders) became a military and aristocratic fashion, shunned by ordinary Gaels. By the 1920s radical politicians and poets who thought of themselves as sternly historical, progressive nationalists were prepared to wear tartan again – though it was discouraged by the early leaders of the Nationalist party. The poet MacDiarmid adopted a cod-Gaelic name and a kilt for his national-revivalist persona. Yet he came from the Borders and did not speak Gaelic. He was tricking himself out in trumpery associated originally with Sir Walter Scott, who was among the Scotsmen MacDiarmid most hated and railed against.

It is a curious phenomenon. Today kilts are worn proudly when the SNP marches, bagpipes playing and saltires aloft. Many of those wearing it, just like the kilt-wearers at innumerable weddings, have no real Highland connections. Indeed, tartan can be viewed most reliably at the balls held for anglicized, aristocratic 'Hooray Hamishes'. Perhaps it is wrong to mock: tartan is a symbol, and all symbols can change their meaning. It meant one thing to its original wearers. It had another, virtually opposite, meaning for the play-actors of Scott's pageant of 1822. Its meaning changed again for the Scottish regiments and had become a simpler symbol of patriotism by the two world wars.

Now it is starting to mean something else. The historian winces at the popularized use of tartan as a general symbol of Scottish patriotism. But there may be more to this than meets the eye: some young Nationalists wear the kilt with a kind of defiant mockery, responding to a century of music-hall and *Punch* caricature. It is a pale reflection of the cultural inversion that causes American radical blacks to refer to themselves as 'niggers' or gays to rechristen themselves 'queer'. Like those words, the kilt is meant to be hard to ignore: at the most basic level, the kilt wearer is nailing his colours to the mast.

Similar twists of meaning can be traced in the attitudes of Lowland Scotland to the Gaelic language. It was mocked in the seventeenth century, persecuted after 1745 and revived in spurious translation during the 'Ossian' episode. In the nineteenth century Gaelic was again being studied in Edinburgh and gathered and written down by folk-song collectors (even as it was being extirpated by ministers and educators in the Highlands). By the turn of the century it was being mocked as a sign of backwardness in industrial Glasgow, yet a generation later the children of the mockers were in Nationalist groups in the city that held compulsory Gaelic lessons for all recruits. In Edinburgh today some of the patriotic middle classes are turning once again to study Gaelic – just like their forebears in the 1820s. The ironies criss-cross and dazzle like the most luridly polychromatic of tartan designs splashed across a shortbread tin.

The Buried History of the Scottish Kirk

In Scotland's history and in its current political battle its national Church, the Church of Scotland or the Kirk, has a special place. According to a detailed poll carried out for BBC Scotland's series *Scotland 2000* in 1987, 64 per cent of Scots described themselves as Presbyterian or Protestant, against 15 per cent for the next group, the Catholics. Although Scots are no longer great churchgoers — membership is down from 1.27 million in 1951 to 787,000 in 1990 — the Kirk retains a vague loyalty among the people that is much more widespread than the reach of the Church of England. Any Scot with a smattering of history knows that the Kirk was a main pillar of nationhood for three centuries. Any Scot who reads the serious papers or watches television recognizes that the Kirk today aspires to play an active, indeed provocative, role in the developing argument about the nation's future.

When the Scottish Constitutional Convention gathered to demand an Edinburgh parliament in early 1989 it was a clergyman (albeit a Methodist), the General Secretary of the Scottish Council of Churches, Canon Kenyon Wright, who challenged the idea that Margaret Thatcher could, as the government, say no: 'We are the people and we say yes.' Around him clerical greys and blacks were prominent: for many middle-class Scots the appearance of so many plump, pink faces nodding on dog-collars gives a reassuring respectability to a movement intended to be subversive of the present order. Many of the most active pro-Home Rule politicians have been, or are, also active Kirk members (often elders). The Kirk itself has been committed to some form of Home Rule since the 1940s. When John Major launched his pre-election assault on independence and devolution one of the first hostile responses came not from an MP but from the Reverend Norman Shanks, convener of the Kirk's Church and Nation Committee. And what is interesting about that is that it surprised nobody.

There are ironies in the Kirk's position. Through much of its Victorian and early twentieth-century history the Kirk was a strongly conservative force, politically as well as socially. Like all national Churches, it contains different, often competing, traditions. The Home Rulers now seem to be strongly dominant at each

May's General Assembly in Edinburgh (when around 1,300 ministers and lay elders from across Scotland gather for the Kirk's effective parliament). Many ministers were genuinely outraged by Margaret Thatcher's address to the General Assembly in 1988 when she argued that capitalist values and Christian ethics were inextricably linked. In 1989 the Kirk's Church and Nation Committee produced a report that attacked the 'elective dictatorship' of the Westminster parliamentary system and issued a call to arms: 'From a Scottish constitutional and theological perspective this English constitutional tradition of state absolutism has always been unacceptable in theory. It is now intolerable in practice.' Yet among the clerical Friends of the People there are still plenty of gentle old dears who desire nothing more than to dress up in knee britches and totter down to the Palace of Holyroodhouse for fish-paste sandwiches with the Queen or her representatives.

The Kirk's struggle to define its own role, which has a real impact on the rest of the Scottish political establishment, is also about rediscovering its own history. Will Storrar, a pro-Home Rule minister from Carluke in Lanarkshire and a church historian who wrote much of the 1989 report, has been proclaiming a hidden, or at any rate under-discussed, history of the Kirk stretching back to its late medieval origins. One of Storrar's heroes is John Major. Not the one with the grin and the glasses, but the earlier John Major (or Mair, in Scots), a brilliant theologian and historian who was born near North Berwick around 1469. His central importance is only now being rediscovered, and a 'Mair Institute for Christian Thought' has recently been founded in Midlothian. Major was, indeed, an extraordinary figure. Apart from writing a history of Britain, sceptically analysing the early Scottish national myths and arguing for some form of union with England, he was a great teacher and radical constitutional thinker. He taught at Cambridge and Paris as well as in Scotland and argued that the power of princes and popes was strictly limited. In the Church, ultimate power lay not in the hands of the Pope but with a consilium, or council of advisers, representing the people; in the secular state too tyrannical princes had no absolute power. Though he was hostile to Martin Luther, Major's pupils included both John Calvin, founder of Calvinism, and Ignatius Loyola, founder of the Jesuits. Both the Calvinists and the Jesuits would later be seen by upholders of royal absolutism as posing a serious and parallel threat: they argued strongly that tyrants could lawfully be deposed.

In Scottish terms, Major's arguments echoed the promise of the Declaration of Arbroath to depose King Robert the Bruce if he turned bad. His Scottish pupils included George Buchanan, the Reformation humanist and poet (a Gaelic-speaker who wrote in limpid Latin and argued in earthy Scots-English), and John Knox himself. Buchanan was the only lay Moderator (or chairman) in the Kirk's history. He was also the tutor of King James VI, the first king of England and Scotland, who once told a flattering female courtier, 'Ye may kiss his arse, Madam, but I ha'e skelped [thrashed] it.' Buchanan defended the rough treatment of James's mother, the Catholic Mary Queen of Scots (on the Major principle), and was a pillar of the Reformation, an intellectual source for the anti-absolutist principle that fed the English and Scottish civil wars.

Although there were Protestants active in Scotland from the 1520s, the Reformation proper began in the 1550s and Presbyterian Scotland finally triumphed only in the 1630s as a full-blown revolution that altered the way Scots thought about almost everything. It has been often, and rightly, said that the Scottish democratic tradition owes more to Knox than to Marx. The first phase of reformation was relatively moderate in Scotland, though Knox was an extremist (he has been described as 'a great public speaker of the Hitler sort' by the Glasgow writer Alasdair Gray, and Gray is probably right). In the Reformation days bishops were retained, monks were left in relative peace and the Calvinists seemed to follow prescriptions about education and moral seriousness not so dissimilar to those of the Catholic reformers – and it is worth remembering that even Knox was a Catholic cleric once.

Also, right from the beginning, the Reformation presented itself as a patriotic Scottish movement. But it was patriotically anti-French, not anti-English. And this was quite a change. Catholic France, which for a time had sent its soldiers to man Scottish castles and its administrators to rule in Edinburgh, was a central link in the continental alliance against the Reformation. Mary Queen of Scots, far from being the Scottish patriot of legend, had signed secret papers before her marriage to the Dauphin handing over

Scotland to the French if she died childless. John Knox, by contrast, had done time as a French galley slave and became closely associated with exiled English Protestants during his time in Switzerland. He probably favoured a full Union with England to create a 'Godly nation' that would lead the battle against continental popery. This novel pro-English bias was confirmed during the Civil War, when Scottish and English Calvinists fought side by side. Even after their falling out and the Cromwellian invasion of Scotland there were Scottish Presbyterians who saw their victory as intimately linked with the success of the Commonwealth. Although the English revolution did not usher in Presbyterianism in the south as the Scots had hoped and urged, the first parliamentary union occurred not, as is popularly supposed, in 1707 but under Oliver Cromwell. This first and, so far, last British republic was a brief and forced affair; even so, in the 1650s, thirty Scottish MPs were sent to Westminster, and Englishmen were appointed judges at the Court of Session in Edinburgh.

But, although it brought England and Scotland closer, the Reformation is important in Scotland's political history above all for its semi-democratic character. This owes something to the pre-Reformation doctrines of men like John Major and was evident well before the civil war. In 1596 Andrew Melville, the preacher whose *Second Book of Discipline* was a fundamental text for Scottish Presbyterianism, confronted King James VI at his hunting lodge and informed him that he was merely 'God's sillie vassal'. With the ghosts of Major and Calvin smiling above him Melville explained that there were two kingdoms in Scotland. One was the secular one, but the other was Christ's, 'and his kingdom the Kirk, whose subject King James the Sixth is, and of whose kingdom [he is] not a king, nor a lord, nor a head, but a member'. Despite having had his arse skelped by George Buchanan (or perhaps because of this), James was unreceptive and later went on to write with flaming passion about his divine right of kingship.

In another mouth, at another time, Melville's challenge might have been a purely theological one. In seventeenth-century Scotland it was direct and practical: his blueprint for the Scottish Kirk, which built on *The First Book of Discipline*, co-authored by John Knox himself, was startlingly democratic for the times and envisaged a

Church that was deeply intertwined with secular life. In every parish, village and burgh the Kirk would educate Scottish children in grammar, so that poor families would be literate and able to read the word of God. (They would read the Bible in King James's English version, however. The lack of a Scots Bible undermined the use of Scots as a prose form and contributed significantly to the cultural identity crisis of Scots in the twentieth century. In the 1970s a fine Scots New Testament was published and became widely available – about 350 years too late.)

Knox and Melville decreed that their Kirk would relieve the poor and establish pensions and bursaries for the wives and children of its ministers. The congregations would elect their own ministers. Melville then went further in calling for Church courts that would have authority over everyone in religious matters. The Scottish ministers and the parish elders (also elected), meeting together in the General Assembly, would have a 'different and distinct' authority from that of the state – in matters of conscience, a higher authority. This was not a mere matter of form of religious worship but a theocracy in the making, a vision of godly society not so very different from that of the Islamic leaders of present-day Iran. The monarchical state realized the threat and made war on the Presbyterian reformers and the Provisional Governments they set up. It was Charles I's prosecution of this battle for ultimate authority that led, indirectly, to the English Civil War. First time around, the Stuarts beat the reformers, but the Melville doctrine soon reasserted itself. Although the Kirk later developed a strong and influential Moderate party of faction, the radical Kirk suspicion of state authority has marked Scotland ever since.

During the Presbyterian wars, and then confirmed by the Restoration, the Kirk unleashed a savage religious revolution, prosecuted by militant cells in every part of the Lowlands. The heroic side of this revolution is symbolized by the persecution of the extreme Covenanters, such as the Cameronians of south-west Scotland, who worshipped outdoors and defied the state's right to interfere. Their story has been long remembered and politically potent. In 1970 Tam Dalyell, the Labour MP, was told when canvassing in the South Ayrshire by-election that brought Jim Sillars to the Commons that he should not visit homes in the south of the constituency.

Why? Because in the 1680s his ancestor, 'Bluidy Tam' Dalyell (a professional soldier who had been the Tsarist army commander at Minsk and is said to have imported the thumbscrew to Britain), led the repression of local Covenanters. South Ayrshire still had 'Covenanting villages', and anyone called Dalyell would be lethal to the Labour Party's cause, Tam was told. They are good grudge-bearers down in Ayrshire.

The dark side of the revolution in the 1600s was seen in the Kirk's repressive laws and wide-ranging, repulsive punishments. These included burning (for adultery or witchcraft) and mutilations, whippings, brandings and public humiliations for lesser offences. This black period in the Kirk's history has provided much of the ammunition for anti-clerical socialist attacks on it during the twentieth century. Tom Johnston, the Labour MP and Secretary of State in Churchill's wartime government, described Presbyterian witch-burning in a history of the Scottish working classes: 'For a century and a half every Burgh and Parish in Scotland seems to have offered to Heaven its regular incense of burning flesh – human flesh, the flesh of the mothers and grandmothers of the labouring poor.' Knox (though personally a more intriguing and complex man than his popular image suggests) was perhaps Khomeini's predecessor in more than dark clothing and beard. Like Islam, militant Presbyterianism was embraced by millions of ordinary people despite, or sometimes because of, its harshness. In England the rigours of the Puritan revolution were ameliorated and then replaced by the Restoration and the relatively lax, pro-establishment Anglican Church. In Scotland the Puritans stayed in charge and won the loyalty of the great bulk of the Lowland people. The value of this inheritance has divided Scots ever since.

The religious revolution did not last in full spate – nothing does – and slowed to a broader, shallower stream. Politically a loyalist Hanoverian current appeared in the Kirk and became dominant after the Church was guaranteed its position in Scottish life by the Treaty of Union in 1707. For as long as the Church leaders could regard themselves as a central part of the Scottish establishment their hostility to Westminster rule remained muted. But the Treaty of Union was understood rather differently by Westminster and by the Kirk, by which it was argued that the Scottish system involved two 'houses' of parliament. One, the conventional parliament, was merged with Westminster. But the other was the Kirk's General Assembly, with its special powers over the nation's spiritual and educational life, and it was unaffected. Like the Scottish universities and the law and the Convention of Royal Burghs, it carried on. Loyal addresses were read to monarchs from time to time, but the Kirk was a separate and alternative state where the English tradition of complete parliamentary sovereignty lost its power and stumbled.

That at least, was how Kirk radicals saw the matter. London rarely did. In 1712, with a Tory majority in the Commons, Westminster passed a Patronage Act that gave back to Scottish landlords the right to impose their choice of ministers in Scottish kirks against the wishes of the local congregations. This measure, intended as a defence of property rights, had the potential to cause a serious constitutional rupture. Why? Because, as Lord Cooper pointed out in 1953, the Scottish constitutional tradition rejected absolute sovereignty (originally royal sovereignty but, by implication, parliamentary sovereignty too). It did not recognize the power of the Westminster Parliament to interfere with the internal workings of the Scottish Kirk. Yet in English constitutional doctrine, as it was evolving from the Glorious Revolution of 1688 towards the now-discredited Victorian theorists like Dicey, Parliament's power was absolute; it could interfere where it damn well liked. The Scots, it seemed, had surrendered their developing doctrine of shared, distributed sovereignty and traded it in for a new kind of absolutism.

This problem, which dives like a hidden crack to the heart of the Union itself, was worried away at for another century or so. Every so often small groups in the Kirk, refusing to recognize the rights of English politicians or the landlords to interfere with their presbyteries' power, would break away. Moderates were lampooned by radicals (including John Witherspoon, who later became a leading intellectual of the American revolution at Princeton and signed the Declaration of Independence). Moderates lampooned back. Schism, indeed, became a way of life. There were splits between 'lifters' and 'anti-lifters' about whether or not the minister should raise up the bread when consecrating it. There were splits about the oaths for burgesses. There was even a split, in an already split-off Kirk, about whether hare soup, used to nourish some congregations at worship, was spiritually unclean or merely tasty. It may seem ludicrous now (and was then), but in criticizing the Scottish love of Kirk schism and dispute it is worth remembering that the old Kirk was not merely a place where you went on the Sabbath: it was the centre of all debate; it ruled the education system to university level; it provided the poor relief; it was the moral law. In the absence of parliamentary debate the Kirk's arguments were a form of national politics.

The constitutional dispute finally blew open in the 1840s, when the most dramatic nineteenth-century event in the Kirk's history occurred – the Disruption. The Kirk's 'Claim of Right' of 1842 blandly stated that any parliamentary Acts affecting the 'government, discipline, rights and privileges' of the Church with which it did not agree were contrary to the Treaty of Union and 'void and null and of no legal force or effect'. In 1843 the Evangelicals broke away from the established Kirk, surrendering their livings and manses in protest at landowners' rights to impose ministers on their congregations. Since landowners' rights had been enforced by Westminster and sanctioned by the Court of Session, this was a rebellion against Parliament and the courts too.

The march of the top-hatted clerical rebels out of the General Assembly was welcomed by cheering crowds in Edinburgh. Across Scotland ministers were faced with an agonizing choice, and congregations and communities were split. The exiles from the Kirk set up the Free Church, dominated by the evangelical Thomas Chalmers, who believed in the parish as the basic social unit where the poor would be helped and the unbelievers converted. Faced with the intimidation and hostility of landlords, the Free Kirkers struggled to raise the funds to build new churches. In many places they spent their first winter worshipping outdoors in the tradition of the old Covenanters. Their refusal to acknowledge state power was widely seen in Victorian Scotland as both a triumph of conscience over patronage and an admirable act of democratic defiance against London and legal tyranny. It was a political act, commemorated in paintings, prints and literature. The Free Kirkers were not in any sense politically leftish – indeed many were strongly Tory, and Chalmers was a fervent supporter of the basic rights of the propertied classes. But they were constitutionally radical: a Presbyterian philosopher, James Ferrier, argued that the Free Kirkers should not have walked out; the Kirk itself as the second house of the Scottish parliament should have defied Westminster directly.

In 1850 one of the Free Church leaders, James Begg, called for a Scottish national revival. Although he started by deploring the rise of drunkenness and Sabbath-breaking and calling for a strengthening of Scottish representation at Westminster, he went on later to attack the Act of Union itself and toyed with the idea of recalling a Scottish parliament. He was joined by other Free Kirkers, some Tory romantics, antiquarians and radicals in the National Association for the Vindication of Scottish Rights of 1853–4, which has been described as the first modern nationalist movement. Despite the holding of big meetings and the circulation of angry pamphlets, however, it quickly lost impetus – the first of many false dawns for post-Union Scottish nationalism.

Even in the old Kirk, meanwhile, hostility to the influence of the Tory landlords was sometimes intense and caused the Conservatives problems throughout the rest of the century and beyond. One account, published in 1912, has stories of congregations pelting the landowner's pet ministers with dung. One of those unfortunate clerics, it was reported, had asked the head of a family the common theological question 'Who made Paul a preacher?' 'But the reply came, snell and sharp, "It wasna the Duke of Queensberry at ony rate."' Hostility to outside power was, therefore, strong throughout both main branches of the Scottish Kirk. And the radicals eventually won. In 1921 a Westminster government with other things on its mind passed the Church of Scotland Act, paving the way for much of the Free Kirk to rejoin the old Kirk. The Act recognized the Kirk's insurgent 'Claim of Right' to complete sovereignty in its own sphere, 'subject to no civil authority'. Westminster punctured its own most sacred doctrine of parliamentary sovereignty. To paraphrase the opening words of the 'Asterix' comic books: today the House of Commons rules all Britain. All? Not quite all: a small village, called the Church of Scotland, holds out (led, of course, by that fiery Celtic warrior Crucifix).

This constitutional independence did not mean the Kirk was progressive in any other sense: far from it. Throughout the inter-war period it was fiercely anti-Catholic and pro-establishment. Under the leadership of John White, a strong Tory Unionist, it allied itself with Conservative leaders and frequently petitioned them to deport Scotland's Irish population. During the Second World War, however, a progressive minister, John Baillie, challenged the White world view and eventually, in 1943, became Moderator himself. Baillie was influenced by the American New Deal theologian Reinhold Niebuhr (who also influenced many post-war socialists, including the Labour politician Denis Healey) and took the Kirk towards the post-war Welfare State consensus. White bitterly opposed all this semi-socialism. On the afternoon he finally lost to Baillie he went home in despair and promptly died of a broken heart – or, more prosaically, a heart attack. From 1948 the Kirk's enthusiasm for social justice was accompanied by backing for Scottish Home Rule, and Presbyterian churchmen were prominent in the quasi-Nationalist Covenant movement of the early 1950s (just as Free Kirkers had been prominent in the Society for the Vindication of Scottish Rights a century earlier). Its Church and Nation Committee gave detailed pro-devolution evidence to the Royal Commission on the constitution in the 1970s, and it was only prevented from telling all its ministers to read a pro-devolution statement to their congregations during the referendum of 1979 by a late fight-back on the part of Unionist clergy. In the 1980s and 1990s clergymen have been prominent in both the Campaign for a Scottish Assembly and the Scottish Constitutional Convention.

So the Kirk has an historical, if not necessarily a theological, basis for its Home Rule faith. It is, in a way, one arm of a broader intellectual movement in Scotland that has produced new historical perspectives about the nation's history and new, sceptical analyses of its various Victorian and provincial cults. The Kirk's constitutional thinking culminated in a 1989 report that stated:

It is not possible to resolve the question of the democratic control of Scottish affairs and the setting up of a Scottish Assembly apart from a fundamental shift in our constitutional thinking away from the notion of the unlimited or absolute sovereignty of the British Parliament, towards the historic Scottish and Reformed (e.g. Presbyterian) constitutional principle of limited or relative sovereignty.

This radicalism was welcomed by pro-Home Rulers: Duncan Forrester, Professor of Ethics and Practical Theology at New College,

Edinburgh, called it a 'welcome return to the earlier Calvinist and Scottish tradition'.

But it was equally strongly opposed by Unionist clergymen, some of whom feared that Scottish independence, if it happened, would lead inevitably to a secular state where the Kirk would have no special place. Given the fall in Kirk attendance and the rising influence of the Catholic Church, which started reviving in Scotland because of Irish immigration, they may be right. Independence (unlike Home Rule) would certainly lead to difficult questions for Scottish churchmen. One senior clergyman, Andrew Herron, who was prominent on the anti-devolution side during the 1979 referendum, has poured public scorn on the idea that his Church is constitutionally on the side of the Scottish Home Rulers: 'I am bitterly opposed to the Kirk's taking sides in the debate on Scottish Nationalism, and that simply because I cannot believe any one side in that controversy reflects the true Christian point of view, the other being less than Christian.'

The Kirk, of course, has had an impact on Scottish thought and language that goes wider than its own political or constitutional struggle. It has given Scots an important part of their own self-image. For generations Scottish radicals have compared themselves with the early Covenanters, who were seen as pure in spirit and courageously unconcerned about tyrannical government. Observers took them at their word: one found that the Clydeside shipyard workers between the wars had 'added to their Socialism not the self-complacent innovations of Lenin but the not less dangerous fire of fierce democratic connections ingrained in their nation and passed down unaltered from generations of bleak Covenanting ancestors'. But even among Leninists it is not hard to hear the echo of the grim fathers of the Kirk. The Clydeside revolutionary John Maclean told a court in 1918: 'No government is going to take from me my right to speak, my right to protest against wrong, my right to do everything that is for the benefit of mankind. I am not here, then, as the accused; I am here as the accuser of capitalism dripping with blood from head to foot.' The self-certainty, even the imagery, are unmistakable: here is the twentieth-century Cameronian, facing down the royal and Popish oppressors (Knoxism–Leninism – it is a fearful thought!).

At the other end of the political spectrum the plainness and hard-working ethic of the Scottish business community has been nourished by the Kirk. From the Victorian self-improvers, with Carlyle in one pocket and a Bible in the other, to the overblown contemporary reputation of Scottish bankers, the Kirk's influence runs deep. In its dour, plain (and sometimes extremist) way, it has seemed to answer something cold and dark-coloured in the northern soul. Writing about Scotland in 1911, and with a rural Scots rhythm to his prose, the great novelist Lewis Grassic Gibbon described the plainness of the kirk of Kinraddie, his fictitious village in the rural Mearns on Scotland's east coast. It is a plainness that goes to the heart of the meaning of the Kirk: 'But the windows of the main hall, though they were coloured, they had never a picture in them and there were no pictures in there at all, who wanted them? Only coarse creatures like Catholics wanted a kirk to look like a grocer's calendar. So it was decent and bare-like . . .'

'Decent and bare-like'. The nationalist historian P. H. Scott wrote in the 1970s of the 'Romano-Scottish ideal', which was 'severitas . . . being stern with oneself', and it is not hard to see the connection with the Kirk. The oft-mocked dourness and caution of the Scots accountant, the abstract fire of the classic Scots lawyer and even the Scottish penchant for deflating, sardonic humour can all be traced to the ministers. Above all, though, the Kirk's enthusiasm for learning and theological argument fuelled the more general Scottish delight in education, speculation and disputation. The Scottish universities have always attracted a higher proportion of the population, and a wider class spread, than the old English universities. Their 'democratic intellect', challenged by anglicization in this century, has been used repeatedly as an example of the Scottish character at its best. Scottish universities had flourished before the Reformation. Yet the reformers − including grim young Andrew Melville − reformed them too, and the connection between them and the Kirk is undeniable. It was the Kirk that fought against the anglicization of the old universities in Victorian times. And no one who has sat through an hour-long sermon in a Wee Free kirk (where they still do these things properly) on the precise nuances and meanings, word by word, of a biblical passage could fail to understand the analytical tradition that is being passed on.

43

So Nationalists and Home Rulers can use, and have used, the history of the Scottish Kirk as proof positive of a national tradition that is distinct from England's and is politically turbulent. Not everyone agrees: Michael Fry argues that the Disruption meant the breaking up of a great Scottish institution and the destruction of a fundamental element of Scottish identity. Certainly, the Kirk lost its administration of poor relief shortly after the great split and its schools in 1872. Yet its influence has been extraordinary; it kept the loyalty of Scots for far longer than the frilly, compromising Church of England managed to appeal to its constituency. But, as with everything in Scotland, the Kirk has its enemies. A rich and powerful anti-clerical tradition in Scotland, which includes Robert Burns, Robert Louis Stevenson and a host of modern Scots like Tom Nairn, has painted the Presbyterian tradition as a perverse example of all that is wrong with Scotland. At a lower level the caricatures are so well known that they hardly need repeating – the deep gloom of an old-style Scottish Sabbath, the hypocrisy and tyranny of some ministers, the sour and dogmatic anti-Catholicism that was so rife in the Kirk until recent times. Burns, quite consciously, returned to a celebratory peasant culture of drink and song and frankness that preceded the Reformation, which the Kirk tried to kill and which survived its repression. The Kirk represented only one side of the Scots character. Those who proclaim the brave history and contemporary radicalism of their Kirk must remember that for many fellow-countrymen the whole business has been an oppressive, gloomy nightmare.

The Myth-bound Nation

The independence wars; the Union; the Highlands; the Kirk. These are four strong threads in Scottish history that affect the way Scots think about themselves today. But before moving on to describe the political battle for Scotland, it is worth remembering that history intrudes into the debate in plenty of other areas too, particularly where the Scottish public world has influenced the nation in its stateless centuries. Scots law, Scottish administration and the Scottish universities are parts of a sort of shadow state, headquartered in Edinburgh. All have their own histories, and all have had some influence on Scottish middle-class opinion, which seems to have become steadily more nationalist – with a small 'n' – since the 1960s.

Scots law is a European oddity because it incorporates elements of European legal tradition, based on Roman law, and of Anglo-Saxon law. The continental parts of Scots law appeared in medieval times and then in the centuries between Bannockburn and the Union. The English parts have mostly come since then. Lord Cooper called it 'the mirror of Scotland's history and traditions and a typical product of the national character . . . just as truly a part of our national inheritance as our language or literature or religion'. Unlike England's, Scotland's law was synthesized in a series of books by three great thinkers – Viscount Stair, John Erskine and George Bell. The first and the greatest of these was Stair, and Cooper described his good book, the *Institutions* of 1681, as 'an original amalgam of Roman Law, Feudal Law and native customary law, systemized by resort to the law of nature and the Bible, and illuminated by many flashes of ideal metaphysic. To this work and its author every Scots lawyer has since paid a tribute of almost superstitious reverence.'

In post-Union Scotland these superstitious natives have wielded great power. For a century and a half administration of government was partly carried out by Scottish lawyers working through undemocratic and nepotistic boards. From a board of manufactures, set up twenty years after the Union, others developed, covering the Poor Law, the fisheries, public health and education. The Lord Advocate was the minister who dealt with Scottish administration (often agreed by Scots in private deals and then carried swiftly through a bored and ignorant House of Commons). To rise in Scottish administration or politics in Victorian times you almost had to be a lawyer first. Some would ask how much has changed. In the absence of much else to challenge them, the Scots judges (including, for civil cases, those grandly titled Senators of the College of Justice) and the lawyers became a central part of the dignity and self-importance of the Scottish capital. The nineteenth-century system was finally challenged by the creation of the Scottish Office in the 1880s and reformed away by a Conservative government in the 1930s. Scottish Labour MPs actually protested, on the grounds that the special power of the boards of Scots lawyers was an integral part of the ancient nation. The pride of Scots law has certainly outlasted the 160 years or so of government-by-board. Today anyone who stands on the Mound in Edinburgh will notice the turkey-cock gait and rich ruby jowls of certain gentlemen progressing up and down from that temple of the Edinburgh establishment, the New Club, to the courts in Parliament House and can see fleshy proof of the persistent and impenetrable self-esteem of Scots law and its judges.

Protected by the Treaty of Union, Scots law has nevertheless been eroded by the stream of all-British legislation from an essentially alien legal culture – Scottish laws have often been tacked-on bits of British Bills, drafted according to English law. This has produced a form of 'legal nationalism' in Scotland that is not necessarily politically nationalist – indeed, is often hostile to political nationalism and was strikingly so during the 1970s. Lord Cooper was clearly a legal nationalist. But legal nationalism is not a simple story; the current Attorney General for Scotland, Alan Rodger, has shown that the pressure for a single British system of commercial law came strongly from Scottish businessmen and lawyers in their Victorian heyday. Still, their successors object today that they often have to treat with the European institutions, whose legal systems are nearer to Scots law than English common law, via English junior ministers. And in Brussels and The Hague the continental lawyers and politicians find it hard to grasp the idea that Britain has separate legal systems; not unnaturally, they tend to focus on the English one, forgetting the Scots system. In 1992 Lord Hope, the Lord President (Scotland's senior judge), criticized the Union Treaty of 1707 at a private dinner of lawyers and described the Scottish legal system as the one 'small spark of light' to survive the Union. He was immediately criticized in turn for making a quasi-Nationalist speech and went to ground (or, more probably, to the New Club).

The lawyers' administrative power has long since passed to the civil servants of the Scottish Office, which, since 1885, has been steadily expanding in Edinburgh and now oversees most of the government's Scottish business. Its 12,000-strong bureaucracy is bigger than that of the European Commission at Brussels. Intended by generations of Conservative and Labour politicians to provide a sop to nationalist feeling, it has probably only fed the desire for a parliament to oversee its workings. This is the foot-shuffling wallflower administration that seems to be for ever waiting for its legislative partner. Labour's devolution proposals in the 1970s set its heart racing; the consummation was devoutly wished but never occurred. Today the bureaucratic class that works in the Scottish Office is a big but mostly silent player in Scottish life; the occasional glimpses of the real views behind the twitching curtain of Civil Service impartiality suggest that many of them are more nationalist than their masters. It was a former civil servant, Jim Ross, who wrote much of the 1988 'Claim of Right' after he had retired from a lifetime of service that had included drafting the Labour devolution legislation of the late 1970s.

Scottish education remains distinctive, though the reforms of the Conservatives have made school education somewhat less so, and the abolition of 'Highers', combined with pressure for a single British curriculum, could one day have an even more dramatic effect. Every educated English person knows that Scottish education is immeasurably superior, and every educated English person, according to the latest Europe-wide research, is probably wrong. This is one area where Scottish conceit has not served the nation well. Among the groups of middle-class dissidents who moved towards Home Rule in the 1980s teachers in the Scottish union, the Educational Institute of Scotland (EIS), and university lecturers were prominent. But politically the case of the universities has been more prominent still.

In Victorian times the Scottish universities had their unique system of education slowly watered down under the pressure of London's desire for uniform standards. The description of this process in George Elder Davie's *The Democratic Intellect* (1960) was a powerful early impetus for the revision of other branches of Scottish history and culture. Davie's argument was that the grounding in basic philosophy given to 15- and 16-year-olds when they arrived at Scottish universities, plus the disputatious, give-and-take teaching style of the best professors, produced a Scottish graduate mind that was a million miles removed from the classically educated English mind of the period. Not necessarily better: just different. What gave Davie's case particular poignancy was that it started to circulate just at the time the 1963 Robbins Report was killing off the separate funding and organization of the Scottish universities. Michael Fry

47

points out that the final bout of the Englishing of the universities came at just the time when the country as a whole was becoming more self-consciously Scottish. Davie's argument that the old Scottish universities had produced a different kind of mental landscape after centuries of development (and that this different landscape was valuable and worth preserving) is strikingly similar to Lord Cooper's argument about Scots law. Both are crucial to the idea of nationalism. Variety is not the spice of life but life itself.

The process described by Davie continued, and in recent years the spate of English students and academics coming to the ancient Scottish universities (notably Edinburgh and St Andrews) has produced a hostile reaction. At times this has led to accusations of racism. Yet at one point the school with the highest number of students at Edinburgh University was Eton College. The argument is less an anti-English one than a debate about the fast eroding distinctiveness of Scottish education and other Scottish institutions. It is no surprise to find that most models of a Scottish parliament would give it responsibility for university education north of the border.

The coded politics of Scots law, the hidden politics of the Scottish Office and the university controversies are, of course, limited mostly to the relevant professional groups and small middle-class coteries around them. Distinctively Scottish businesses, such as the big life-assurance associations or the investment-trust movement, tend to be fiercely Unionist and regard constitutional change as bad for confidence and bad for profits. As we shall see later, contemporary nationalism is not a simple affair. The middle-class varieties are important, but working-class nationalism in the housing estates seems to have growing influence – and that probably terrifies a lot of middle-class nationalists.

Meanwhile other bodies also act as occasional ventriloquists for Scotland's nationhood. The Convention of Scottish Local Authorities (COSLA), set up in 1975 as an amalgam of local council associations, including the medieval Convention of Royal Burghs, is treated with a respect that its sister bodies in England never seem to summon up. In industrial Scotland the Scottish Trades Union Congress (STUC), with its different system of organization from the TUC's in England and its more radical tradition, has enjoyed (and sometimes used) a strong influence. Occasionally, the Scottish Development Agency (now Scottish Enterprise) and the manager-and-union body, the Scottish Council for Development and Industry, have been listened to as if they spoke for Scotland. Westminster bodies, by contrast, have never been taken terribly seriously – even on the relatively rare occasions when they have met in Edinburgh, as in 1942 and the 1980s. Before the 1992 election the Labour and Liberal Democrat-dominated pro-Home Rule body, the Scottish Constitutional Convention, which uses the imagery and language of the Kirk disruption and the Covenant, achieved high, if transient, status.

This chapter has been about Scottish history and its tenacious myths. Scotland is bound by them and littered with them – strong, wiry myths, often contradictory, complex and fankled. Some even say that the last remaining element of real Scottishness is an obsessive interest in Scottish history, a grisly intellectual autopsy of dead dreams and stinking ancestors. Maybe. But Scottishness continues to be defined as much by culture and history as by anything else, and historical truth matters. It is certainly preferable to historical lies. Who are the Scots? Are they, as some English critics believe, a race of northern starvelings stuck in the cold, stagnant pools of their past failures, those bloody old boglands, fuming with ancient humiliations? Are they, as the Nationalists believe, a unique and ancient people with a unique democratic tradition to offer the new Europe? Or are they, less dramatically, just another small European people in an interdependent world who need to recover a measure of statehood in order to stop looking over their shoulders?

2

New Dreams in an Old Land:
the Origins of Modern Nationalism

Though Scotland has not been a nation for some time, it has possessed a distinctly marked style of life; and that is now falling to pieces, for there is no visible and effective power to hold it together . . . What stands in the way of Home Rule for Scotland is simply apathy, the apathy of England but chiefly the apathy of Scotland. Consequently the Scottish Nationalist movement at its present stage is mainly a movement to rouse Scotland from its indifference . . .

Edwin Muir, *Scottish Journey*, 1935

The real question for Scotsmen is not whether an independent Scotland would be viable, but whether it would be bearable . . . it is not the wild men of Scottish Nationalism who are to be feared: it is the dull men of unchanging Scotland.

Arthur Marwick, in *Memoirs of a Modern Scotland*, 1969

Home Rule and the Revolution:
Labour Fails to Deliver

Scotland became pregnant with modern nationalism soon after the 1914–18 war. The country had lost about one in ten of all its men aged between 16 and 50, 20 per cent of the total British losses and more, proportionately, than any other country in the Empire. At home there had been serious labour unrest on Clydeside, where militant workers were imprisoned after organizing a series of war-time engineering and rent strikes. The shock of the war, followed by the shock of the economic depression that soon followed it, changed utterly the political mood in Scotland. That war gave birth to many new countries in Europe; despite the burnishing that victory gave to the idea of Britishness, some Scots, demobilized from the kilted regiments or from the munitions factories, began to feel that their nationhood should be expressed too.

Before the war nationalist feeling had largely been subsumed in the Home Rule movement. Although Home Rule was a principle of the Scottish Liberals, it had arrived in Scottish politics in a big way only in the 1880s, on the coat-tails of Gladstone's policy of Home Rule for Ireland. Scottish Home Rule was part of a wider strategy for dealing with the Irish question by devolving power to all the nations of Britain – Gladstone had been unimpressed by the idea until he was led towards it by the Irish crisis. Even so, it seemed likely that the Liberals would sooner or later legislate for a parliament in Edinburgh. The Scottish Liberal Association, under radical influence, voted for Home Rule in 1888. From then until the First World War a steady stream of Home Rule Bills was presented to parliament. As we have seen, the Liberal Prime Minister Asquith envisaged Home Rule for Scotland as part of a wider federal reform of the United Kingdom. By the 1910s Home Rule seemed merely a question of time, and in August 1914 a Scottish Home Rule Bill passed its second reading in the Commons before being abandoned because of the war.

A lesser, political, war had produced another strand of Home Rulery. The land wars in the Highlands, pitting angry, land-hungry crofters against landlords (and, in Skye, soldiers), found political expression through the Highland Land League and the Crofters' Party. Its more radical proto-nationalism was based on common Scottish and Irish Gaelic interests and tactics. Although this too was a phenomenon of the 1880s, anti-landlordism resurfaced again after the First World War, when demobilized Highland soldiers came home looking for a livelihood on the land. Sympathy with the crofters was traditional and widespread among urban agitators and helped to ensure that Home Rulery became part of the bag and baggage of Scottish lowland radicalism. By the early years of Labourism a mix of the old Liberal heritage and Highland radicalism had seen to it that the Independent Labour Party was staunchly in favour of a Scottish parliament. In 1915 Ramsay MacDonald argued that the weakness of the Labour movement in Scotland before the war had been partly because it 'had not been Scotch enough'. Tom Johnston, the Labour politician and journalist who later became Secretary of State for Scotland under Churchill, even published a blacklist of anti-Home Rule MPs in his famous Labour paper 'Forward'.

Until the Liberal collapse most Unionist critics regarded Scottish Home Rule very largely as a defensive measure designed to maintain Liberalism's powerful Scottish base – the same charge made against Labour Home Rulers a century later. Other Unionists were less sure, and some (like John Buchan, the Tory novelist) favoured Scottish Home Rule inside the Empire, part of the creation of a worldwide imperial block surrounded by tariff walls. Its effect was not so different from the current fashion for 'independence in Europe'; like the European Community, the Empire would provide a bigger, warmer grouping, protecting Scotland from the chilliness of total separation. But, as the Empire collapsed, so did the possibility of that kind of Home Rule. The end of Empire had a contradictory impact on Scottish national sentiment. On the one hand, the emergence of 'Britain' had coincided with the creation of the Empire, and when that common project started disintegrating some Scots began to feel that the British side of their dual nationality was diminished. That helped to foster Scottish nationalism. Yet, at the same time, the end of Empire meant the end of the possibility of Home Rule inside it – which may have made Scottish nationalism seem less attractive to the very same people who were feeling more Scottish than ever before.

Unlike Ireland, Scotland had remained closely integrated with the British political system. From 1885 onwards the country's rickety administration in Edinburgh was rationalized with the appointment of a Scottish Secretary of State. Calls for political devolution to match this growing state power had grown steadily louder but did not seem to threaten Scotland's status as part of Britain. This was, after all, the British agenda of Liberalism. Through most of the Victorian period Scotland had provided the Liberals with a loyal regiment of silent, dough-faced MPs, rather like the unimpressive Scottish Labour contingent of the 1950s. By the early 1900s Scottish constituencies seemed cosy havens for ambitious English Liberal politicians such as the Prime Minister, Asquith, and (rather later) the young Winston Churchill. At the beginning of the century, when the Liberal MP Augustine Birrell was standing on top of a hill overlooking Fife and East Lothian, he was able to exclaim cheerily (to Asquith among others): 'What a grateful thought that there is not an acre in this vast and varied landscape which is not represented at Westminster by a London barrister!' By 1906 the vast bulk of Scottish MPs lived in England; many were English. But a Liberal split between Gladstone's supporters and the Unionists, and then the party's dramatic decline, marked the end of the English domination of Scottish electoral politics. Among the scores of Scottish Liberal casualties between the wars were Churchill and Asquith.

The strange death of Liberal Scotland is a huge and complicated subject in its own right – and beyond the scope of this book. But because it was paralleled by the emergence of Scottish socialism it did not seem at first to remove Home Rule from the political agenda. Labour's newly formed Scottish Council carried its first Home Rule motion in 1916. At the end of the war there were Labour calls for independent Scottish representation at the Versailles peace conference, and Labour's 1918 Scottish manifesto made an Edinburgh parliament one of the party's priorities (along with the nationalization of land and prohibition of alcohol – like Home Rule, both pre-war radical Liberal demands too). Nor was this simply routine waffle: a year later Labour's Scottish executive threatened mass strikes if Westminster ignored Home Rule. Initially, though, the issue was derailed by the continuing Irish crisis. In 1919 a Speaker's Conference at Westminster did some preliminary work on the creation of national assemblies for Scotland, Ireland, England and Wales. It recommended a Scottish parliament the following year, but there was little interest at Westminster, and, not surprisingly, the 1920 Government of Ireland Act dominated the constitutional debate.

The Irish issue influenced Scottish politics in another way: after it was resolved it allowed the huge reservoir of Catholic Irish votes in Scotland to flow from Irish nationalist politics into the Labour movement. John Wheatley, the brilliant Catholic socialist whose later Housing Act was one of Labour's few inter-war triumphs, was the man who did more than any other to propagandize for Labour – and was abused by the priests and mobbed by irate Catholic workers for his pains. The loyalty of the Catholic vote came to matter a lot to Labour: the Scottish electorate tripled as a result of the 1918 Reform Act, and Catholic voters were concentrated in constituencies particularly affected by the wider franchise. They were often the seats where Labour first broke through. In 1918

Labour's vote was ten times bigger than it had been in 1910, and in 1922 Labour boosted its Scottish representation from seven MPs to twenty-nine.

The reasons for the advance of Labour, and for its attitude to Home Rule, were economic as well as straightforwardly political. Before the First World War Scotland had been no paradise. But it had been industrially vibrant. On some measures it was the richest nation in the world, and its industrialists and middle classes were self-confident. In 1913 the Clyde had launched more new shipping than the total output of either Germany or America – about a fifth of the world's total emerged from that one estuary. In textiles, steel, iron and coal Scotland had been a big and expanding international producer. Scottish lowland agriculture, based on the big 'ferm touns', was advanced. In the post-war boom of 1919–20 Scottish industrial self-confidence seemed to have recovered, and few would have suggested that the country could not stand on its own feet. Many socialists and Liberals thought that the creation of a powerful Scottish parliament to harness the powerful Scottish economy would be essential in order to clear slums and raise wages: Home Rule was a sign of economic confidence, not pessimism.

During the war Scottish socialists had been gripped more strongly by social questions than by constitutional ones. The 'dilution' of labour in munitions factories – lower-paid workers doing skilled workers' jobs, threatening their economic position – and racketeering by private landlords in the Glasgow slums (some of the most stinking, leprous housing to have existed in any modern country) provided good recruiting issues. Lloyd George had been worried enough to come to Glasgow to calm the workers in 1915: he received such a vulgar and derisive response to his patriotic pieties that a sanitized account of the meeting had to be handed out to the newspapers. Tom Johnston's socialist paper *Forward* got the real story, though, and printed it, rude heckles included. Offended, Lloyd George had the paper closed down and seized, which caused such ridicule in Scotland that he was forced to summon Johnston to London and apologize.

But the wartime industrial troubles were only a tremor compared with the agitation and industrial decline that came later. When the 1919–20 post-war boom ended Scotland's aged heavy industry stumbled and crashed. The inventiveness that had produced the steam turbine and new shipbuilding techniques seemed to have gone; management was complacent; there was a glut of shipping. For the first time in many people's memories Scottish workers started to be worse paid than their English counterparts. Their forward march to greater wealth was halted. The newly enfranchised voters demanded action over the disease, malnutrition, child deaths and alcoholic violence that were endemic in the closes and tenements of Scotland's cities. For anyone with eyes to see the condition of the poor was the most glaring problem facing the country.

The 1920s and the 1930s were decades of sudden, alarming decay. After 1919–20 Scotland went into faster, deeper industrial decline than did England. In the later 1930s it recovered more slowly than England. There is a wealth of grim statistics to demonstrate this. The tonnage of ships launched on the Clyde fell catastrophically, and by 1933 nearly seven out of ten of the insured workers in the shipbuilding and repair yards were on the dole. Steel production was nearly halved as a proportion of the total UK output. The coal industry contracted by a third, and the countryside started to empty as farm prices plummeted. This decline weakened the Scottish economy so that it was particularly badly hit by the international slump of 1929. Not surprisingly, many Scots left. Between 1921 and 1931 there was a net loss to Scotland from emigration of eighty in every 1,000 people. That compared with five in every 1,000 in England. Most countries would make up the difference with a rising birthrate, but Scotland's total population actually declined during the 1920s for the first time since records began in 1801. Net emigration from Scotland continued until the late 1980s.

Those who stayed faced longer bouts of unemployment and lower wages when they worked. Between 1931 and 1936 unemployment among insured workers was never less than 23 per cent, and, the Commons was told later, 'It was always from five to seven in every 100 workers worse than in England and Wales.' The new motor and light-engineering industries that sprang up across the Midlands and around fast-spreading London were not matched in Scotland. In the five years from 1932 3,217 new factories were built in the United Kingdom, but only 127 of them were in Scotland, and, since 133 closed in the same period, Scotland actually suffered a net loss. For those in work, average wages were also lower than in England – in 1933, 14 per cent below the English and Welsh average. Economic collapse, combined with a growing conviction that the only escape was via central planning directed by a more intervention-ist Labour government, undercut the self-confidence of Home Rulers in the Labour Party and is the central explanation of why they lost interest in the issue as the decade went on. Tom Johnston, whose blacklist of anti-Home Rulers has already been mentioned, was able to write later: 'What purport would there be in getting a Scots parliament in Edinburgh if it has to administer an emigration system, a glorified Poor Law and a graveyard?' As in the 1970s, Scottish self-determination was boosted by economic strength and undermined by economic decline.

The cold statistics explain not simply the behaviour of the Labour radicals but also the seeping away of confidence among middle-class Scots who had become used to seeing their country as a dynamo of the Empire. Their mood of lassitude was well conveyed by Edwin Muir, the poet, when he toured Scotland in 1935:

They are not English, and they are ceasing to be Scottish for lack of encouragement. They live in the sort of vacuum which, one imagines, exists in the provincial towns of Austrian Italy, or of German Poland: in places that have lost their old life and have not yet found a new one. A certain meaninglessness and despondency hangs round such places; they are out of things; they do not know the reason for their existence; and people emigrate from them readily, without knowing why.

It was against that sense of despair that the Nationalists and the Scottish Renaissance writers reacted.

Turning back from the economics to the new politics of national-ism that emerged in the 1920s and 1930s, we must return, briefly, to the last of the old-style Home Rulers. Robert Bontine Cunning-hame Graham often seemed to have galloped out of a particularly lurid Victorian boy's story book. Described by the poet MacDiarmid as 'incredibly romantic', he was an impoverished aristocrat, political rebel and man of letters who claimed descent from early Scottish kings. A radical Liberal and then a founder of the Scottish Labour Party with Keir Hardie in 1888, he had been arrested at a riot in Trafalgar Square during a dockers' strike, had offended and amused the House of Commons and had written some fine short stories. Some of these were set in the pampas of Argentina, where he had lived as a gaucho and was known as Don Roberto. He went on to become the first president of the Scottish National Party. In 1918 Cunninghame Graham took a leading role in the re-establishment of the Scottish Home Rule Association (SHRA). In its first incarnation this had appeared in 1886 and was supported by Gladstonian Liberals and early socialist trade unionists. One of its leaders had been the future Labour Prime Minister Ramsay MacDonald, who wrote to Keir Hardie when he was fighting the 1888 Mid-Lanark by-election: 'Let the consequences be what they may, do not withdraw. The cause of Labour and of Scottish Nationality will suffer much thereby. Your defeat will awaken Scotland, and your victory will reconstruct Scottish Liberalism. All success be yours, and the National cause you champion.' MacDonald's letter, apart from demonstrating that the emotional, windy style he was later ridiculed for started early, shows how intertwined Labour, Liberalism and Scottish Home Rule had been before the war.

In 1918 the reformed association promised to champion 'the Scottish demand for Scottish self-government in respect of Scottish affairs'. Although the SHRA had more than 300 organizations affiliated to it, not all of them took it terribly seriously, and it was never a mass movement; at its peak in 1927 it had only 3,100 individual members. That did not mean that Home Rule itself was not taken seriously, just that for many Scots the Labour and Liberal parties still seemed to be perfectly adequate vehicles for it.

Meanwhile Scotland seemed to some people to be lurching towards revolution. The wartime Clydeside unrest had been followed by angry mass meetings in Glasgow city centre and calls for a general strike in support of a shorter working week. In January 1919, responding to pleas from a frightened Lord Provost of Glasgow, the Cabinet ordered English troops north to quell what the Scottish Secretary feared was a 'Bolshevist rising'. (Winston Churchill was popularly, but wrongly, blamed for the decision.) The London government had decided that Scottish troops in the city's Maryhill barracks should be locked in before they too joined the revolutionaries. Machine-gunners from English regiments established posts in Glasgow's big hotels; six lumbering tanks arrived in the city's Cattle Market; and field guns were positioned in George Square, outside the grandly gothic City Chambers.

In the 1980s and 1990s there has been a lot of learned argy-bargy about whether 'Red Clydeside' was an overblown myth or whether there really was a potential revolution waiting to occur. When they grew old the socialist leaders tended to play down the matter in their memoirs, but by then most were wholly respectable and had an interest in minimizing their earlier actions. To middle-class Scots at the time the tanks in the streets did not seem an outlandish over-reaction. For instance, they knew from their newspapers that one of the militants, the schoolteacher John Maclean, had been elected an honorary president of the First All-Russian Congress of Soviets, along with Lenin and Trotsky, and appointed Bolshevik Consul in Glasgow. Maclean had been arrested twice for sedition during the war, held closely guarded in Edinburgh Castle and twice convicted, serving harsh sentences of penal servitude at Edinburgh's Calton Gaol, later the site of the Scottish Office. A letter in a Glasgow evening newspaper in 1922 fulminated: 'Those who advocate Home Rule are principally Socialists, Communists and Irish, whose aim is to establish Russian rule in Scotland.' Maclean was indeed fascinated by the Irish socialist rebels of 1916, but, despite his best efforts and those of hundreds of other working-class agitators, the revolution failed to occur. The majority of Clydeside socialists were reformers, not revolutionaries – as they would soon prove.

The socialist leaders, who had inherited some of the baggage of radical Liberalism, were almost all Scottish Home Rulers. Maclean himself would later try to form an independent Scottish communist movement, despite Lenin's opposition. He referred derisively to Willie Gallacher, the Scottish communist leader who carried the irate messages from Moscow, as 'Lenin's gramophone'. Maclean, by then an extreme Marxist-nationalist, established a short-lived party dedicated to creating a Scottish workers' republic. Standing as a candidate in the Gorbals district of Glasgow in 1923, when he had been released from his fifth term of imprisonment, Maclean announced that the social revolution would be possible sooner in politically advanced Scotland than in England: 'This policy of a Workers' Republic in Scotland debars me from going to John Bull's London Parliament.' (He was proved right, since only 4,000 people voted for him, against 16,500 for the Independent Labour Party man, George Buchanan.) His mix of nationalism and communism appealed strongly to the poet Hugh MacDiarmid, who in the 1940s helped turn Maclean, who died young from privation, into a martyr of the Scottish left. Admired by Lenin (despite their quarrels), he featured on a Soviet postage stamp as late as the 1970s.

A little closer to the mainstream, the Clydeside MPs of the Independent Labour Party who were elected in 1922 had gone to London, from Glasgow's St Enoch's Station, with 'The Red Flag' echoing in their ears. One of them, Tom Henderson, protested to the crowd that he wished he was going to the parliament in Edinburgh. The rest would have agreed; almost all the twenty-nine Labour MPs elected in Scotland that year were committed to an Edinburgh parliament. There was, of course, the issue of emphasis: socialist first or nationalist first? To start with, it hardly seemed a problem: Robert Burns, a poet of occasional nationalist views (though he could play the Unionist when it suited him) and internationalist sentiment, was routinely claimed as an early socialist. The Glasgow MPs considered their Scottishness and their socialism to be richly and sentimentally interwoven. The haunted, accusatory Jimmie Maxton had promised the St Enoch's crowds that they would see 'the atmosphere of the Clyde getting the better of the House of Commons'. Maxton became famous throughout Britain as the conscience of the left; his campaigns against slum housing and poverty wages, and his staring eyes, lank hair and denunciatory forefinger, made him a staple of cartoonists and writers – the agitator as caricature. But Maxton's attitudes to Scotland epitomized the difficulty faced by any Labour Home Ruler. After a year he returned to Glasgow to tell a meeting of Scottish teachers that he found it humiliating to be working for 'a policy of fundamental change for the benefit of the Scottish people and to find the Scottish majority [at Westminster] steadily voted down by the votes of the English members pledged to a policy of social stagnation'. The argument was echoed in the 1980s by Scottish Labour dissidents.

The argument drove Maxton and other Independent Labour Party MPs quite close to full-throated nationalism. They fulminated and sang at patriotic rallies at Bannockburn and Elderslie, William Wallace's birthplace. Labour's front-bencher Gordon Brown, in his biography of Maxton, quotes him in full spate at a rally called in 1924 to support a Labour Bill for Home Rule to be presented by George Buchanan, Maclean's old adversary in the Gorbals. Maxton told the meeting in St Andrew's Hall, Glasgow, that he asked for no greater job

than to make English-ridden, capitalist-ridden, landowner-ridden Scotland into the Scottish Socialist Commonwealth ... Give us our Parliament in Scotland. Set it up next year. We will start with no traditions. We will start with ideals. We will start with the aim and object that there will be 134 men and women, pledged to 134 Scottish constituencies, to spend their whole energy, their whole brain power, their whole courage, and their whole soul, in making Scotland into a country in which we can take people from all nations of the earth and say: This is our land, this is our Scotland, these are our people, these are our men, our works, our women and children: can you beat it?

Yet by the 1940s he was equating Scottish nationalism with the rise of Nazism in Germany.

The gap between Maxton's rhetoric in Scotland and what actually happened to the Bill he was supporting is instructive. There had been earlier Scottish Home Rule motions and Bills – in 1894, 1895, 1908, 1911, 1914 and 1920 – but the Buchanan one had a special significance. It was the first parliamentary expression of the Scottish Labour demand for Home Rule. Buchanan told the Commons that his Bill was 'representative of Scottish Labour opinion'. He ridiculed the idea that English MPs were about to vote on a measure concerning the reunion of Presbyterian Scottish Churches and that he, as a Glasgow Gorbals MP, was expected to vote on the London Traffic Bill. But one of his central arguments was that unless Parliament agreed to 'this mild, meagre measure', it would eventually be forced to yield to more extreme demands, as it had over Ireland. The Marxist John Maclean, Buchanan reminded the House, had polled over 4,000 votes in the Gorbals (three times as many as the Liberal candidate) for a 'complete, separate, Scottish Free State'. The Irish parallel suggested that if moderate Home Rulers did not prevail, 'catastrophe' would follow. Buchanan was proved wrong, of course: Irish parallels have proved notoriously slippery. It comes as a shock to the modern reader to find that in 1924 Northern Ireland was regarded at Westminster as a model of good government: 'Does anyone in this country hear of bad government in Ulster?' asked one Home Ruler during the same debate.

Buchanan also argued that Home Rule and Scottish working-class poverty were closely linked. Since it expresses clearly why, for the first generation of Scottish Labour MPs, Home Rule was not a side-issue, his argument deserves to be heard again:

[In Glasgow] you have the tragedy going on day after day, a death rate of four times the number of children than the death rate in a well-to-do division, and that is not because our people are poor, or Scottish, or Irish, or drunkards. It is not even because this Parliament is brutal towards our people. It is because this Parliament cannot devote the time to the work, and furthermore because it has no knowledge of the problems with which we are confronted.

The debate saw many arguments raised on both sides that would become familiar later. Could Scotland afford to break free? And, as in 1914, what would be the position of Scottish MPs at Westminster if there were an Edinburgh parliament? The debate was notable too for an argument about where the new Scottish parliament should be sited. The Unionist MP for Perth and Kinross, the Duchess of Atholl, argued that a new building would be too costly but that there was no appropriate building in Edinburgh to be taken over. David Kirkwood, the Independent Labour Party MP, who, like Maclean, had been imprisoned during the war in Edinburgh's Calton prison, sprang up. Hansard records:

MR KIRKWOOD: What about Calton Gaol? That is empty.
DUCHESS OF ATHOLL: If the hon. Member would like to be returned as a representative of his constituency to the Calton Gaol, he is quite welcome to do so.
MR KIRKWOOD: I have been there before.
DUCHESS OF ATHOLL: The hon. Member speaks then from personal experience of the amenities of the building. I have no such experience, but I am inclined to think that the building is hardly adaptable to Parliamentary purposes.

(Kirkwood later became a highly respected figure and friend of Churchill, while the Duchess joined forces with the anti-fascist Popular Front, resigned from the National Government Parliament and lost her own seat as an anti-appeasement candidate during a filthy by-election, becoming known as 'the Red Duchess'.)

Punctuated by such surreal pleasantries, the 1924 debate meandered on for hours. Relatively few Unionist MPs turned up, and the Home Rulers were convinced that they were winning the argument. Then the Speaker betrayed them: he reneged on an earlier promise that he would end the debate and hold a vote. Instead he allowed the measure to lapse for lack of time. This prompted furious protests from Buchanan, Maxton and Kirkwood, and the Speaker eventually suspended the sitting because 'Grave disorder has arisen in the House.' The surging rhetoric of big public meetings in Scotland had been easily diverted by Westminster shenanigans – not for the last time.

Three years later, backed by the Scottish Home Rule Association, another Labour MP, the Revd James Barr, brought in his Government of Scotland Bill. It was supported by the Scottish Convention, a gathering of Scottish MPs, trade unionists, Royal Burghs and local authorities. It was a radical Bill, since Barr proposed that all Scottish MPs should quit Westminster for a new Edinburgh parliament. Thereafter defence and Imperial issues affecting Scotland and England jointly could be decided by an 'Imperial Council'. Yet again, the optimism and mass meetings in Scotland were easily rebuffed by the indifference of the English and Unionist MPs. Barr told the Commons that he was attempting to restore to Scotland its parliament, which dated back to 1326 and had been undermined by the Union of the Crowns when King James the VI and I went south to London. From there the king had said: 'Here I sit and govern Scotland with my pen. I write and it is done; and by the Clerk of the Council I govern Scotland now, which others could not do by the sword.' The present Scottish Secretary, said Barr, was the King James of his day. The Bill was seconded by Tom Johnston, but the debate had hardly got under way before it was cut short by lack of parliamentary time. It been squeezed in after a debate on environmental hygiene, and one Labour journalist complained that 'The claims of Scotland had to come after Bugs, Fleas and Vermin.' Whatever happened to the fleas, the Scottish Bill was again easily talked out.

After that the Home Rule case went into a steady and deep

decline in the Labour Party that lasted for forty years. Although Labour continued to be formally committed to Home Rule until the 1930s, its next minority government ended in a catastrophic split and the formation of the Unionist-dominated National Government. Home Rule slipped down the rump Labour Party's list of priorities, particularly after 1932, when the more pro-Home Rule Independent Labour Party split away. The rest of the Labour movement seemed less and less interested in the subject as the country was confronted by slump, mass unemployment and the general strike. The threatening Clydeside MPs developed into well-behaved, House-trained ex-radicals – to the extent that Churchill could say in the mid-1930s that Kirkwood, was 'a grand fellow, if handled in the right way' and that the gaunt Maxton was 'the greatest gentleman in the House of Commons'. But, as far as Labour was concerned, Scottish Home Rule had been lost somewhere on the path to respectability.

The National Party is Born: There are Four Proud Parents

This trend had been spotted as early as 1927 by a young Labour supporter, gifted with a brilliant speaking style, called John MacCormick. He had tumbled into Labour student politics almost by accident (he had wanted to speak in a student union debate at Glasgow University and found the Labour benches emptier). Tramping around the island of Mull on a propaganda tour with a senior Labour speaker, John Kinloch, MacCormick found the groups that gathered to listen were more interested in Home Rule than socialism. Given the intertwined early history of the Labour Party and the pro-Home Rule Land League, and the revival of the issue when landless soldiers returned to the Highlands in 1918–19, this was hardly surprising. But MacCormick noticed too that his older friend had little belief that Labour would carry out its Scottish promises. He urged MacCormick to give the party a chance: 'If people like ourselves keep prodding from behind, we can keep the Party up to its promises. Besides, there's no other way.' The keen-eared law student heard the pessimistic tone more clearly than Kinloch's overt message and drew his own conclusions. He decided to leave Labour and devote himself to Home Rule. Back in Glasgow, his mother scolded him: 'Home Rule, indeed! That died at Culloden. You'll be daft if you throw your future to the winds chasing that old dream.' But then she added that it would be a great thing 'if only we could get it'. To the unprejudiced observer, anyone devoting himself to Scottish nationalism in 1927 would have seemed half crazy. Fortunately for MacCormick, he was not the only dreamer.

The 22-year-old MacCormick formed the Glasgow University Scottish Nationalist Association a few weeks later, in September 1927. He and two friends scribbled its constitution in a café in Glasgow's Sauchiehall Street one evening. The minutes were recorded on the back of an envelope, and its first membership card stated its object to be 'To foster and maintain Scottish Nationalism by (1) securing self-government for Scotland and (2) advancing the ideals of Scottish culture within and without the University'. It must have seemed no more than a half serious student joke of the kind that happens in cafés and pubs in dozens of ancient university cities every evening. But it led the romantic-minded law student into an extraordinary political career, bouncing from the left of the spectrum to the right, into ferocious battles about the meaning of nationalism and periodic alliances with all other parties, before forming a large extra-parliamentary movement in the 1940s. Yet in 1927 so tiny was the world of Scottish nationalism outside the Independent Labour Party and radical tradition that MacCormick himself had not realized the existence of the Scottish Home Rule Association. It heard of his student group and got in touch. Although Cunninghame Graham was its flamboyant president, the organizer was Roland Eugene Muirhead, the well-off owner of a tannery from Bridge-of-Weir. He became one of the founders of the new party, which was lucky for it.

Muirhead, who lived until 1964 and founded his last nationalist organization as late as 1950, is an underrated figure in the history of Scottish politics. Yet without his successful little business and his generosity much of the propaganda of the Independent Labour Party and then of the Nationalists would not have been possible. He paid for the socialist newspaper *Forward* (and Tom Johnston admitted to persuading it to become more pro-Home Rule as a result). He paid for the *Scots Independent*. He paid for most of the pamphlets and booklets that spread the Nationalist cause during the inter-war years. It would be hyperbole to say that without Muirhead Scottish Nationalism would not have happened, but the movement would certainly have been a lot quieter. When MacCormick met him he must have seemed a bit of a crank. As a youth he had decamped from the family tannery and gone to live in an anarchist commune in America (his brother was a friend of Prince Kropotkin, the famous Russian anarchist) before joining the Young Scots Society and the Highland Land League. He was a dour fellow, as dull and obsessive-seeming as Cunninghame Graham was flamboyant and grasshopper-brained. MacCormick said of him: 'He is as difficult to negotiate with as granite is to carve . . . He was of the calibre of the old Covenanters who defied the Government's dragoons and gladly died for their faith. Like them he made up in sincerity what he lacked in humour and, although he was a wealthy man, he always dressed shabbily in a kind of hodden grey.' Everyone commented on his shapeless suits, stuffed with press cuttings. During the Second World War he was raided (absurdly) as a potential Nazi sympathizer and had a nineteenth-century sporting rifle confiscated. He was the first of scores of amateur politicians to keep the Home Rule movement alive when professionals seemed inclined to forget about it: he is, in that respect, the grandfather of the men and women who formed the Campaign for a Scottish Assembly in the 1980s.

Back in 1928 the Scottish Home Rule Association, with its pro-Labour bias, did not join the new Nationalist party. Without Muirhead and his money it fell to pieces instead. But Muirhead, with the student Nationalists, was an essential catalyst for other groups that eventually fused at a rally at Bannockburn in 1928 to form the National Party of Scotland. These groups were unimpressive. One was called the Scots National League, which was hot for a Gaelic revival and Highland land reform. One of its founders was the Honourable Ruaraidh Erskine of Marr, the Brighton-born son of the fifth Lord Erskine. In the early years of Scottish Nationalism some odd types turned up, but none came odder than Erskine. He learned Gaelic from his nanny and his politics from Sinn Fein. A fervent Scottish revolutionary and admirer of Lenin, he managed to be a monarchist and a (Protestant-hating) Catholic at the same time. He was, in colloquial terms, something of a nutter. But Scottish left-wing politics was relatively tolerant of eccentric aristocrats (it still is), and Erskine worked from time to time with such serious politicians as John Maclean, the MPs Maxton and Kirkwood and Tom Johnston himself. Later Erskine became a friend of Hugh MacDiarmid, who published articles in his *Pictish Review* and eventually dropped out of the Nationalist movement, decamping to the Mediterranean in disgust when it became offensively moderate.

The League itself was not as nutty as Erskine, though it had plenty of other strange members. It never had more than 1,000 paid-up supporters, and much of its activity was in London, where it was supported by bagpipe-listening, Jacobite-song-singing exiles. In terms of its politics, its greatest difference from the Scottish Home Rule Association was that it was avowedly separatist – the distinction between separatism and Home Rule, which had periodically worried Labour MPs and was to split the Scottish National Party itself, was there from the start. The League's newspaper, *Scots Independent*, had a wider circulation and eventually became the quasi-official voice of Scottish Nationalism.

The last parent of the new party was called the Scottish National Movement. It was a small, Edinburgh-based outfit dominated by the talented Scots poet Lewis Spence. Spence was described by MacCormick as looking like a cautious lawyer: 'He habitually wore spats and a bowler hat which, to my youthful mind, detracted greatly from his literary reputation.' Spence was a crackling essayist but no great politician and performed exceptionally badly when he became the new party's first by-election candidate. The much greater poet MacDiarmid fell out with him (not in itself a bad sign, since MacDiarmid fell out with most people) and described Spence a few years later, when he was identified with the moderate camp in the Nationalist movement: 'The blighter has no standing and has lost any potentiality he ever had of doing any useful work in a hopeless mixture of conceit, cant, venom and verbiage. His very physical appearance reminds me of a pig's carcass in a butcher's shop' (which was probably unfair).

In 1927 moves had started to bring all these groups together. There had been sporadic calls for a Scottish National Party in the 1890s and then in 1923–4, but, as we have seen, first Liberalism and then Labourism had seemed likely to carry through the Home Rule project instead. By 1927 the Liberal Party was already in catastrophic decline, and Labour, as we have seen, was losing interest too. So in January 1928 MacCormick's student Nationalists convened a joint meeting. It included moderates and extremists, socialists and right-wingers, Home Rulers, Imperialists and outright separatists, workers and aristocrats, poets and lawyers. They bickered and haggled over the new party's aims and constitution, finally deciding that its purpose was to 'secure self-government for Scotland with independent national status within the British group of nations'.

The new party, a puny, wailing thing, was born in April. All political parties have to start somewhere. But most eyewitnesses of the bunch of youths and oddities who founded the National Party of Scotland would have given it zero chance of success. It grew very slowly and endured many false dawns. Yet it did grow and has exercised a profound influence on the course of Scottish politics this century. And, through the unlikely medium of Glasgow University's rectorial election of 1928, the new National Party enjoyed an immediate oxygen blast of publicity that prevented it from being stillborn.

The Perils of Respectability

Students from the older Scottish universities have the right every few years to elect a rector, the titular head of their university. These elections have often functioned as political dogfights and have sometimes been rowdy. In modern times students have elected rock musicians, political dissidents, journalists and so on. But the 1928 contest in Glasgow was one of the first of its kind and shocked the Scottish press. The Nationalists, who were virtually unknown, persuaded Cunninghame Graham to stand for them. The Tory candidate was the Prime Minister, Stanley Baldwin. Conservative Central Office therefore took the occasion somewhat seriously and sent up organizers, various party bigwigs and even ministers to speak on Baldwin's behalf. Against them, apart from the Labour and Liberal candidates, the Nationalists could pit one well-known but eccentric aristocratic story writer, a few students, plus a clutch of novelists who had heard about the contest and turned up for some fun. To the amazement of Baldwin and everyone else, Cunninghame

Graham came within sixty-six votes of beating him. It was the first time, but not the last, that the Conservatives were to underestimate the hidden potency of Scottish Nationalism. It was a minor occasion, but it gave rise to glorious visions among the optimistic Nationalists: in his biography of the novelist Compton Mackenzie, Andro Linklater says: 'Suddenly it seemed as though nationalism must exist, like a huge artesian well beneath the crust of existing politics, waiting to be tapped.' Years later, it would be.

Perhaps the most significant aspect of the first years of the National Party of Scotland was that it swiftly left behind the left-wing Labour tradition that had helped to create it. The activities of the working class Home Rulers, whether they were Marxist revolutionaries like John Maclean or Independent Labour Party MPs like Maxton, seemed almost irrelevant to the middle-class men who took over the new party. And *vice versa*. A month after the new party had been founded the poet Hugh Macdiarmid hoped that Nationalists, the Independent Labour Party and the Labour Party might run joint candidates in some constituencies: 'Although certain Socialist members may not be willing to come out as Nationalists, others can do so without being any the less Socialistic and even on the grounds that Scottish independence is a short cut to Socialist Government in Scotland, and that therefore a group of candidates who are definitely Nationalist-Socialists is quite a reasonable proposition.' MacDiarmid, anticipating the Trotskyist entryists of more recent times, also proposed 'little groups acting as Nationalist "caves" in each of the three existing parties'. But no serious attempt was made on either side to bridge the divide.

The National Party's founders were mostly well outside mainstream Labour politics socially, imaginatively and geographically. Once the National Party got under way, it was quick to bracket Labour with the rest of the unacceptable London-based parties. A pamphlet from the early 1930s makes the point: 'Class antagonism is a thing quite foreign to the Scottish spirit. It was unknown here until it was imported from England . . . In Scotland there is no such inherent feeling of separation between classes.' A copy of this leaflet loaned to this writer by the Labour MP John Maxton had been annotated in pencil by his uncle, Jimmie Maxton. On its back Maxton the elder had scribbled his disagreement: 'Still experimenting – but *socialism* all the time – no man exploiting his fellow man.' Maxton said later, in 1943, looking back to that critical year of 1928, 'When the Scottish nationalists came to us, who were the supporters of International Socialism, and told us that if we were to secure their support we would have to place nationalism in front of international socialism in our programme and in our activities, I declined to do it.'

The geography of early nationalism underlines the point: Glasgow, including its university (often described as the most Scottish in Scotland), was the city where the movement started. But its leading lights tended more and more to live and work in the anti-socialist parts of Scotland – Edinburgh or small towns on the east coast or in the Highlands. Contemporary fictional accounts of the nationalist upsurge tend to be set in Edinburgh, Fife or Inverness. And many of the early Nationalists were notable for failing to slot neatly into the clichés of class politics – they were intellectuals, journalists, students, small businessmen, provincial lawyers or aristocrats down on their luck. For the working-class politicians the National Party never provided a serious alternative to Labour. Its membership figures were unclear (another tradition that has survived to modern times) but probably fluctuated between 5,000 and 8,000.

Even now the Scottish National Party (SNP) attracts a kind of floating, in-between political class, rather as Liberalism does. Millions of Scots were born into Labour-voting traditions, and the SNP has had to struggle not to seem alien to them. Bob McLean, one of the founders of the pro-Home Rule group Scottish Labour Action in 1988, has explained the political gulf between socialism and nationalism in personal terms: 'I had been an enthusiastic Home Ruler from as early as I could remember, and this led me into the ranks of the SNP, as soon as they would take me, in the early 1970s. However, born into a Labour tradition and imbued with the movement's collectivist values, I was always uncomfortable with the tenor of the sectarianism between Nationalist and Labour activists.' Encounters with a Labour MP persuaded him to switch parties, but he found the transition caused agonizing 'personal *Angst*'. Current Labour MPs are inclined to describe the Nationalists as vicious and irresponsible, while the SNP has tagged Labour as Quislings and Uncle Toms. The gap between Labour socialists and SNP socialists remains a deep and jagged fissure in Scottish politics. This is often explained as the fall-out from the devolution years of the 1970s. But it goes right back to the origins of the Nationalist party in the 1920s.

So does the long, though so far fruitless, Nationalist courtship of the Scottish establishment. The early leadership of the National Party, though surrounded by kilted poets and left-wing aristocrats notable for their exuberant facial hair, tried painfully hard to seem moderate and respectable. Despite the presence in the party of some militant Catholics – such as Erskine of Marr and Compton Mackenzie – its leadership seemed to mimic the plain ethos of the Church of Scotland. Kilt wearing was, in the early days, regarded as a music-hall perversion. Bowlers and dark suits were *de rigueur*. Members were periodically warned against drinking or shouting. An internal party pamphlet of the 1930s allowed the use of slogans chalked on walls but not of 'loud controversy in tram-cars and public places – especially in Edinburgh, where people travel silent'. More seriously, MacCormick's reasons for wanting the National Party to merge with the right-wing, pro-Home Rule Scottish Party, which it eventually did in 1934, to form the Scottish National Party, included the fact that the latter could boast a few prominent Liberal and Conservative businessmen and the Duke of Montrose. The Duke eventually became honorary president, and the merged party diluted its aims from the National Party's 'self-government for Scotland with independent national status within the British group of nations' to the 1934 policy for 'a Parliament which shall be the final authority on all Scottish Affairs'.

The merger was preceded by a purge of about 20 per cent of the original National Party's membership, in May 1933, to make it more moderate, less separatist and generally acceptable to polite drawing-room opinion. Even MacCormick found the patriotic speeches of some of those whom he expelled rather moving. But he was determined to push the national movement further into the mainstream. This did not seem an impossible ambition. Scottish politics was then, as it is now, a small world, where many Nationalists were on friendly terms with Liberals, Conservatives and socialists and most felt themselves united by a vague but profound Scottish patriotism. Take one small network: the Unionist

Bob Boothby, who was a Tory Aberdeenshire MP and ally of Churchill, was also a close friend of the Scottish Nationalist novelist Compton Mackenzie. In 1935 Boothby attacked the failure of the English-dominated Commons to deal effectively with Scottish business and called for all Scottish MPs to meet in Edinburgh at regular intervals instead. Boothby's cousin, the Liberal journalist Ludovic Kennedy, was both an admirer of Boothby and strongly attracted to the SNP. Boothby's hero, Churchill, flirted with Scottish Home Rule both as a Liberal and as a Conservative. Labour's Tom Johnston was an early Home Ruler and was also supported by both Boothby and Churchill. As we shall see, the pro-Churchill newspaper tycoon Beaverbrook backed MacCormick, and MacCormick conspired with the Liberals. In this tangled mix of mutual acquaintance and well-meaning patriotism it did not seem impossible to make Home Rule the consensual belief of most mainstream politicians.

But for MacCormick the first problem was the extremism, and propensity to argue, of some of his own party. One of the most eloquent explanations of the position of the MacCormick-supporting moderates was made by the Highland novelist Neil Gunn, who was a mainstay of the National Party's active Inverness branch and acted as a go-between in the negotiations with the right-wing Scottish Party (see below). Gunn's novels emphasize spirituality and inwardness. Although he wrote profound political allegory, he was essentially a lyrical and contemplative writer, not a natural combatant in public affairs. But that gave him a detachment that made his judgement of the internal feuds of the Nationalists acute — and depressing. In a letter to one of the Nationalist die-hards, Gunn chided him:

That extremism in general stands for purity and courage is a species of self-delusion . . . Division has been Scotland's arch-fiend and has always stood on 'doctrinal purity'. It may be that we [the Scots] are like that and therefore any hope of our ever misgoverning ourselves may mercifully never be realized . . . At any rate we should by this time have learned from our history that if ever we are going to achieve a national aim, it can only be by a major harmony that refuses to be wrecked by minority discord. Now I maintain that this harmony can be achieved in Scotland today but it can be achieved only on a basis of broad principle . . . it's rather

disheartening to think of our efforts resulting in no more than giving
satisfaction to extremists a century hence as they proceed, complete with
sporran, to lay wreaths on Scotland's final Culloden.

Gunn's syntax suggests he was scribbling this in an emotional,
overwrought mood, doubtless reflecting the political crisis of 1933.
But his fear of Scottish disputatiousness remains relevant. In today's
debates between the SNP hard-liners and those who stress cross-party
and national consensus there is no doubt where he would have stood.

In the 1930s, however, the attempt by Gunn and the Nationalist
leadership to create a more popular, respectable movement proved
futile. The membership of the right-wing Scottish Party, which
they spent so much energy wooing, probably never rose above 100.
After the merger the new Scottish National Party was no more
popular with the voters than the old National Party of Scotland.
Less so, indeed: the 1935 general election showed a dramatic slide
in support in industrial towns – in the case of Kilmarnock, from
17 per cent before the merger to just over 6 per cent. The *Scots
Independent*, the main, though unofficial, voice of Nationalism,
blamed the fusion of the two parties for 'the resignation from the
Party of a number of hard-working and enthusiastic Scottish Nationalists, the expulsion of others and the incoming into the SNP of
some very moderate Nationalists'. It also attacked the presidency of
the Duke of Montrose, 'a member of the Scottish aristocracy, that
relic of the past', and he resigned shortly afterwards.

And the Scottish Party, though more moderately pro-Home Rule
than Nationalist as such, failed utterly to bring over many
Conservatives. It drew heavily on Tory Imperialist dissidents from
Cathcart in Glasgow and thus bolstered in the SNP a strain of
Scottish sentiment that makes much of Scotland's historic role as a
'Mother Nation' of the Empire – a favourite phrase among early
Nationalists. At its best, this was merely the expression of a small
country that had exported many of its best sons and daughters to
Canada, Africa, Australia and New Zealand as missionaries, engi-
neers, farmers and so on. At its worst, this Scottish imperial pride
came down to a belief that the highest expression of Scottish political
culture was a bearded man in a kilt, bearskin and red tunic poking
his bayonet through a 'Fuzzy-wuzzy'.

A more sophisticated, though sentimental, Imperialist supporter of Nationalism was the newspaper magnate and Churchill-backer Lord Beaverbrook. In 1932 his *Daily Express* (shortly afterwards Scottified north of the Border as the *Scottish Daily Express*) carried this open letter from Beaverbrook:

As for Scottish Nationalism I am, of course, strongly in favour of that movement. It is a sound movement and it is not made unsound because some of its supporters express extreme views. The movement that has no extremists has no promise of development and growth. Scottish Nationalism would give Scotland control of her domestic policies while securing her in her present share of Imperial concerns. That is a splendid project.

As it happens, Rupert Murdoch agreed in 1992 that the Scottish version of his *Sun* newspaper should convert to Nationalism – there were, as we shall see, some parallels with the Beaverbrook incident.

Writing in the 1960s, the left-wing author Tom Nairn found 'an evil mélange of decrepit Presbyterianism and imperialist thuggery' still solidly represented in the SNP. Nairn had some rude fun at the expense of those who see Scotland as a colony:

Scotland is not a colony, a semi-colony, a pseudo-colony, a near-colony, a neo-colony or any kind of colony of the English. She is a junior but (as these things go) highly successful partner in the general business enterprise of Anglo-Scots imperialism. Now that this business is evidently on its last legs, it may be quite reasonable for the Scots to want out. But there is really no point in disguising this with heroic ikonry. After all, when the going was good, the world heard very little of the Scots' longing for independence.

One of the achievements of the current leadership of the SNP is to have ousted and sidelined the sentimental-imperial strain from the party; but the whining about being a colony continues.

Whether or not he recruited any Imperialists, MacCormick's wooing of the establishment did the movement little good in the 1930s. The real establishment was larger and less easy to pin down than a few big names. The loose network discussed above, of Mackenzie–Boothby–Churchill–Beaverbrook–MacCormick, was, after all, also a network of 'unsound' outsiders, a lot of people who were considered dangerous at the time. As Boothby said about

73

another of his networks in a letter to Oswald Mosley explaining why he would not join his new party, people might say, 'By God, now all the shits have climbed into the same basket, so we know where we are.' The Scottish Party had itself provoked an angry backlash from Glasgow Tories, who issued a Unionist manifesto proclaiming that all sections of industry, commerce, agriculture, banking and the professions in Scotland were against a Scottish parliament because Scotland and England had become closely and intricately interwoven and were, indeed, 'indivisibly one'. An historian of Scottish Nationalism, Jack Brand, notes that the signatories of this counterblast included '456 Scottish notables including six dukes, three marquesses, nine earls, three viscounts, ten lords, fifty-seven knights, two ladies, two Highland chiefs, four senior clergy, seventy-six justices of the peace, eleven professors and thirty-nine gentlemen with military titles'. Montrose and a clutch of Liberal lawyers were hardly a royal flush compared with that lot. Even today, when Unionism seems in such decline, the SNP has been little more effective in gaining prominent establishment recruits. It has seen itself as a reformist party that ought to be taken seriously by the political right and as a progressive party that ought to appeal to many on the left. But the right has always regarded it as extremist, and the left has mostly seen it as an irrelevant, though dangerous, diversion.

So the Nationalists became, unwillingly but inevitably, a group apart. Their project was seen as both extreme and eccentric. While the Labour Party, the Conservatives and even the Liberals had their natural, historic supporters, the SNP, which was meant to be the political embodiment of Scottishness, managed to seem somehow alien. It was off cavorting in a faintly ridiculous tartan ghetto. Serious modernizers wanted nothing to do with it. All small groups risk attracting more than their fair share of eccentrics, and the SNP was not an exception. Lewis Spence, the poet MacDiarmid's 'pig's carcass' and the first Nationalist by-election candidate, exploded with frustration in an article in 1928 that sums up, brutally, some of the problems of an enthusiasts' party – even a poets' party:

I am all for the new nationalism, but at the moment it presents to me a maelstrom boiling and bubbling with the cross-current of rival and frequently fantastic theories, schemes and notions, riotous with tumultuous personality and convulsive with petulant individual predilection . . . If Scotland is to survive as a nation a strong curb must be put upon the blatant egotism of many of her protagonists . . . Every month produces its harvest of new 'poets', critics, and theorists, political and literary, until the mind reels before the kaleidoscopic confusion displayed by their multi-coloured and frequently absurd doctrines.

The dottiest of those doctrines mentioned by Spence – the dream of Jacobite restoration, or a Presbyterian theocracy, or a national Scottish–French *rapprochement* – have long died in the SNP. But the bucking forces of egotism and rancour that he diagnoses, and that worried Neil Gunn so much too, have stayed with the party through its life. The SNP's very smallness led to personality feuds and ideological rows, in the 1980s as in the 1920s, 1930s and 1940s. Many Scots drew the gloomy conclusion that the SNP was indeed a microcosm of Scotland – a living museum of the country's bloodthirsty, romantic and self-divided past, which decent folk would do better to forget. In recent years this has started to change, for reasons we will discover later.

The story, then, of the parties and groups and movements and associations of early Nationalism is an important one. Alert contemporary readers will have heard uncanny and sometimes alarming echoes of today's politics. The waning of the Home Rule cause in the Labour Party, then the politics and splits of the new Nationalists, created the conditions for Scottish politics after the war and up to the present. But enough, for now, of the body. It is time to turn to what has been called literary nationalism – to the spirit, the ferment of ideas and images that bubbled up in Scotland between the wars. Without ideas, politics is a meaningless grappling for power. Without dreams, it is a dull and purposeless ritual.

Everyday Life in the Poets' Party

The giant of literary nationalism was Christopher Grieve, better known by his *nom-de-guerre*, Hugh MacDiarmid. A poet who, at his best, ranks with T. S. Eliot and Ezra Pound among the giants of modernism, MacDiarmid's politics were extreme, often contradictory and almost entirely devoid of common sense. In the stuffy world of Scottish public life in the 1920s that was part of their attraction. For a few years MacDiarmid was a fervent proponent of Social Credit, an obscure economic doctrine that hinged on an international financiers' conspiracy and the need of governments to take over banking. MacDiarmid's theories drove his fellow Nationalists mad – as one of the novelists who dabbled with Scottish Nationalism, Eric Linklater, later explained. Linklater fought one of the National Party's early disastrous by-election campaigns in East Fife in 1933 and used the experience for his novel *Magnus Merriman*, which came out the following year. In it he painted a thinly disguised portrait of MacDiarmid as the poet 'Hugh Skene' who,

with burning intensity, declared that he was a Communist. But he also referred, with dark elusive details, to some private economic policy of his own which was, apparently, neither communistic nor capitalistic, but ideally suited to modern conditions. He refused to explain the system because, as he logically declared, an explanation would be wasted on people still ignorant of its fundamental hypotheses. Those hypotheses they must discover for themselves.

The wildness and arrogance were pure MacDiarmid. What Linklater cannot convey by pastiche is the man's literary achievement: MacDiarmid's poetry remains a vast and little colonized continent of wonders, glittering views and strange formations, which everyone with the requisite supply of synapses and a little common courage should visit.

A founder member of the National Party, MacDiarmid managed to get thrown out of it in 1934 for his communism, and then thrown out of the Communist Party in 1938 for his 'nationalist deviation'. Four years later, when the Nationalists had split and swung under left-wing pacifist leadership, he rejoined them. Then he resigned again. In 1956, when droves of British communists were leaving the Party because of the Soviet repression in Hungary, MacDiarmid rejoined that, snarling about the need to put down revisionists (a somewhat strange position for a self-professed Nationalist). When the world was crowding through the exit, MacDiarmid was fighting to get in. Any would-be practical politician looking for a guru (Scots especially) should run a mile from his gigantic presence. John MacCormick said of Grieve/MacDiarmid:

Although I have no doubt that he has done invaluable work in the whole field of Scottish literature I am certain that C. M. Grieve has been politically one of the greatest handicaps with which any national movement could have been burdened. His love of bitter controversy, his extravagant and self-assertive criticism of the English, and his woolly thinking ... were taken by many of the more sober-minded Scots as sufficient excuse to condemn the whole case for Home Rule out of hand.

Absolutely true: yet today tens of thousands of unsober-minded Scots, who have never even heard of the ever-respectable MacCormick, read MacDiarmid for inspiration.

MacCormick's terror of the poet was wholly understandable. For although MacDiarmid provided much of the bright spirit of Nationalism, he was a prince of its darker aspects too. The 1920s were the innocent days when Adolf Hitler was an unknown conspirator. Then progressives, as well as blimpish reactionaries, found race a useful concept. MacCormick, who was no anti-English zealot, said in his autobiography, *The Flag in the Wind*, that even as a child he believed that the Scots were racially unified. He had 'a proper pride in race ... but the race to which I belonged was dispossessed and the Scotland of which I read in school was not my people's inheritance'. His enemy MacDiarmid also harped on the alleged character of the Scottish race. In 'Cencrastus', his long and not wholly successful poem written while he was heavily engaged in propaganda for the new National Party, MacDiarmid wrote:

> The Unconscious Ideas that impel a race
> Spring frae an ineffable sense o' hoo to be
> A certain kind o' human being – Let's face
> This fact in Scotland and we'll see
> The fantasy o' an unconquerable soul
> Neath nations' rivalries, persecutions, wars,
> The golden casket o' their Covenant, their goal.

This mystical belief in racial destiny is one that Europe has learned to fear. In a letter written to the novelist Compton Mackenzie in 1929, as the National Party was taking shape, MacDiarmid announced with relish: 'The party is steadily eliminating the moderatist, compromising, democratic element and all the young people are coming round to the realization of the need of – and readiness to institute – a species of Scottish Fascism.' Aside from MacDiarmid's insatiable desire to make flesh creep, it is important to understand that his notion of fascism in the 1920s (it surfaced as early as 1923 in one article) was a vague amalgam of anti-capitalism and a desire for strong Scottish leadership. It was emotional, meaning no more than his espousal of Social Credit. By the mid-1930s, when the nature of continental fascism was clearer, and when MacDiarmid was posing as a bloodthirsty communist, he used the term 'fascist' as one of uncomplicated – even routine – abuse.

A fascination with racial theories was not the prerogative of a handful of wild literary enthusiasts. Indeed, the nastiest aspect of early SNP politics was bound up more with the party's legalistic right wing, and the Church of Scotland, than with the stormy petrel MacDiarmid. It was, essentially, anti-Catholic and anti-Irish propaganda. This was a particularly bizarre trend in a party that had included prominent Catholics among its founders and had early on been influenced by the Irish independence movement. But as the Catholic vote had gravitated to Labour and the Protestant backlash had filtered through the Scottish establishment, any attempt to move the SNP to the mainstream right would sooner or later come up against the Irish question. This was the period of fervent anti–Irish repatriation motions in the Kirk's General Assembly. The Nationalist attempt to hitch itself to racism is best seen in a pamphlet produced by the SNP in 1937 on 'Scotland's Dilemma'. At one point it tries to deal with the smear that Home Rule would mean rule by the Irish. In a section entitled 'The Green Terror' the pamphlet says that Nationalists sympathize with the fear that 'Scotsmen will be dispossessed of their own country by immigrants and their children'. But, says the author, that can be prevented by a Scottish government with a strong immigration policy: 'The menace of Irish domination lies in the future. But it is certain that, unless measures are taken to arrest and control immigration and to put into the hands of the Scottish people the key to the racial destiny of their country, there will be inevitably a race-conflict of the most bitter kind.' And that was in the dark year of 1937! Scottish nationalism has taken on the colour of many different periods – from Roman Catholic Jacobitism in the 1740s and French revolutionary republicanism in the 1790s to anti-Labourism in the 1960s and anti-Thatcherism in the 1980s. It would be idle and dishonest to deny that Scottish nationalism had also, for some years, a distinct racist undercurrent. MacDiarmid posed problems for the new National Party that were more profound than his spasms of fascist rhetoric. Two, in particular, go to the heart of the National Party's reason for existing. First, he had no interest in Home Rule but was an out-and-out separatist. MacCormick and the party leadership, as we have seen, were keen for Home Rule compromises, and MacDiarmid's deep contempt for their position is shown in a letter he wrote in 1935, a year after he had been expelled from the SNP. He fumed that the party leadership and the Duke of Montrose's Scottish Party Home Rulers were 'pseudo-nationalists – Anglo-Scots with no real knowledge of the Scottish language or literature – insulated from it by English and from the fact that they are cut off from the Scottish proletariat'. By then the politics of separation versus devolution had become deeply entangled in MacDiarmid's literary battle, to defend the use of synthetic Scots, his poetic language made up of ordinary spoken Scots and words pillaged from a dictionary of Old Scots, against the majority who found it stunted and barely comprehensible. (Predictably, the literary quarrel, mainly with the poet Edwin Muir, produced invective that was even more poisonous than the political quarrel.) Later MacDiarmid compared himself with the sun in a poem that predicted that the MacCormick leadership of the National Party would 'vanish, like mists'.

While this was characteristically arrogant, MacDiarmid was, after all, proved right. Although the separatists have tended to be regarded as woolly-minded extremists compared with the Home Rulers and devolvers, it should be pointed out that the latter failed to achieve anything either. All the various schemes for Home Rule, right up to the present day, have crumbled when faced with Westminster resistance. On this question of holding out for separation rather than compromising, MacDiarmid's ghost and the SNP hard-liners can at least ask why they are seen as impractical dreamers while the other lot are applauded as practical-minded achievers. The 'extremists' scare off many Home Rulers, but without them the Scottish national question would have ceased to be asked seriously decades ago. This is yet another paradox embodied in the life and work of MacDiarmid.

The second challenge posed by MacDiarmid in particular and the literary nationalists in general concerned socialism. He had a deep and justifiable contempt for trinket nationalism, the sentimental obsessions with flags and forms of addresses that characterized some right-wing nationalists. In his great work 'A Drunk Man Looks at the Thistle' MacDiarmid writes:

> And O! to think that there are members o'
> St Andrew's Societies sleepin' soon',
> Wha to the papers wrote afore they bedded
> On regimental buttons or buckled shoon
>
> Or use o' England whaur the UK's meent,
> Or this or that anent the Blue Saltire,
> Recruitin', pedigrees, and Gude kens what,
> Filled wi' a proper patriotic fire!

He was attacking those same traditionally militaristic Scots who had supported the Scottish Party before the merger with the National Party. As so often, he was more perceptive when attacking than when creating a coherent philosophy of his own. His greatest humanist poems were more socialist in inspiration than nationalist:

> Now more and more on my concern with the lifted waves of genius
>   gaining
> I am aware of the lightless depths that beneath them lie;
> And as one who hears their tiny shells incessantly raining
> On the ocean floor as the foraminifera die.

Instead of trinket nationalism MacDiarmid argued for an ideological nationalism, one based not on Scotland's history, or simply on its people's right of self-determination, but on a potential Scotland of the future, which would be intellectually richer and socially more egalitarian. We have seen how the first Nationalist leaders turned their backs on Labour, but the argument has rumbled on through the subsequent history of the SNP. Should the party try to stay outside the left–right divide, try to make itself a congenial home for Scottish patriots of all views, or should it be an ideologically committed left-wing party? This debate led to expulsions in 1933–4 but to expulsions in 1982–3 as well. Since most socialists were in the Labour movement or the Communist Party, it was hardly surprising that MacDiarmid and the other leftists found themselves in a minority. Again, Eric Linklater's *Magnus Merriman* conveys some of the flavour of the time. Skene/MacDiarmid explains:

I don't believe, as an ultimate thing, in small nationalism. I want to see the creation of a world state. I'm a Communist. And I'm a Scottish Nationalist because I believe that if Scotland were independent we could do a great deal towards establishing a central state in Western Europe.

This outburst provokes the book's hero to put the right-wing case for nationalism:

I am a Scottish Nationalist because I am a Conservative. I believe in the conservation of what is best in a country . . . and I believe that small nations are generally more interesting, more efficiently managed, and more soundly established than big ones. I am not a Communist, Socialist or a Pacifist and I strongly protest against the association with Scottish Nationalism of any tenets of Communism, Socialism or Pacifism. Communism is an Oriental perversion, Pacifism is a vegetarian perversion and Socialism is a blind man's perversion. There are two essential factors in any national movement: a leader . . . and a sufficient number of people who can be persuaded or compelled to follow . . . At present, Scotland possesses neither of these factors.

Once again (partly because I have unfairly quoted from a novelist's caricature of MacDiarmid, not the man himself – but only partly), the poet seems on the silly side of the argument. Yet the history of the SNP has shown all too clearly that it is not easy to have a successful party whose members disagree about fundamental things like the role of the state, whether or not politics are based on class and which other nations provide good models for the future. For the time being, the SNP has settled this by moving decisively to the left. But the party membership still seems rather more divided and confused than its leadership about the importance of left–right politics.

Among MacDiarmid's literary colleagues was another of the upper-class romantics who gave early Scottish nationalism its gamey flavour – Boothby's friend Compton Mackenzie, best known today as the author of such satirical novels as *Whisky Galore* and *The Monarch of the Glen*. The son of an English-born comedy actor and an American actress, Mackenzie was linked to Scotland only weakly by blood but strongly by instinct. He was a Roman Catholic convert and serious novelist (talented enough to impress Conrad) who became, as 'Captain Z', a British spy in Greece during the First World War. His reports were, according to military attachés, made up of a mix of hysteria and gossip.

Compton Mackenzie's nationalism was a deeply romantic creature. He noted the pro-Turkish views of English homosexuals in
British intelligence and developed a theory that nations had a gender:
England and Turkey were male, but Scotland was female. This
gives, I fear, a genuine flavour of Mackenzie's political thought. In
the year of the National Party's birth he demanded that every
intelligent Scot should devote himself (*sic*) to political independence:
'All the dreams that haunt us – the salvation of Gaelic, the revival of
Braid Scots, a Gaelic University in Inverness, the repopulation of
the glens, a Celtic federation, and a hundred other things, will only
embody themselves when we have a Scottish Free State under the
Crown.'

Mackenzie's biographer comments on this outpouring, which is
reminiscent of that other English-born aristocrat Erskine of Marr,
by citing yet another Scottish novelist of the 1930s, Lewis Grassic
Gibbon. Gibbon, a socialist, described Mackenzie's vision as 'a Scots
Catholic kingdom, with Mr Compton Mackenzie Prime Minister
to some disinterred Jacobite royalty, and all the Scots intellectuals
settled out on the land on thirty-acre crofts or sent out to re-colonize
St Kilda for the good of their souls and the nation'. Gibbon showed
what he thought of this prospect by moving instead to Welwyn
Garden City, where he died young.

But Mackenzie, despite his dottiness, proved a tireless propagand-
ist for Scottish Nationalism – even occasionally against painful
personal odds. When he spoke for Cunninghame Graham in the
Glasgow University rectorial election in October 1928 he had recently had all his teeth pulled out and was just learning to manipulate
a set of false ones. One observer found this made him look 'as
harmlessly sinister as Captain Hook'. A lesser man would have
declined to speechify to a crowded meeting of sceptical students,
but he persevered and swung round his audience. Six years later
Mackenzie was back, this time standing as rector himself in a contest
that he won handsomely – the Nationalists' first electoral victory of
any kind. Among those he defeated was Oswald Mosley.

In the meantime Mackenzie and MacDiarmid, together with
wild Erskine of Marr, planned to form a secret, law-breaking,
consciousness-raising group, Clann Albain (or Children of Scotland).
Mackenzie said that its members would be 'pledged to do all they

could to foster the Celtic Idea with a vision, on a far distant horizon at present, of rescuing the British Isles from being dominated by London'. MacDiarmid engaged in a flurry of letter-writing to younger activists and issued dark hints. It seems that they talked of occupying Edinburgh Castle, or the Island of Rhum, or seizing the Stone of Destiny, the boulder on which Scotland's medieval kings were crowned at Scone near Perth, which was stolen and taken to Westminster Abbey in 1296 by England's royal kleptomaniac, Edward I. The law-abiding Scottish Nationalist leadership found out and quarrelled publicly with conspiracists. It is unlikely that MacDiarmid himself thought of Clann Albain as more than a pressure valve for his periodic bursts of frustration with the sober souls who led the party. In a letter sent in 1931 to Neil Gunn in Inverness, MacDiarmid's postscript ended: 'Fed up with SNP policy altogether – and SNP personnel. Nothing for it really but Clann Albain.' But, like all other forms of conspiracist illegality in the recent history of Scottish nationalism, Clann Albain got nowhere. MacDiarmid used the title for his projected five-volume poetic autobiography. Glittering fragments of this exist, but it was never completed – one of the greatest Scottish poems never written.

It is hard to resist the thought that Mackenzie drifted away from active nationalism when the movement grew too serious for juvenile wheezes. But he put the Stone of Destiny idea into his 1945 novel *The North Wind of Love* and was gratified when, on Christmas Day, 1950, some young Nationalists abducted the sacred lump. This faintly surreal adventure persuaded the Special Branch to investigate Mackenzie, who had once been its ally as a member of British Intelligence. Ironically, given the hostility of the Nationalist leadership to Clann Albain, MacCormick himself was much more deeply involved in the Stone of Destiny seizure – his historical romanticism and nose for publicity getting the better of his respectability. Mackenzie's greatest contribution to the nationalist movement was neither his political vision (which was cheerfully batty) nor his strategy (which was equally so) but his propaganda, verbal as much as written. He was too witty a novelist to be quite sure about whether he was propagating Scottish patriotism or sending it up – rather like Eric Linklater himself. A brilliant story-teller and radio broadcaster, his platform performances thrilled the blood. At the 1933 commemoration of the Battle of Bannockburn he inspired some young Nationalists to invade the near-by Stirling Castle and haul down the Union Jack. In his semi-autobiographical novel *The West Wind of Love* Mackenzie's *alter ego* is told: 'When you were seventeen you could carry off your romantic individualism . . . At that age your Jacobitism and Chopinism and Byronism added to your charm, but now at thirty-nine you're going to a fancy-dress ball in an unsuitable costume.' Another character defends him: 'But even butterflies have their uses. They fertilize many flowers during their beautiful existence.' It seems a fair epitaph for the nationalism of one of Scotland's most popular and eccentric writers.

Peace or War? Towards the Great Split

By the mid-1930s it was fairly clear that the first Nationalist upsurge of 1928–33 had petered out. The Nationalists had a few solid achievements to chalk up. They had survived as a party. Above all, they had made Scotland talk, and think: the Scottish press had become fascinated by the arguments and personalities of the movement and argued the toss about Home Rule, separation and Unionism, vociferously, month after month. In a more book-centred culture than today's a spate of novels, poems, articles and pamphlets had alerted the middle classes to Nationalist arguments. The literary revival had given Scots a feeling that their small country could still produce surprises. On a political level the Nationalists had learned a little from their early and amateurish attempts to build an organization. They had formed branches across Scotland, fought by-elections and some general election seats and seen one of their number elected as Lord Rector of Glasgow University.

But these achievements were, in truth, puny compared to the debit side. After managing to attract just 5 per cent of the votes in the two seats the National Party fought in 1929, its share in five seats in the 1931 general election rose to 13 per cent. But the 1935 election had been, with the exception of a 28 per cent vote in the Western Isles, pretty disastrous. Nor was there any sign that the Nationalists had been able effectively to concentrate their resources on by-elections to produce more of a breakthrough. MacCormick's account of the party's first attempt, the 1928 North Midlothian by-election fought by Lewis Spence, is either hilarious or depressing, depending on your point of view. The Nationalist 'organizer' proved to have a particular talent for summoning speakers to the wrong places on the wrong nights, and the candidate failed to improve his chances by delivering, instead of his eve-of-poll address, a long Burns Night oration in Middle Scots.

By 1933, when Eric Linklater fought the East Fife by-election, things were barely any better organized. In his fictionalized account of it the cheerful but incompetent agent Captain Smellie absconds with the SNP's deposit, posters and speakers fail to turn up, meetings turn rowdy and the candidate clearly has no taste for electoral politics. Linklater's description of one of the audiences of the Nationalist candidate, Merriman, at the Fife village of 'Pitsharnie', is such a wonderful piece of rhetorical anti-elector savagery that it deserves quotation in full:

There was an ill-washed, ill-favoured boy sitting beside a rat-mouthed mother. There was a coarse lumpy woman, dressed in the dark, who showed eight of her badly-assorted teeth when she yawned. There was a brace of loutish hobbledehoys, and an old man with a dribbling nose, an ear-trumpet, a dirty beard and a noisy habit of breathing. There was a rough sneering red-faced slit-eyed cattle-dealer, all whisky and lechery, and a plump blouse-full of girl hotly aware of him in the seat in front. There was a smug trim smooth little minister, making three hundred a year pimping for a God in whom his heart was too small to believe; an angry impotent schoolmaster who made rather less by petty sadism and failing to educate children whom – in his favour be it said – no power on earth could educate; and a rickle of rural inanity behind.

Unsurprisingly, given the tone of this, Merriman responds to one heckler later in the campaign who asks what he is doing with a snarled 'Wasting my time.' In Linklater's novel the Nationalist comes last with only 608 votes. In Linklater's real election, which was complicated by the intervention of a Beaverbrook candidate standing for Imperial Preference, the result was little better. He came last with 1,083 votes. The SNP leader, MacCormick, felt that the novelist had been baffled by the campaign. On the back jacket of an early edition of *Magnus Merriman*, where the by-election is described, the blurb says of Linklater: 'He has dabbled in politics, and repented.' If the SNP found there were drawbacks in the membership of communist poets, it did little better out of repentant novelists.

As the SNP struggled through its by-elections, clearly failing to maintain the momentum of its earliest years, MacCormick became ever more convinced that the real problem was the movement's isolation from the rest of Scottish politics. It had to reach out, even if that meant compromising its aims. Merger with the Scottish Party had failed to do this, so it was time to go further. Perhaps a broad coalition with all Scottish Home Rulers would be the thing. After the expulsions of 1933–4 MacCormick was in effective control of the party and began campaigning for this. Labour, which had once more been advertising its Home Rule credentials in the 1935 general election, was one possible partner. But he decided to start by approaching the Scottish Liberals, with their long history of federalism, with a view to an electoral deal. Later MacCormick said blandly, 'It began to seem to many Nationalists that in the future we might make common cause with the Liberal Party.' *Many* Nationalists? MacCormick did not bother to get formal authorization for this move from the SNP's ruling National Council and relied instead on the ex-Scottish Party clique around him. Their enthusiasm for the Liberals was unsurprising: many of the leaders of the Scottish Party had been Liberal politicians themselves, and the Duke of Montrose was shortly to take the Liberal whip in the House of Lords.

MacCormick was also just a bit of a snob and was tickled by the idea of entering into discussions with Lady Louise Glen-Coats, the key Home Ruler in the Scottish Liberal Federation. His account of their first meeting, at the Glen-Coats' Hollybush House in Ayrshire, is characteristic:

It was a large and lovely room and, at what seemed to me to be an immense distance away, the dinner party was seated around a long and beautifully polished table. To my further consternation the gentlemen were immaculate in dinner jackets and Lady Glen-Coats was wearing a shimmering silver-grey evening gown. I was in a shabby office suit from which I had only been able partially to brush the considerable quantity of good Ayrshire soil which had accumulated upon it. Never in my life had I felt more nervous and embarrassed nor more unworthy of what should have been an important occasion. I was, of course, received by Lady Glen-Coats and Sir Thomas with perfect hospitality . . .

It was all rather far removed from the abrasive left-wing National-ism of, say, John Maclean in the Gorbals or Hugh MacDiarmid who, impoverished, unpopular with the critics and divorced, was by then fuming noisily on the Shetland island of Whalsay. Later during his meal with the Glen-Coats MacCormick dropped a pea from his fork, and it bounced on the table: 'I gazed at it in a final horror of discomfiture.' The things a man will do for his country! Perhaps because of MacCormick's enthusiasm for the Liberal quality and the weak position of the Liberals across most of Scotland, a deal was eventually struck, with both parties working on a joint Home Rule declaration and the Liberals agreeing not to put up candidates against twelve seats to be fought by the SNP at the next election.

Castle-creeping was not the only way the SNP attempted to extend the appeal of Home Rule in the late 1930s: it also tried to woo trade unions and Labour supporters. The Aberdeen branch of the party issued a leaflet appealing for left-wing support with an argument that became a staple throughout the Thatcher years: 'Scots voters in 1935 gave a majority for Labour, Liberal and other Progres-sive parties. We always do . . . Stafford Cripps supports Home Rule for Scotland. Do you? Why be ruled by a Tory Gang you don't elect?' Since so much of the SNP's propaganda in the later 1930s was about Scotland's steep economic decline relative even to Eng-land's (between the wars around 600,000 Scots left Scotland), it sometimes found itself talking the same language as Labour and the communists, who also supported Home Rule and, indeed, on at least one occasion marched with tartan sashes and placards of Robert the Bruce.

As MacCormick and the SNP leadership tried to build bridges across the Scottish political world, the more extreme Nationalists broke off into shadowier and sillier groups. MacDiarmid, as we have already seen, was on for any silliness going. Another prominent founder of senseless organizations was Wendy Wood, who finally left the SNP in the 1950s to form the Scottish Patriots. This still exists, just. She had been one of the tearers-down of the Union Jack at Stirling Castle under the influence of Compton Mackenzie's Bannockburn rhetoric. She set up a number of outfits, such as the Scottish Watch, a youth organization; the Democratic Scottish Self-Government Organization; and the Scottish Defence Force, which, apparently, was the proud possessor of a hidden rifle range and 'a few picked officers'. Professor Brand, the historian, says of Wendy Wood that it would be very easy to dismiss her as a buffoon or trouble-maker, 'but that would be too facile a judgement'. Would it? She was an attractive, courageous and publicity-conscious woman, but she was a gadfly, not a politician. Other bizarre groups included the League of True Scots, the Scots Guard and the Scottish Front.

Compton Mackenzie himself, in his Highland farce *The Monarch of the Glen*, which he wrote in the bleak winter of 1940–41, includes a satirical swipe against such movements. The MacDonald of Ben Nevis, a vast Anglo-Scottish laird of equally low boiling-point and intelligence, whose fight to keep the National Union of Hikers out of Glenbristle and Glenbogle forms the centrepiece of the farce, has a robust, establishment view of the independence movement: 'Scottish Nationalists? I regard Scottish Nationalists as worse than hikers. To me they hardly appear human. They should be stamped out like vermin.' It is a fair bet that Lady Glen-Coats had a few real-life Ben Nevises in her social circle. In the novel Ben Nevis is reconciled by the help some young Nationalists give him against the English hikers. The patriots belong to the 'Scottish Brotherhood of Action', which spends much of its money on paint for smearing English and Gaelic slogans on public buildings (this may have been based on the author's own boyish dreams or on a Glasgow National-ist youth movement, Fianna na h-Alba, which was addicted to hill-walking and compulsory Gaelic lessons). In Mackenzie's novel the Scottish Brothers have come to Glenbristle in pursuit of the magnifi-cently ox-like Ben Nevis, as they explain to the book's heroine, Carrie Royde:

'You weren't going to kidnap Ben Nevis?' Carrie gasped.

'Only as part of a general campaign for kidnapping lairds,' the bard explained. 'But don't worry, Mistress Royde. There are plenty of others. We'll leave Ben Nevis out of the general campaign, at any rate for this year.'

'I'm afraid you'll think me terribly dense,' said Carrie. 'But I wish you'd explain just exactly what would be the practical value of kidnapping lairds.'

'The creation of a state of uneasiness amongst the landed class,' James informed her. 'The same with the rich business men. We aim to kidnap quite a few of them. Trades-union leaders too. Ministers. Sheriffs. School-masters. The editor of the *Glasgow Herald*. The editor of the *Scotsman*. The general idea is to shake up complacency . . . [And as for Ben Nevis himself] think how much being kidnapped would widen the point of view of a landed proprietor like that. Men of his type require mental shocks imagina-tively applied.'

Mackenzie's satire can be regarded as the last word on the various para-military and secretive organizations that sprang up around the SNP in the 1930s. This present book does not describe the revival of Scottish country dancing. It will not spend much time on the fantasists either.

Much more important for the SNP was the looming war. The party now regarded itself as moderate and progressive on economic policy (though still strongly anti-immigration) and was quite clearly hostile to fascism in all its forms. But there had been, going back to the First World War, a strain of Scottish radical nationalist opinion that held that London governments had no right to conscript Scots or to declare war on their behalf. It was the polar opposite, in the nationalist spectrum, to the enthusiastic imperialism of some of the Scottish Party group. In the shadow of the Second World War it reappeared. In MacCormick's words, 'Once again, a real and funda-mental cleavage both of sentiment and opinion began to make itself evident.' MacCormick and the centre-right leadership of the SNP had some strong arguments. First, the Nationalists were in a small minority in Scotland and could hardly claim that most of their fellow-countrymen were unready to fight for Britain. Scots might not have liked the 1707 Union but had acquiesced in it. Second, what claim would the SNP have to being a progressive party if it failed to stand up to Nazism?

But the anti-imperialist left wing of the SNP had been working hard to dissuade the party from going to war for London (as they saw it) since 1936, and at the party's conference the following year the SNP declared itself 'strongly opposed to the manpower of Scotland being used to defend an Empire in the government of which she has no voice'. All male members of the SNP of military age were committed to refusing military service until the party's programme of self-government had been fulfilled, and the confer-ence criticized the 'apparently purposeless' amassing of arms by the

British government. The Scots Neutrality League was founded by a former journalist to secure Neutrality in the coming war and to oppose conscription. It was assisted by the fact that R. E. Muirhead, the 'hodden grey' financier whom MacCormick had approached to help found the National Party ten years earlier, was a convinced moral pacifist. He allowed the Neutrality League space to put its arguments in the *Scots Independent*, which he controlled.

As the true menace of Hitler became clearer, however, the majority of the SNP had second thoughts. In 1938 the party announced that Scots would fight alongside Englishmen for ideals that appealed to them, such as liberty and democracy, but that the SNP would 'resist all propagandistic efforts to march our people to an imperialist war'. The foreign-affairs manifesto that contained this formulation was written to paper over widening cracks. It was meant to move the SNP into a more clearly pro-war position without offending the anti-war faction in the party, which remained powerful and articulate, particularly among those separatists who had always been hostile to Home Rule-style compromises.

By September 1939 the SNP accepted both the war and conscription, though it argued that the definition of conscientious objection should be widened to include 'objection based on profound political conviction' – in other words, Scottish Nationalism. Although Nationalists, like others, flooded into the services, the party leadership kept up its attacks on the government over specific issues like the conscription of Scottish girls to work in England – an issue that aroused anger in Scotland throughout the war – and the apparently poor quality of Scottish defences against air attacks. The first few Nationalists who refused to be conscripted on political grounds were imprisoned. They included a tall, bearded Aberdeen University Greek lecturer, Douglas Young, who was already known as a poet in Scots. He would soon challenge MacCormick's leadership head-on. The party was still divided. But then, in different ways, it always had been. In April 1940 the SNP exploited the fact that it was not a party to the war-time truce agreed by Labour, the Liberals and the Conservatives, and it put up a candidate for a by-election in the sprawling Highland constituency of Argyll, which (MacCormick noted with his characteristic romanticism) covered most of the ancient Scottish kingdom of Dalriada.

The SNP closed ranks for the campaign and seemed to be doing well when, just two days before polling, Hitler's armies attacked Norway and the Low Countries. The Phoney War had ended and, as a crescendo of patriotic, pro-Government feeling swept the country and the press, the SNP's progress was stopped. Even so, the party's candidate, a 69-year-old journalist called William Power, won 7,300 votes against 12,300 for the Conservative (government) candidate. The SNP campaigners gathered, quite pleased and united, in the Stag Hotel, Lochgilphead, to celebrate. They had, they felt, much to look forward to. They were wrong. It was the last gasp of the old SNP. The party was about to be torn apart by a savage row that would change the course of Nationalist politics for a generation.

3

The Union Comes in Pink or Blue: Scotland 1942–68

The spirit of the age has manifested itself in one of those recurrent crazes for the sinking of differences, the obliteration of individual characteristics, and the absorption of small units in even larger amalgamations, as if a special virtue resided in mere size.

Lord Cooper, Scotland's Lord Justice General, 1949

– Weary with centuries
This empty capital snorts like a great beast
Caged in its sleep, dreaming of freedom
But with nae belief,
Indulging an auld ritual
Whase meaning has been forgot owre lang,
A mere habit of words – when the drink's in –
And signifying naething.

Sydney Goodsir Smith,
'Kynd Kittock's Land', 1965

The Nationalist Split: Low Road and High Road

The arguments that broke the SNP into two at its 1942 conference were the same arguments that had plagued Nationalism from the beginning and carried on doing so during the high tide of modern British Unionism – from the war to the late 1960s. The excuse for the SNP rift was wartime conscription. But it was really about other things – above all whether the Nationalists should be an independent political party, fighting all other parties in order to win separation through the ballot box, or whether they should work with and inside other parties to generate the maximum amount of enthusiasm for Home Rule in Scotland. Both strategies had disabling flaws.

If the SNP took the low road of party politics, opposing itself to the rest of the Scottish political parties, it risked the ghetto. It had to face the fact that although most Scots wanted Home Rule of some kind, they rarely thought it the most important thing. They were not oppressed, and they were just as concerned as English voters about Britain's standing in the world, the Cold War and Britain's post-war economic crisis. So while the SNP's claim was principally constitutional, it relegated itself far down most voters' priorities. It developed policies on many things, some sensible, others less so (Scots were to be obliged to eat more cured herrings, for instance, and chain stores 'under alien control' were to be banned). But such policies did not fire the nation. As Labour and the Conservatives fought about the kind of country post-war Britain would be, the SNP found itself drifting into irrelevance. Many voters who might have been happy to see Home Rule on another party's wider menu of policies declined to stop at the SNP's Tartan Diner, which offered only unseasoned constitutional change (and cured herrings). They were Scots first, but Scots patriotically, not politically.

Yet if the Nationalists took the high road, turning their back on party politics and trying instead to get the greatest possible agreement among their fellow compatriots, they got equally stuck. They ran up against the Westminster Parliament, where MPs declined to take seriously any form of political expression other than their good selves. In a parliamentary democracy signing mass petitions is no substitute for Members. That was the problem the Home Rulers discovered in the 1920s, and it was the problem the 'Covenanters' rediscovered in the early 1950s. Exactly the same problem confronts Home Rulers today: what happens when Westminster says no? The importance of the 1942 split was that it produced two opposing Nationalist strategies – the small sect and the broad church – and then conclusively demonstrated the weaknesses of both. In politics it is not always true that somebody wins. The wartime Nationalist split produced only two competing sets of losers.

At the SNP's 1942 Glasgow conference an anti-leadership group that included prominent pacifists put up Douglas Young, the Aberdeen poet, against MacCormick's candidate, the aged journalist William Power. On a stiflingly hot June day, by a mere two votes. Young won. It had been an ill-tempered debate, and MacCormick was in no doubt that it was he who was the real target. He described his party as 'this rabble' and stood up to announce his resignation from the SNP. Thirty or forty other delegates did the same, and MacCormick, as he was leaving the conference hall, shouted that they should follow him to a near-by hotel to decide what to do next. Not only did many SNP members object to his moderate line and his enthusiasm for links with other parties, but they also felt (rightly) that he had been leading the party autocratically. His hostility to the pacifist camp was merely the excuse for the break. In his autobiography, written many years later, MacCormick justified himself in words that echoed those of Neil Gunn. The pacifist and separatist hard-liners were 'wild men' who were by nature intolerant: 'As individuals they were no doubt excellent people who held sincerely and courageously to their opinions, but each was a party in himself and all lacked the power to cohere in a common cause. The very word "compromise" was anathema to them, yet compromise, up to a proper limit, is the essence of all successful political endeavour.' The irony was that Douglas Young, though ready to serve prison sentences to demonstrate his rejection of the right of the British state to conscript Scots, was not a hard-liner on the Home Rule issue. Constitutionally and strategically he was nearer Mac-Cormick. Indeed, he left the SNP after the war when it voted not to allow dual membership with other parties.

What mattered was that MacCormick took his organizational genius and energy outside the SNP to set up a new campaigning group, the Scottish Convention, while the SNP itself lost support and trudged off into the wilderness. There, for many years, it existed rather than lived. The rest of the war, however, was an unreal period for both kinds of Nationalist. The SNP, still outside the anti-politics deal agreed by the big parties, fought by-elections. Douglas Young, in and out of prison, campaigned and pamphleteered. As has been noted briefly above, one of the most sensitive issues was the conscription of Scots girls to work in under-staffed English munitions factories (some 200 a week were being sent south by the middle of the war). The SNP complained bitterly about the plight of these 'young girls, [sent] far away from their homeland to forced labour in a foreign land'. The mixture of pacifism and nationalism was taken rather too seriously by the government: there was some evidence of mild harassment by undercover British agents who were pursuing Nationalists in the hope of discovering treachery. The Nazi leaders in Berlin too became over-excited by the prospect of a latter-day Jacobite rising and established 'Radio Caledonia' in the hope of fomenting anti-English feeling.

At Motherwell in 1945 the SNP's next leader, a young Presbyterian doctor called Robert McIntyre, became the first Scottish Nationalist to win a parliamentary seat – though he lost it a few weeks later in the general election. The party was small and lacking in talent, but it was now firmly focused on independence both for itself and for Scotland. Its new leaders, including McIntyre, put together a fresh statement of aims and policies that was eventually adopted in December 1946. It starts: 'The people of Scotland, as members of one of the oldest nations in Europe, are the inheritors, bearers and transmitters of an historic tradition of liberty.' The paper outlined the development of a planned economy based on 'the diffusion of economic power'; a State bank; and a general opposition to private or state monopolies. Schemes for everything from the electrification of Highland railways to the future of forestry were noted. It was in many respects an anti-statist 'small man's manifesto', though the small man had his moments of crankiness. But the SNP's dreams dwarfed its organization. In the years immediately after the war it gained derisory numbers of votes and had a tiny membership. Douglas Young, in a later book, said of McIntyre that 'his concept of a narrow and exclusive nationalist party is in the tradition of past Presbyterian sects.' Cruel: but in the 1950s and early 1960s the SNP did seem more of a sect than a party.

The Convention

The Scottish Convention looked nothing like a political party either, but it was much more than a sect. Its name was supposed to signify a coming together of the Scottish people, and its aim was to 'seek to discover the highest common factor of national agreement on the reform of Scottish Government' and achieve it. It would not fight elections, but in the wartime atmosphere its non-partisan tone appealed to many Nationalists. Within weeks it had a membership of more than 1,000 and had formed branches across Scotland. Throughout the rest of the war it held meetings at a Glasgow cinema and issued various pamphlets. MacCormick himself finally joined the Liberals and, indeed, stood unsuccessfully as a Liberal candidate in the 1945 general election. Once the war ended he flung himself with characteristic optimism into creating a Scottish consensus for Home Rule. Another flurry of supporters was recruited, and MacCormick began to lay plans for a 'Scottish National Assembly' to meet in Glasgow in March 1947. More than 600 delegates from Churches, trade unions, town councils and other bodies turned up, leading the *Scotsman* to describe it as perhaps the most representative meeting ever held to discuss Scottish affairs. Three resolutions were put to it, ranging from one expressing satisfaction with the status quo to another, overwhelmingly supported, that called for a Scottish parliament within the UK. The meeting set up a forty-five-strong committee to carry the thing on and to try to lobby the Prime Minister, Clement Attlee.

Its proposals became known as the 'Blue Print for Scotland'. There would be a single-chamber Scottish parliament with authority over most matters except the currency, foreign affairs, defence and the crown. This was agreed at the second national assembly in March 1948, which also swiped at the centralizing tendencies of the Attlee government. The next problem was to find a way of carrying on the campaign without attacking political parties or standing in elections. MacCormick's idea proved a huge success: it was to return to the old Presbyterian tradition of a 'solemn league and covenant' that would express Scottish opinion. In April 1949 the assembly's committee and some sympathetic journalists met in a hotel in Aberfoyle and drafted the famous Covenant. It seemed to betray a touching belief that ripe and stately language might help impress the parliamentarians:

We, the people of Scotland who subscribe this Engagement, declare our belief that reform in the constitution of our country is necessary to secure good government in accordance with our Scottish traditions and to promote the spiritual and economic welfare of our nation.

We affirm that the desire for such reform is both deep and widespread through the whole community, transcending all political differences and sectional interests, and we undertake to continue united in purpose for its achievement.

With that end in view we solemnly enter into this Covenant whereby we pledge ourselves, in all loyalty to the Crown and within the framework of the United Kingdom, to do everything in our power to secure for Scotland a Parliament with adequate legislative authority in Scottish affairs.

It was presented to the third national assembly on 29 October 1949, when 1,200 people crowded into the Church of Scotland Assembly Hall on the Mound, Edinburgh. Like the launch of the second Convention at the same venue in 1989, it was a fine, Scottish affair. Nevile Davidson, the minister of Glasgow's Cathedral Church, opened the assembly with an impromptu prayer. Then streams of dark-suited delegates proclaimed their readiness to sign MacCormick's covenant. MacCormick described the scene thus:

Unknown district councillors rubbed shoulders and joined in pledges with the men whose titles had sounded through all the history of Scotland. Working men from the docks of Glasgow or the pits of Fife spoke with the same voice as portly business-men in pin-striped trousers. It was such a demonstration of national unity as the Scots might never have hoped to see, and when, finally, the scroll upon which the Covenant was inscribed was unrolled for signature every person in the hall joined patiently in the queue to sign it.

The Duke of Montrose was the first to sign, followed by Mac-Cormick and a stream of civic, Church and business leaders, followed by 'those more humble people who in Scotland, where we are all Jack Tamson's Bairns, are the salt of the earth'. MacCormick had no doubt that 'it was one of the great occasions in the long history of our nation ... a turning-point in the life of our people from which there will never be any going back'. The Covenant sparked a firestorm of enthusiasm across Scotland, gaining 50,000 signatures in the week after the assembly meeting. Copies for signature were stacked in bakers and fish-shops, university halls and city offices. It was carried far beyond Scotland; the journalist Neal Ascherson, then a young National Serviceman, remembers optimistically toting a copy around Malaya to be signed by sceptical Scottish rubber-planters. The Covenant eventually attracted 2 million names, though there were said to have been a few Mickey Mouses and Donald Ducks, and some people signed more than once. Even so, it was quite an achievement. Yet MacCormick was entirely wrong about its impact. To understand why, it is necessary to go back two years to a small mistake he made that reveals the flaw in his entire strategy.

Although he had started his political life – almost, remember, by accident – as a supporter of the Labour Party, MacCormick had been drifting rightwards for a long time. His wooing of the Liberals, then his decision to join that party, were consistent with his view that all good patriots should work together for Home Rule. The Liberals had, after all, been the first party of Home Rule and were still remembered as such across much of rural Scotland. But by the late 1940s the party was facing oblivion, in Scotland as in the rest of the country. The Liberals who, thirty years earlier, had had the vast majority of Scottish MPs – fifty-nine of them, against only nine Tories and three socialists – had failed to win a single Scottish constituency at the 1945 general election. Small wonder that they too were casting around for a broader alliance. In an era dominated by Labour centralism and corporatism the Liberals looked first to the more liberal wing of the Conservatives. Some of the latter had published a pamphlet designed to appeal to the old-fashioned anti-statist Liberals. There had even been tentative talks that were intended to bring about a merger of the Liberals and the Tory Unionists in Scotland.

The plans were interrupted when, in December 1947, the former Tory Prime Minister Stanley Baldwin died and his son, who was the socialist Labour MP for Paisley, succeeded to his father's earl-dom. MacCormick had already been chosen as the Liberals' prospective candidate for this seat. The Unionist–Tory camp agreed that they would not stand against him. MacCormick would describe himself as a 'National candidate' and would be backed by Unionists, Liberals and Covenant members against Labour's Douglas Johnstone. A joint declaration was put out stating that Scotland's national existence would be threatened 'if the process of centralizing the economic control of Scotland in Whitehall is allowed to continue'. By this, naturally, MacCormick's anti-Labour alliance meant the post-war nationalization programme. Although, both then and since, Conservatives have used quasi-Nationalist arguments against socialist planning from London, the idea that they had been converted to Home Rule was fatuous. They were using MacCormick as a handy stick to beat Labour. It is a measure of MacCormick's naïvety that he was able to find 'quiet pleasure' in standing on the same platform as Tory MPs who had 'hitherto been distinguished as immovable opponents of Scottish Nationalism'. Hitherto and henceforward also! The Conservative Party in Scotland was still, after all, officially called the Unionist Party. MacCormick failed to win the by-election. But he gave Labour a nasty shock that the party did not forget.

It would have been a reasonable and entertaining escapade for MacCormick to indulge in, except that it proved yet again that party politics would always get in the way of his Covenant dream. The Unionists saw the election in party terms. So did Labour. Even MacCormick's old Liberal friends denounced the pact. Only Mac-Cormick himself seems to have thought that his actions would not queer his pitch with the Labour government. In his autobiography MacCormick explained that he had never been able to understand party loyalty: 'It can only lead to an unthinking acceptance of slogans instead of ideals and to the prostitution of political endeavour to the satisfaction of mere personal ambitions.' Fine words for a private citizen; but they betray a strange lack of understanding for a politician. In MacCormick's defence, the late 1930s and the 1940s did engender a vague, cross-party Scottish patriotism that produced groups such as the National Trust for Scotland and the Saltire Society and led to a wartime suspension of Labour–Tory antagonism under the rule of Tom Johnston. This could have been mistaken for a move away from London-centred party politics. The Covenant might have seemed part of this. But party politics was only in suspension. MacCormick's candidacy had ensured that the Labour government would dismiss his great Scottish Convention petition as the work of its enemies.

Even that, however, cannot excuse the reaction of the then Scottish Secretary, Arthur Woodburn, to the launching of the Covenant. A disciplinarian and unimaginative party organizer, he was a shadow of earlier Scottish Labour leaders. In an evening debate in the Commons a fortnight after the mass signing in Edinburgh Wood-burn responded to the Covenant with a speech that was incoherent, indeed witless, but deserves to be remembered as marking the conversion of Labour in power to complete and uncompromising Unionism. He said that for nearly a thousand years the Scots had resented any attempt by others to impose their will on Scotland, but this view was mostly unjustified:

Arising out of this feeling, I think that it is true to say that if asked, 'Do Scots prefer to make their own decisions?' the answer, undoubtedly, would be 'yes'. Such questions are quite unrealistic and have no reference to the practical application of such a sentiment. The answers which they automatically provoke are quite valueless.

Eh? Woodburn went on:

So far as the economic situation is concerned, our very survival depends upon the position which Britain holds in the opinion of the world. This depends first and foremost on its ability to maintain its moral leadership in the eyes of world democracy. It would be the height of unwisdom at such a time to suggest that the unity of Britain was even questioned by separatism or divisions within our own country. It is true, of course, that these demands are at the moment presented in the most harmless language . . . but when one realizes that the Communist Party is one of the parties which places itself behind this demand it will be seen that this tactic is entirely in accordance with their customary strategy.

Woodburn then further distinguished himself by suggesting that MacCormick had advocated bombing Downing Street and had used the word 'bomb' on three occasions in his recent speeches. In fact, MacCormick had said that although Scotland might become independent more quickly if someone exploded a bomb in Downing Street, Scots preferred the slower but more radical methods of considered argument. He had also jocularly promised that, if elected at Paisley, he would carry no Scottish Nationalist bomb into the Commons. Challenged by other MPs about his allegations against MacCormick, Woodburn rumbled on vaguely about agitators, dangerous talk and irresponsible elements. The idea that the cautious businessmen, staid town councillors and elderly churchmen who had signed the Covenant in the Church of Scotland Assembly Hall were the followers of bomb-throwing communist revolutionaries is, and was, laughable.

But there was a more serious side to the debate that followed the Covenant. Woodburn had made much of the government's almost obsessive belief in central planning ('In a short time we will have a soil survey which will give us better knowledge of our soil than has been available to any other Government'). Walter Elliot, the Scottish Tory leader, attacked him with the now familiar argument that 'The increasing control, which of recent years has been more and more centralized in Whitehall, inevitably produces a sense that power is moving from Scotland to England.' Even he, however, stressed that Scotland was a nation 'which by its own choice has agreed to work with the great nation south of the border' – a classically Unionist formulation from a Tory who had stood alongside poor MacCormick at Paisley two years earlier.

So while Scots queued for hours in the streets of Glasgow and Edinburgh to sign the Covenant, and were just as enthusiastic in small towns like Kirriemuir and Galashiels, their leader's strategy was an entirely hopeless one. Even as MacCormick was rhapsodizing about the strength of support, the chairman of the Scottish Unionist MPs was writing to him to explain, dismissively, that complex matters such as Home Rule could not be determined by plebiscites or the numbers of signatures on a document but only by voting for MPs: 'The constitutional methods by which the people in our democracy can make their wishes known and effective are well understood, generally respected, in constant use and available to all shades of opinion.' The trouble was that where an issue like Home Rule was neither acceptable to the English leaders of the main parties nor the most important single issue for most voters, the system kept it off the agenda at Westminster. Only the conversion of the major parties, or unrest in Scotland, would change that. To break through the electoral barrier, Home Rule had to be not only a vaguely popular sentiment (as the Covenant proved it was) but deeply popular too – not just on everyone's list of ten good things but near enough the top of the list to convince political parties to promise it. This problem re-emerged in the devolution arguments of the 1980s: opinion polls regularly showed that four Scots in five wanted either devolution or outright independence. But what the polls did not show was *how much* they wanted those changes; the lack of widespread popular discontent tended to confirm the view of Unionists (pink or blue) at Westminster that Scots were not as bothered as the opinion pollsters, and Scottish journalists, suggested.

The Covenant movement carried on but had nowhere to go. There was an attempt to change its policy so that it would put up parliamentary candidates against any MP who did not agree to support Home Rule. But party-political loyalties were too great for the Covenanters themselves, and the idea was dropped. That was the end. MacCormick himself was involved in the romantic escapade of the seizure of the Stone of Destiny from Westminster Abbey and its smuggled repatriation to Scotland – it eventually turned up again at Arbroath Cathedral, draped with the Scottish saltire – and with unsuccessful legal challenges to Queen Elizabeth's right to style herself, 'the Second' in Scotland. Postboxes with the QEII symbol were blown up, though not by MacCormick or the SNP, and this was commemorated in song. MacCormick died in 1961, a sincere partisan of Scottish government, tinged with brilliance, who had tried various strategies but found them all to fail. By then his last throw, the Covenant, was drifting into half-forgotten history. How many Scottish political activists today even remember the great Covenant that, one day in Edinburgh, had seemed to portend a revolution in their nation's politics?

From Johnston to Ross-Shire: Labour's Unionist Heyday

Back, then, to the mainstream. Only two parties really counted in Scotland in the 1940s and 1950s. The first, Labour, was entering the promised land of power after decades of division and frustration. Its changed attitudes to Scottish Home Rule are symbolized by Tom Johnston. He is such a giant figure in Scottish politics, and his turning away from Home Rule was so clearly thought out, that he is worth considering in some detail. The clue to Johnston lies in his early training on the Kirkintilloch town council in 1914–18. To a modern observer the range of successful municipal enterprises engaged in by Johnston and his cronies in that ancient but semi-industrial town outside Glasgow seems incredible. They boosted higher education by holding popular boxing and dancing classes for those who also agreed to study English or mathematics; they formed a big, long-lived municipal bank to invest local money in building waterworks, gas and roads; they set up a municipal cinema, built municipal showers and houses, and bought bulk orders of English suits and baby food and sold them on at cost price; and they pasteurized milk and improved the food supply for the poorest children, halving the infant mortality rate in three years. This was municipal socialism of ambition and variety that made the Greater London Council of the 1980s look timid and conservative.

Although Johnston eventually became a more conventional Westminster parliamentarian – to the extent that he was seen by many in the 1930s as a serious alternative to Clement Attlee as Labour leader – he never quite lost his enthusiasm for the practical, rolled-sleeves approach of his early civic training. So when Churchill asked him to become first the Regional Commissioner for Scotland, in charge of civil defence, and then the Secretary of State for Scotland in the wartime government, Johnston seized his chance to try practical reforms on a grander scale. Slumped sleeplessly on overnight trains between Edinburgh and London, he dreamed of creating 'Scotia Resurgent' with reforms of almost everything. His mental activity seemed ceaseless, and his range of interest was extraordinary. Johnston's wartime priorities included a programme to bring new technology industries north; the creation of the North of Scotland Hydro-Electric Board to revive the Highlands and provide cheap electricity; the reduction of hospital waiting lists; reform of the school curriculum; projects to boost forestry and hill farming; and programmes against juvenile delinquency and VD. He even proposed a fish-farming industry and expressed great frustration that technology had not advanced sufficiently by the early 1940s to build an industry he was sure would have a big future (it now employs more people than disappearing industries such as steel-making or coalmining).

This explosion of activity, which continued after the war when Johnston left politics to run the Hydro Board and work for the Forestry Commission, seemed to offer the purpose of political life – getting things done – without its wearisome argumentativeness. Yet this was a quirk of wartime conditions; Churchill in effect made Johnston Scotland's benign dictator during hostilities, and for a few years he ran the country through a 'Council of State' including all the pre-war Secretaries of State. Johnston was not constitutionally dictatorial – he attempted a grand committee meeting of all Scottish MPs in Edinburgh, but it proved an anti-climax – but he was a natural doer, not a talker or a thinker. His ideas for industrial regeneration and social reform were infinitely more important to him than the principle of Home Rule. Yet he did not consider himself a whit less Scottish because he abandoned his old faith; he had a deep knowledge of Scottish history and could quote writers ranging from the Renaissance humanist George Buchanan to the contemporary Marxist Hugh MacDiarmid with accurate fluency. By any reasonable measure, he was remarkably successful. Like the most energetic of his successors, Johnston was determined to show that administrative devolution, through the Scottish Office, could do as much for the country as its own parliament. Like all of them, he used the threat of Nationalism as a cudgel to be waved in Cabinet.

His consensual wartime style is vividly demonstrated in a debate in the Commons a month before the SNP split, when Johnston said explicitly that his Council of State functioned as a pro-Scottish lobby in Whitehall, 'so that we could pool our joint efforts and enable me to speak with much greater backing than any of my predecessors'. He told MPs that the Council had been earnestly seeking to discover whether there had been discrimination against Scottish wood-working firms, had challenged the decision to print Scottish telephone directories in England and so on. In that debate, despite some sarcastic interruptions from pro-Home Rulers, speakers from all sides stressed the need for Scottish cooperation with the war effort. The Scottish Tory leader, Walter Elliot, agreed that there was an 'out-of-focus approach to Scottish problems' in White-hall and appealed for solidarity among Scottish politicians: 'Argument to the Scot is a vice more attractive than whisky. We would carry argument to the point of plunging ourselves into poverty as we have often, in the past, plunged ourselves into civil war.' And Johnston himself, when challenged about Home Rule by the West Fife communist MP Willie Gallacher, retorted that the issue was 'a hopeless irrelevance'.

After winning power in 1945 Labour moved smoothly from the Johnston era to become a classic centralizing reformist government. The last fiercely Scottish bastion of Home Rule socialism, the Independent Labour Party, had died. Throughout Britain corporate solutions were in vogue; in Scotland the Johnston era had already powerfully demonstrated their strengths. The new Unionism was not immediately obvious to all Scottish Labour MPs – the party's 1945 Scottish manifesto still stressed Home Rule, and Hector McNeil, later a Labour Scottish Secretary, half jocularly challenged his Tory opponent to strip off his kilt if he was not fully committed to a Scottish parliament. But although activists used Labour's Scottish conferences from 1945 onwards to make repeated attempts to get Home Rule back on the party's agenda, they were always rebuffed by the Labour leadership, which argued (at times quite openly) that Home Rule no longer mattered much now Labour had won power in London. Sadly for Scotland, Johnston's successors in the Scottish Office, including McNeil, had far less energy and imagination than he, so the administrative alternative was pursued with less enthusiasm too.

A 1945 internal Labour inquiry into Home Rule was sidelined by the party bosses, and the anger of activists was turned aside by appeals for pre-election unity. Attlee's government offered only legislative trinkets and extensions of its planning philosophy to Scotland – including a 'Scottish Economic Conference' to exchange information. The economic crisis, nationalization and rehousing were all far higher priorities. In the immediate aftermath of the war Scottish voters probably agreed wholeheartedly. The elation of victory, the prominent part played by Scottish regiments and the mingling of Scots with the other nations of Britain in the common cause had strengthened the feeling of a mutual Britishness – a theme rammed home in wartime propaganda, often brilliantly and movingly. The anti-war Nationalists were out on a very weak and lonely limb. The Scottish Trades Union Congress, which had been fiercely pro-Home Rule in its earlier days, partly reflecting the views of independent Scottish trade unions or of awkward-squad Scottish sections of British unions, had changed its mind too: in 1950 a motion from the miners for a Scottish parliament was crushed by a huge majority. And in 1950, for the first time, Labour went into the general election without a manifesto commitment to Home Rule. Even though the party was sliding from power, the loss of support in Scotland was less than in England.

The 1950–51 Labour administration appointed a fact-finding committee on Scottish economic statistics, and the 1951 Conservative government followed this the next year with a Royal Commission on Scottish government whose remit was to gather evidence and report on changes short of Home Rule. It produced virtually nothing. With Labour in Opposition, the same Unionist trends continued. Scottish party activists still voted for Home Rule motions, but the leadership was wholly opposed to change. In 1956 Hugh Gaitskell finally confirmed what had been utterly clear to all observers for years and formally told the Scottish party that Labour was now Unionist and against Home Rule for the Scots. The Scottish Labour membership obstinately passed a contradictory motion, but, year after year, the Home Rule cause declined. In 1959 the Scottish conference itself repudiated devolution. The reasons are not hard to grasp. The Scottish economy had started to perform badly again compared with the British economy as a whole; as in the 1920s, this made Scottish politicians sceptical about going it alone. Second, Labour believed strongly that it would win again at Westminster and felt that the experience of the wartime government and the Attlee administration had demonstrated its case that all-British policies were the best way to benefit Scotland. Scotland, in turn, would be vital to Labour's advance at Westminster. Although the middle of the decade saw the Conservatives getting an overall majority of the Scottish popular vote, Labour was advancing steadily throughout the 1950s.

As the 1960s opened Labour in Scotland was chalking up strong swings (better than in England in both the 1959 and the 1964 general election, despite the fact that the Conservatives were led by Harold Macmillan and then Alec Douglas-Home, two Scottish-blooded aristocrats). Labour was doing this on a shoe-string: in 1962 it had five full-time agents compared with fifty-five for the Unionists. In the two-party race of the 1964 election Labour won decisively in Scotland, taking forty-three seats to the Unionists' twenty-four and the Liberals' four. Harold Wilson was in power, thanks to Scottish votes. In 1966 Labour won an extra three seats in Scotland and came within an inch of winning 50 per cent of the total vote; the Conservatives were down to twenty seats. The Nationalists had won 5 per cent of the poll, or nearly 15 per cent in the seats that the SNP had actually fought. This was interesting, and a premonition, but was little noticed at the time.

This was the Willie Ross era in Scotland, dominated by the

stern-faced and authoritarian Presbyterian conservative who ran the country like a personal fiefdom for Harold Wilson. A former school-teacher and an elder of the Kirk who had served in the war as a major under Mountbatten, he was a savagely satirical and feared debater. He intimidated journalists: he would read out the names of political reporters at Labour's annual Scottish conferences and give them headmasterly reports of the old type: 'Jones, oh, Jones [long sigh]. No' very good at all. Must do better [weary shake of head].' But Ross was a straight, honest and privately humorous man, remembered with affection by some of his political enemies and civil servants too. When a particularly detailed negotiation about spending or drafting had ground on too long for his taste, he would announce, 'Right, I'm invoking the Athine formula.' If an incautious soul raised an eyebrow, Ross would solemnly explain: 'Ach, Tae Hell, It's Near Enough.' His combination of wit, ruthlessness and self-certainty helped him to outmanoeuvre political opponents inside the Labour Party and outside it. He probably rather frightened Harold Wilson, and he won a series of industrial presents for his supporters, including the Dounreay nuclear reactor, the Highlands and Islands Development Board, the rescue of Fairfields Shipyard on the Clyde and the Invergordon aluminium smelter. If Scotland later came close to being seen as an interventionists' economy, dependent on subsidy and corporatism, it was Ross who was partly to blame.

Devoted to economic planning and subsidy, his most enduring and successful creation was probably the Scottish Development Agency (today known as Scottish Enterprise). Within a few years of Labour's taking office, public spending in Scotland was a fifth higher per head than in England. Yet Ross's raids on the Exchequer and his interventionism were only logical extensions of the planning ethos of others who may be remembered more kindly, such as Wheatley and Johnston. He was even following the previous Conservative administration. Indeed, he was inclined to appoint Tories to his unelected boards: on one famous occasion he curtly informed Labour's Scottish conference at Perth that this was because, in his view, the Labour Party people did not have enough brains. The councillors and trade-union leaders were doubtless hurt and certainly grumbled. But they did so quietly: Ross's paternalistic politics were, at least to start with, extraordinarily successful with the voters.

Much of what he did seemed intended to build a one-party state; the 1969 report into the reform of local government, creating seven regions in Scotland, was seized upon by Ross partly because the giant Strathclyde region, covering half the Scottish voters, would clearly become a nigh impregnable Labour fortress. And the centralist one-party Scotland of Ross's imagination had as little place for National-ists as for Tories. He was for ever fulminating blackly about the dastardly ways of 'the Nats' at Cabinet meetings. Interestingly, Labour MPs on both sides of the devolution argument believe that Ross's contemptuously anti-SNP line (he invented the phrase 'Tartan Tories' for them) did his party no service. One pro-Home Rule Scottish politician, Harry Ewing, who was appointed to Ross's team as devolution minister by Harold Wilson without Ross's knowledge, believes that Ross scared many of the Scottish MPs, including the party's Scottish executive, into a Unionist position: 'I think the executive was just afraid of Willie Ross.' After 1966 Ross presented a face of uncompromising self-certainty to Scotland. But it was shortly to crack – and not into a smile either.

The Real 'Tartan Tories'

A myth has grown up about the Conservatives in Scotland. It is sometimes said that they used to be Scotland's great national party but that they have suffered a catastrophic decline since the 1950s because they have been seen more and more as an alien, anglified organization. There is a grain of truth there. It is hard to be a successful right-wing party without wrapping yourself in the flag, and the problem of 'which flag?' has never been quite resolved by the Scottish Tories. But the emphasis is all wrong. First, there was no 'Conservative Party' in Scotland between 1912 and 1965, only the Scottish Unionist Association. The distinction (even though the Unionists managed to produce a Conservative Prime Minister) was more than semantic. 'Unionist' referred not to the Scottish and English Union but to the Irish one.

A prime source of working-class support was the Protestants in sectarian Glasgow and Dundee. After Gladstone's conversion on Irish Home Rule in 1886, the big Liberal Unionist breakaway group began a long courtship with the Tories, which led to fusion

in the autumn of 1912 and eventually to the extinction of the
Liberal Unionist tradition – though there were Scottish MPs who
insisted on being described as Liberal Unionists or National Liberals,
not Tories, until the 1960s. In 1912 the Unionist title had been
agreed on partly because the Conservative or Tory label was considered a handicap in Scotland. The Conservative cause had been a
hard one ever since the 1830s, when the Tory landlords' opposition
to parliamentary reform helped to turn Scotland into a Liberal
fiefdom. The first Reform Bill had a proportionately greater impact
in Scotland than in England, raising the number of voters from just
4,500 to nearly 65,000, an increase of 1,400 per cent. Tory opposition
to it was consequently bitterly resented; the Duke of Buccleuch's
carriage was stoned in Edinburgh in 1832, and the Tories had to
field pro-Reform candidates to stand any chance of winning Scottish
seats. Although the Tories regrouped and made progress, suspicion
of them persisted.

Fewer Scottish than English voters were dependent on the patronage of Tory landowners, and the independent-mindedness of Scottish Presbyterianism hardly helped. A typically hostile analysis came
from the great Whig lawyer Lord Cockburn, who blamed a Tory
win in a by-election on a 'confederacy of Lairds to domineer over
their dependents. It is the victory of the owners of the soil achieved
by the forced services of their helots and serfs.' And when the
Scottish Conservative Association was formed in 1835 the (then
teenage) *Scotsman* newspaper predicted that its main purpose would
be bribery and intimidation. Dusty, irrelevant stuff? More than 150
years later, in 1992, a prominent Scot who had served in Margaret
Thatcher's Cabinet was still analysing the weakness of his party in
Scotland in terms of the lack of a wealthy farming tradition (except
in Dumfriesshire and parts of the north-east) and the over-reliance
of the Tories on a very few lairds!

But their electoral failure and the taint of landlordism did not
mean that they were seen in the last century as an alien party. Sir
Walter Scott, the most famous nineteenth-century Scottish Tory,
was a deep patriot whose complex and anguished sense of history
remains a strong influence today. The myth of Scott the anti-Scot
has been effectively demolished by the revival of interest in the
novelist's furiously patriotic attack on London currency measures.

In his first 'Malachi Malagrowther' letter of 1826 Sir Walter Scott complained that English ministers inflicted on Scotland 'experiment and innovation at our expense, which they resist obstinately when it is to be carried through at their own risk' – a complaint that was echoed during the poll-tax saga of the mid-1980s. Yet the backward-looking, sentimental Toryism of Scott's followers and the Highland cult, discussed in Chapter 2, was never translated into votes.

Apart from occasional eruptions of good fortune, the Tories languished as a minority Opposition party in high-mindedly Liberal Scotland until the Liberal split over Ireland. When Randolph Churchill arrived in Scotland in the 1880s to advertise his 'Tory democracy', the incorporation of the working-classes into the party, he found the aristocratic and urban leaders of Toryism unpleasant and uninterested. In 1880, in a joke with a curiously modern ring, the Scottish Conservative MPs were said to be able to travel south in one six-seater first-class rail carriage. Lord Salisbury's Scottish weakness in seats was unmatched by any leader until Margaret Thatcher's middle years. Unlike her, he chose to acquiesce in majority Scottish opinion – agreeing, for instance, to revive the Scottish Secretaryship of State, a measure demanded by leading Liberals, like Rosebery. Tory near-impotence in Scotland was ended by another Liberal, Gladstone, when he became enamoured of Irish Home Rule. The Orange Order had been reviving in Scotland since the 1870s and was explicitly pro-Tory even before the great Home Rule crisis reintroduced religious bigotry into Scottish politics in a big way. An historian of the period, I. G. C. Hutchinson, captures the mood of Protestant Tory Orangeism in Scotland by quoting part of a speech by Provincial Grand Master MacLeod in 1874: 'They had got a good sound solid Conservative Government [cheers] in place of a mixty-maxty government of Churchmen, Ritualists, Quakers, Jews, Infidels, Papists . . . every sound Orangeman was a Conservative and if there were any radicals in their ranks they were as rare as black swans.'

Irish Home Rule changed the whole scene, and from 1886 onwards the Protestant working classes (especially in religiously divided and pro-imperialist Glasgow) started coming over to Unionism. The split in Liberalism also undermined its old moral authority, perhaps best exemplified by Gladstone's famous Midlothian campaign. By the 1890s the Liberal Unionists (against Irish, but not necessarily Scottish, Home Rule) were sitting with the Conservatives at Westminster. The Scottish Unionist party of modern times had been born. Yet the Liberal influence still seemed daunting right up to the war. John Buchan, the novelist and Tory MP, penned the finest description of the Scottish anti-Tory mood in his haunting 1940 autobiography, *Memory Hold-the-Door*:

Now that the once omnipotent Liberal party has so declined, it is hard to realize how formidable it was in 1911 – especially in Scotland. Its dogmas were so completely taken for granted that their presentation partook less of argument than of tribal incantation. Mr Gladstone had given it an aura of earnest morality, so that its platforms were also pulpits and its harangues had the weight of sermons. Its members seemed to assume that their opponents must be lacking either in morals or mind. The Tories were the 'stupid' party; Liberals alone understood and sympathized with the poor; a working man who was not a Liberal was inaccessible to reason, or morally corrupt, or intimidated by laird or employer. I remember a lady summing up the attitude thus: Tories may think they are better born, but Liberals know that they are born better.

The condescending tone was flung back. The first Unionist reform for Scotland, though accomplished with strong Liberal support, was the creation of the Scottish Secretaryship of State in 1885 (still seen by some modern Tories as the start of the rot). But a letter written by the Conservative premier Lord Salisbury to the Duke of Richmond and Gordon, offering him the first Secretaryship of State, has become notorious for its bluff and cheery cynicism: 'The work is not very heavy – the dignity (measured by salary) is the same as your present office – but measured by the expectations of the people of Scotland it is approaching the Arch-angelic ... It really is a matter where the effulgence of two Dukedoms and the best salmon river in Scotland will go a long way.'

Against the background of the Liberal hegemony, then the Labour Party's success in spreading its gospel through working-class Scotland, the notion that the Scottish Conservatives and Unionists were ever the great party of the country starts to look pretty threadbare. Their successes between the wars and in the 1950s (in 1955 they got 50.1 per cent of the Scottish vote, the only party ever to have done so) became not the norm but the lucky tactical exceptions, to be remembered in a blue-and-gold-tinged haze. The Unionists of the 1920s and 1930s benefited both from strong anti-Catholicism and from the Labour split at the time of the National Government.

In the 1920s the Unionists still had strong connections with the Grand Orange Lodge and picked up support at the same time as the Scottish Kirk was campaigning against Irish Catholic immigration. More positively, after 1931 the National Government pressed ahead with the devolution of Scottish administration to the Scottish Office. The system of appointed boards to run things, which was old-fashioned, dominated by Scots lawyers and corrupt, was reformed by Unionists against sentimental-patriotic Labour opposition. The symbol of Unionist reform was the building in Edinburgh (after a bitter architectural feud), on the site of the old Calton Gaol, which had held the Red Clydesiders, of St Andrew's House as the headquarters of the Scottish Office. The building was completed and opened in 1939 and is one of the country's most famous Art Deco constructions, though an Edinburgh architectural guide complains: 'It has the brooding, authoritarian characteristics of the secure headquarters of an occupying power.' Occupying or not, the work done by Unionists on the repatriation of Scottish administration from 1884 onwards gave them their own distinctive agenda.

After the war the Unionists were again able to mobilize special factors to help them overcome the relatively smaller size of the Scottish middle class. They periodically called for, and commissioned, more or less meaningless reports into the economy and government of Scotland and carried on an effective propaganda campaign against Labour nationalization. In the light of the closures of the 1980s and 1990s it is interesting to reflect that if the post-war Tory Unionists had had their way, nationalization would have produced two separate entities – Scottish Coal and a Scottish Steel Corporation. Throughout this period too the dramatic Liberal decline meant that Scotland had only two real parties. Austerity, nationalization and the lack of any commitment to Home Rule made Labour unpopular with millions of Scots, and those protest voters had nowhere to turn but the Unionists. The brightest of the Scottish Tories, like Walter Elliot, played the Scottish card very cleverly against Labour, as we have seen. Perhaps the most famous example of Tory Unionism bedecking itself in tartan came from Churchill himself, who told a meeting in Edinburgh in 1950 that Labour centralization in Whitehall was contrary to the spirit of the 1707 Act of Union: 'If England became an absolute Socialist State, owning all the means of production, distribution and exchange, ruled only by politicians and their officials in the London offices, I personally cannot feel Scotland would be bound to accept such a dispensation.'

The thirteen-year Tory rule of 1951–64 saw Scotland run by a team of consensual managers, often aristocrats. There was Churchill's old drinking partner and confidant, James Stuart. There was the future Prime Minister, Lord Home, who had been asked by Churchill to see if he could get rid of 'this embryonic Scottish nationalist thing'. (Yes, the same Churchill who had draped himself in tartan rhetoric when Labour was in power, the same Churchill who had said in 1911 in Dundee that a Scottish parliament would mean 'a great enrichment not only of the national life of Scotland but of the politics and public life of the United Kingdom'.) There was Michael Noble, later Baron Glenkinglas. All seemed rather better at downing partridge than downing socialists. The Unionists had their own quasi-corporatist tradition, represented by Bob Boothby and Elliot himself, and in the later 1950s they started to drift into industrial interventionism to try to correct economic decline. If there were a few industrial turkeys tethered to Scotland by the Labour regime of Willie Ross, the Conservatives can claim the credit for the British Motor Corporation at Bathgate (1961 – gone), and the Linwood car plant, where the Hillman Imp was built (1963 – gone). The Ravenscraig steelworks (1958 – going) was no turkey, but it was yet another example of the failure of transplanting industry, particularly when its central managers are hundreds of miles away.

It has become a routine of English Conservative analysis to see Scotland as a subsidy alcoholic – poor and too dazed by wee nips of intervention to rebuild its own prosperity. This belief seems to be a mix of two things: the English folk memory of impoverished Scotland going back over centuries, and the sight of higher spending and failed interventionism there since the 1950s. Yet through much of its history Scotland has been wealthy; before the First World War it was measured as the world's richest country. For reasons we have seen the inter-war years were disastrous, but the economic pain was expressed in lower wages and emigration. The period of Scotland, the industrial welfare recipient, is a recent and historically brief one, for which Labour and the Conservatives must share equal credit or blame.

In its active, policy, phase it started in about 1958 and was over by the early 1970s. Because Scottish Secretaries in the Cabinet were always able to threaten their colleagues with nationalism and were working with an historically higher budget, the impact of interventionism was stronger in Scotland than in much of the rest of the United Kingdom. At the time it felt good and helped to sustain a Unionist consensus. But when the economic growth slowed the consensus started to come apart. Since then Scottish economic politics has been largely about coping with the hangover from that fifteen-year experiment. Perhaps we should call it the Toothill era, after the report on the Scottish economy that called for more industrial planning and led to the formation of the Scottish Development Department in 1962. Sir John Toothill, the chairman of Ferranti in Edinburgh, in fact produced a more progressive and sophisticated analysis of what was wrong with Scotland's economic infrastructure than has sometimes been acknowledged – he was unimpressed by attempts to prop up old industries and keen on drawing in new ones, later the main *raison d'être* of the Scottish Development Agency. Maybe, then, a fairer name for this era would be the McButskellite phase, merely a northern variant of the consensual Whitehall strategies of the period, overseen by a florid, complacent fellow in bowler hat and trews.

Although they were a little better organized than Labour, the Unionists had perennial problems with recruiting activists, particularly in the rural areas. The farmers tended to be poorer. The Liberal tradition persisted. The Tories' rural roots were shallow compared with those in most of rural England. One working-class woman Tory office-bearer in Perthshire in the early 1960s confessed that, although she was happy to work for the party, she could not vote for it. Her taken-aback colleagues asked why and were told firmly: 'Because the family was aye Liberal.' Another anecdotal example of the rural Tories' lack of self-confidence came in the mid-1980s, when a Tory local candidate began a leaflet with the defensive thought: 'Although I am a Conservative, I care a lot about local people . . .' Their membership was too old and too amateur. Throughout most of the modern period the Scottish Tory Party has contained a high proportion of upper-class Scots who have sounded English and English incomers. Some of its candidates did not even use the words 'Unionist' or 'Conservative' when campaigning but hid behind words like 'progressive', 'local' or 'independent'. All of these points are worth remembering when considering the Nationalist surges of the 1960s and 1970s. They were a reaction to Labour failure, and in most parts of Britain protest votes might have gone to the rival big party. But in Scotland by the mid-1960s the Tories were weaker than they looked, poorly organized and too often perceived as somehow anti-patriotic. And, as we shall see, the SNP vote seemed a good alternative.

Sober Men and the Thistle

Perhaps the first member of the Scottish pro-Union consensus to take the threat of Nationalism seriously in the 1960s was the Labour anti-devolutionist Tam Dalyell. Best known to a wider public for his dogged and solemn pursuit of Margaret Thatcher over the *Belgrano* and Westland affairs, Dalyell is one of the great originals of Scottish politics. In 1962 this Old Etonian schoolmaster and local laird was the successful by-election candidate at Labour's safe heartland seat of West Lothian. The area, which includes the old town and palace of Linlithgow, had become one of the centres of a modest and largely unnoticed Nationalist revival. The year before, an Ayrshire farmer, Ian Macdonald, had won 18 per cent of the vote in a by-election in the Labour stronghold of Glasgow Bridgeton, but a combination of local factors had been used to explain this away. Macdonald, however, was stirred by his relative success (relative to the daunting unsuccess of SNP candidates from 1945 to 1961, that is) and decided to devote himself to the Nationalist cause full-time. The first talented organizer the party had had since the 1930s, he travelled to West Lothian to campaign for the SNP candidate there, a scoutmaster and manufacturer called Billy Wolfe.

Wolfe, who later became the SNP leader, fought a strong campaign under the slogan 'Put Scotland First' on issues such as the threat to the local shale-oil industry. The Conservative candidate, by contrast, a bald and chilly lawyer, found that the new-fangled television coverage was doing him no favours. Dalyell quickly became alarmed by what he was hearing on the doorsteps and told Labour's then Scottish Secretary, Will Marshall, that he feared the SNP would win 10,000 votes. Marshall eyed Dalyell contemptuously and retorted that he had thought he would make a reasonable Labour MP, but if that was an example of his judgement, the party had clearly made a mistake. Since the war West Lothian had seen pretty standard Labour–Unionist battles, but in 1962, the Labour vote fell by 6,000. (Dalyell comments: 'I wasn't exactly everyone's cup of tea.')

Rather more dramatically, the Unionist vote slumped from more than 18,000 in 1959 to just 4,784; Billy Wolfe came second with 9,450, not far short of Dalyell's predicted 10,000. This result was no inexplicable freak. Macdonald, now working full-time for the SNP, had assembled an enthusiastic local team and whipped up a fierce campaign. In the early 1960s he criss-crossed Scotland helping to set up and organize local SNP branches, so that, when disillusion with Labour became widespread after 1966, the SNP had the membership and organization to start to offer an alternative. Before 1962 there were fewer than twenty active SNP branches in the country and only about 2,000 members. Three years later there were 140 branches, and by 1968 there were 484 branches with up to 120,000 members in total. It was an astonishing expansion.

And the expansion changed the character of the party. Back in the 1950s, as the SNP leader of the period, Arthur Donaldson, later told Wolfe, 'all the activists of the SNP could have been the complement of a small passenger aircraft, and had they flown together and crashed without survivors, the cause of independence would have been lost to view for many years.' In those days the smallness of the party had encouraged sects and breakaways, some of them pretty unpleasant. One group's pamphlet was titled 'The English: Are They Human?' and apparently concluded that they were not: 'Rotten with class privilege and class war. Putrid with sexual perverts and shameless adulterers in high places.' As the SNP started to grow, however, it attracted a core support of more serious souls. What kind of people? Most of the evidence is anecdotal, but it suggests that the revival of Nationalism appealed to the kind of skilled working-class and lower-middle-class voter who disliked the somewhat authoritarian nature of the Labour movement but had no feeling for the Tory cause either – the sort of mildly stroppy individualists who, in other parts of Britain during the 1960s, gravitated to Liberalism.

Wolfe's list of his campaign workers at West Lothian in 1962 is no scientific sample, but it gives the flavour: there were a couple of steel- and paper-mill workers, a salesman, a bank teller, a jeweller, a painter and decorator, a merchant seaman, a surveyor, a draughts-man, a clerk, a publican and a student. It was a group strikingly different from the upper-class lawyers, poets, intellectuals and aristo-crats who had dominated Nationalism a generation earlier. This was, granted, a largely working-class constituency (where the only aristocrat, Tam Dalyell, was on the other side). But the SNP's relaxed leadership of the time was not so dissimilar: lawyers, farmers, small businessmen, clerks. A far cry from 'A Drunk Man Looks at the Thistle', these were more sober types, less interested in poetry than in digging out figures on the Scottish economy.

The party's internal story was one of steady advance. It was an unheroic history of fundraising, finding cheap printers, compiling policies at long meetings, relentless membership recruitment and the establishment of research departments – the behind-the-office-door tale of any modern party anywhere in the world (and of interest to nobody outside it). The SNP did the things one would have ex-pected it to – expended energy on better propaganda, hired staff, published leaflets and policy statements for the 1964 and 1966 general elections. In 1963 party members were impressed with the then ubiquitous symbol of the Campaign for Nuclear Disarmament (CND), and the SNP's equally recognizable thistle-loop symbol was created and disseminated. (It was finally killed off in 1991 and replaced by a sharper-edged, more geometric version, which some party members complained looked like a right-wing South African emblem.) Much thought went into ways of expanding the party's influence – sometimes unsuccessfully, as in a brief courtship with the Scottish Liberals. Wolfe was a leading light on the SNP side, and both David Steel and Ludovic Kennedy, the campaigner and broadcaster, were intrigued by the idea on the Liberal side, but the talks came to nothing. Sometimes the search for new outlets was successful; a long battle for air time and party-political broadcasts finally got the Nationalists on television and radio. Alongside traditional Nationalist themes, mostly economic, SNP activists became involved in the new politics of the 1960s, protesting against the Vietnam war and *Polaris* nuclear bases, opposing hereditary titles and pushing for the single transferable vote.

The SNP was, perhaps unconsciously, positioning itself as a classic protest party, as natural a haven for those disillusioned with the two-party system as was Jo Grimond's Liberal Party. Its political philosophy, outside Nationalism, was of a familiar 'plague-on-both-your-houses' sort, in favour of worker representatives on company boards and cooperatives and of citizen-volunteers running social services. It evolved during the 1960s into a mixture of individualistic, anti-state leftism that mirrored the Liberal revival in England. Apart from Billy Wolfe, other new-generation leaders, like Winnie Ewing and Margo MacDonald, emerged. A Nationalist pools system – Alba Pools – was devised to bring in funds. The party started to put up more candidates too – fifteen candidates and 64,000 votes in 1964, twenty-three candidates in 1966. In the 1967 Glasgow Pollok by-election a Nationalist vet, George Leslie, gained more than 10,000 votes, dishing the Labour candidate and letting the Conservative win. In the local election of that year the party won 200,000 votes and gained sixty-nine county and burgh seats. With hindsight, then, the bombshell of the 1967 Hamilton by-election could have been predicted. The early self-assurance of Willie Ross, who routinely dismissed the SNP as mere 'tartan Tories', had perhaps mesmerized political journalists and other observers. Still, all the policy papers, branches and saved deposits in the world register as nothing on the political seismograph compared with an actual parliamentary victory.

And it came in Hamilton, a small industrial town near Glasgow with its own rather fine racecourse and a long radical tradition based on coalminers and steelworkers. Hamilton had been a staunchly Labour seat – indeed, on paper the party's safest one in Scotland. In October 1967 Tom Fraser, the sitting MP, resigned to take over the chairmanship of the Hydro Board. The SNP, though it had only a small local organization, brought in party workers from Glasgow, Edinburgh and West Lothian – and even managed to get the help of some Welsh Nationalists. The SNP fought a classic by-election campaign. Its candidate was a young, telegenic Glasgow solicitor, Winnie Ewing, who out-campaigned and out-argued her Labour opponent, Alex Wilson. Among those who came to speak for her was Ludovic Kennedy, who resigned from the Scottish Liberal Party to do so. She won with 46 per cent of the vote, seized the headlines and was taken in triumph to London on a train packed with Nationalists before being driven to Westminster in a scarlet Hillman Imp from the Scottish Linwood assembly plant. Her victory gained her television and press coverage the like of which the SNP had only dreamed of: Wolfe reckoned it was as much as the small party had received in the previous twenty years. Ewing's exposure, including a column in the mass-circulation *Daily Record*, must have contributed to the party's even more impressive performance in the local elections the following May, when the SNP got 34 per cent of the votes cast, beating the other parties and making 101 net gains against eighty-four losses for Labour. Although Labour won Hamilton back in 1970, Mrs Ewing's two years in Parliament did her party a great service.

The reasons for Hamilton and the local election victories are not hard to spot: disillusion with the Wilson government, which had failed to build the shiny new economy it had promised four years earlier; Tory and Labour uninterest in Home Rule; and the SNP's hard grind to make itself an effective vote-gathering outfit. The Nationalist gains were being made mostly at Labour's expense and mostly in the smaller industrial towns and the central-belt New Towns; the party won control of Cumbernauld in 1968. It was proving an attractive protest vehicle for working-class voters outside the big (and politically more conservative) cities. No doubt it was also attracting tactical votes from Tories in strong Labour areas, as happened later in Dundee East, where the SNP's future leader, Gordon Wilson, was returned on Tory votes for years.

The successes of 1967–8 were early skirmishes between the SNP and the big Unionist parties. There were many reverses and disappointments to come. But their real significance was seen inside the Conservative and Labour leaderships, where the unexpectedness of the Nationalist challenge produced panic. They had been used to fighting one another, knew the rules, could calibrate their responses. But the Nationalist threat took them by surprise, and both Edward Heath and Harold Wilson moved far faster and more dramatically to counter it than they would have done faced by a more conventional challenge. Within a year of Hamilton both parties set in train committees and commissions that would lead to proposals for Scottish self-government. Both parties disinterred arguments they thought they had buried for good in the early 1950s, and both parties then split over how far to go. Intellectually the first puff from the Nationalist wolf had set the Unionist house rocking; in London, at least, no one seemed to be able to remember quite why a Scottish parliament was so unacceptable. Nationalism was seen as a decentralist philosophy rather than a left-wing political threat to London. Support came from strange places: in his diary for 1968 the Labour politician Tony Benn recorded a lunch conversation with the Duke of Edinburgh: 'We talked of the institution of Government and he said he thought it was a mistake to overcentralize, warmly supporting Welsh and Scottish nationalism; and so do I.'

So there began a headlong and somewhat undignified retreat from straightforward Unionism. It turned the 1970s into the decade of 'devolution'. Today devolution seems as dated as kipper ties, 'Ally's tartan army' and the Bay City Rollers – and, for many, marginally less alluring. There was still no Scottish parliament by the time Margaret Thatcher terminated the 1970s. But those years proved to be important ones for Scotland, bringing hallucinations of optimism, sloughs of black despair and mind-numbing periods of national frustration. At times Scottish politics would seem less about power than about identity crisis – Caledonia foetal and girning on the therapist's chair. If so, the devolution therapy changed Scotland; it emerged from the next decade looking rather more than ten years older.

4

The Devolution Years

There has been a qualitative change in the call for devolution. In the early twentieth century the demand for a separate Scottish legislature was the result of national sentiment. That national sentiment still exists, but added to it is the need for good government, good administration and a better deal for the Scottish people within the United Kingdom.

Malcolm Rifkind, after resigning from the Conservative
front bench, December 1976

An Assembly! we shout,
then vote the thing out
and get back to the business of girning.

Maurice Lindsay,
on what happened afterwards, 1980

To understand the 1970s in Scotland it is necessary first to remember that devolution was mostly cooked up in London by busy politicians with only one eye on the pot. People began to talk about the break-up of Britain for the first time since the Irish crisis of the 1920s. But it was the metropolitan establishment, not the Scots, who seemed the less committed to the status quo. And it was the Tory Unionists in Glasgow, and the Labour Party's Scottish leadership, who were outraged to discover that Home Rule for their country was back on the agenda. Who most wanted devolution? At first a few and relatively obscure Scottish politicians but, above all, the Yorkshire-man Harold Wilson, the Kentish Ted Heath and the Welshman Jim Callaghan. As they did so, 100-carat Scots like the Calvinist Glasgow Tory Teddy Taylor and Labour's headmasterly Willie Ross looked on in disbelief. The reason was that, from London, the Scottish Nationalists looked more threatening yet easier to deal with than they seemed in Scotland. They were an unknown and puzzling quantity for the Westminster village, whose great men found it hard to take their measure. Wilson and Heath decided that a bit of

Home Rule, a toy parliament, albeit with working and satisfactorily noisy parts, would end the Scottish tantrum. And, it has to be admitted, the judgement of the Prime Ministers was better than that of their Caledonian lieutenants: devolution did stop the SNP bandwagon, which was its primary purpose. It did not produce a Scottish assembly, but then that was its secondary and lesser purpose.

Had London politicians been concerned first and foremost with the good governance of Scotland, they might have produced a different scheme and then campaigned for it with greater vigour and conviction. But, however much time devolution took up, they felt always that they had bigger problems to worry about. Inflation, slowing growth, trade-union militancy and political sclerosis seemed to be easing the whole island of Britain into a slithering, irreversible economic and political decline. North Sea oil offered a respite for the nation, so Scotland's continued membership of the London club seemed important in the metropolis. But none of the political leaders had the energy or inclination to philosophize seriously about the British constitution and how best to reform it. The post-1707 settlement was not, they felt, a Union made in Heaven. Devolution was an attempt to settle the Scottish Nationalists' hash without the bore of resorting to a tough or principled defence of the status quo. But, like other clever wheezes of that era, it turned out to be a doomed compromise between irreconcilable principles – in this case, parliamentary absolutism on the one hand and self-determination for Scotland on the other.

The very word devolution means the impermanent passing down of powers still held in principle by the superior body. Enoch Powell's aphorism 'Power devolved is power retained' sums up that side of the affair. But because it was born of weakness, mainly the weakness of the 1974–9 Labour government, devolution was a slippery concept. Ominously, it meant entirely different things to different people. London liked devolution because it didn't seem to mean a dramatic shift in the way Britain worked. In Scotland Nationalists were attracted to it for just the opposite reason: they thought it was obvious that it would lead to the break-up of Britain. In 1977 Jim Sillars, then a Labour-Nationalist, happily rechristened the Scotland Bill the 'catapult to Scottish independence Bill'. Many Scottish Unionists feared it for the same reason: the compromise with Scottish Nationalism looked horribly like betrayal. Eventually every party became divided about devolution's true message: neo-Nationalism or a more stable form of Unionism?

The failure of devolution has been almost universally explained as a failure of nerve by the Scottish people when they declined to endorse it by the required margin at a referendum one wintry day in 1979. But its failure had as much to do with its political purpose. It was a mere phase in the game at Westminster, one tactical stratagem among many during 'a low, dishonest decade'. It was not all-important for most of the parliamentary players. A few years on, it had become only half remembered history, as irrelevant as the Lib–Lab pact or the European referendum campaign of 1975. That would not have mattered much except that in Scotland it left painful psychological wounds the country could have done without, a long period of self-doubt and even self-disgust. It itched away in the national memory, reinforcing, for some, the conviction that to be Scottish was to fail at some crucial moment. But it had other deep effects that have not been fully disentangled even today. It let Scots know that the Union was not a sacred cause in London and, to that extent, it changed the political music of the country, if not its political architecture. Writers had patriotically imagined the Union as a cage, imprisoning the Scottish lion. The devolution years showed that the cage door was no longer locked (if, indeed, it ever had been). The only question was, did the lion want out?

A Grocer in Tartan

Edward Heath had been worried about Scotland before the National-ists seized Hamilton. The Scottish Tories, for reasons discussed in the previous chapter, had been sliding downhill since the mid-1950s. The 1959 'You've never had it so good' election, which took place in Scotland against the background of rising unemployment, saw the Unionist MPs reduced from thirty-six to thirty-one. The 1964 election saw their seats cut to twenty-four, and by 1966, Heath's first election as leader, they were down to twenty. This may seem not so bad compared with the 1987 and 1992 general election results, but it was downright humiliating for a party that had been dominant in Scotland only fifteen years before. So the rise of the

Nationalists offered Heath both a challenge and an opportunity. The Scots both wanted greater autonomy and were clearly kicking against the failure of the Wilson government. If he offered devolution, might that take the steam out of Nationalism, and at the same time give the Scottish Conservatives an attractive, patriotic banner around which anti-Labour Scots could unite? Heath, whose political success had been founded on his detailed but abrasive style at Westminster but who had little experience of Scotland, decided it was worth a try.

There was something a little awkward about a party that called itself Unionist peddling Home Rule, even in the homeopathic doses being considered by Heath. The Tories had, however, been here before, immediately after the war. Indeed, throughout the century there had been a small and intellectual strain of Tory thought that was downright federalist. Although there is no evidence that the ordinary Conservative supporters were attracted to devolution at this time, some of the party's younger and more thoughtful members were. The Thistle Group was formed in November 1967, after Hamilton, and its founders included the future Scottish ministers Michael Ancram and Peter Fraser, later Lord Fraser of Carmyllie. He, despite losing his East Angus seat in the 1987 election, again became a Scottish Office minister following the 1992 election. Older dogs now, they were young pups then, and sounded it. Their first pamphlet, published by Ancram (a good man who re-emerged in 1992 as the MP for the English seat of Devizes), announced that 'A basic aim of the Thistle Group is to stir things up.' Stirring things up is, of course, what Conservativism is meant to be against. On Scotland the group was unequivocal: 'We are convinced that a measure of devolution over her domestic affairs is essential . . . In the eyes of any Scotsman, Scotland is The Priority; and it is only by concentrating on priorities that any political party can hope to gain the confidence of the electorate. This the Scottish Tory Party has failed to do.' The Thistle Group even envisaged a Scottish parliament that raised its own taxes and looked after its own monetary policy.

It was, among other things, a ginger group for federalism, the traditional creed of the Liberals from Gladstone and Asquith onwards. Federalism had long attracted the classier type of thinking

Tory. One classy Tory, Malcolm Rifkind, became chairman of the Thistle Group in 1969, was Scottish Secretary from 1986 to 1990 and is still intrigued by federalist theory, if not practice. Mr Rifkind has always been considered a little too clever for a real Tory. He probably reads books and certainly makes speeches without notes in the House of Commons, where his fluency is regarded with some suspicion. Anyway devolution and federalism were in the Edinburgh air by the late 1960s. A series of *Scotsman* articles advocating them were popular enough to be reprinted as a two-shilling pamphlet called 'How Scotland Should be Governed'. In February 1968 the newspaper tackled head-on the likelihood of a cynical conversion to devolution by the party leaders:

Mr Wilson and Mr Heath will surely decide to risk annoying some of their doctrinaire supporters by making major changes in their parties' policy. Such belated conversions based mainly on expediency may embarrass those who undergo them, upset the guardians of traditional doctrine and cause mockery and amusement among the previously converted. But in this particular case, a change in outlook . . . would be most commendable.

The newspaper itself had no doubt where it stood: 'Government of the people by and for the people should to the largest possible extent be where the people are, so that they can keep an eye on it and take an interest in it.' So when Heath started to revive the argument used by Churchill and Elliot twenty years earlier − that nationalization and the centralization of power in London were threatening Scotland's survival − he was not raising a wholly unfamiliar idea. And, as we shall see, there was a certain amount of federalist immorality in the Labour Party too.

Heath called in a brewer. Sir William McEwen Younger was a leading Unionist and pillar of the Doric establishment − good war, chairman of Scottish & Newcastle Breweries and on the boards of companies like the British Linen Bank and Scottish Television. He had already been asked by Heath to chair a small committee to review the government of Scotland, and he started work a few weeks after the Hamilton by-election. Sir William and his committee decided that a Scottish assembly should be part-elected, part-nominated but should be clearly subordinate to Westminster. This was weak beer by the standards of Sir William's company, but it was just what Heath had ordered. Now he had a devolutionist plan and resolved to make it party policy. Heath was rarely incapacitated by self-doubt and, being right so regularly compared with lesser fellows, saw little need to consult his party in Scotland. In May 1968 he announced to a stunned conference of the Scottish Conservative and Unionist Party in Perth that he was moved by the clamour for change in Scotland. Clamour? What clamour? The doughty Tory matrons and sober Glaswegian Unionists listening to his 'Declaration of Perth' (as it was swiftly dubbed, an ironic allusion to the Arbroath one of 1320) were both surprised and offended to find themselves being treated as Home Rule shock troops by an Englishman. They did not understand, because no one had bothered to explain to them, why he was suddenly parading himself as a demi-Nationalist. Heath applauded the Younger proposals, which only a handful of his audience had read, and announced that he was submitting them to a grand-sounding 'constitutional commission'. This would be chaired by the former Prime Minister and local Perthshire grandee Sir Alec Douglas-Home and would draw up plans to reform Scotland's government. A year later, at the 1969 Scottish Tory conference in Leith, some outraged Unionists had recovered enough to pelt Heath's proposals verbally, declaring his commission merely a pretentious gimmick.

The Douglas-Home commission was set up a couple of months after Perth. It met every four weeks or so for eighteen months and completed its report, *Scotland's Government*, in March 1970. Among its advisers was Sir Robert Menzies, the former Australian Prime Minister, who suggested that Scotland and Wales should be governed by 'regional provincial councils' with an override for the central Parliament on matters of national importance – a proposal, he revealed, that was based on the successful political experience of South Africa! The commission put only a little thin flesh on the recommendations of the Younger committee and proposed an elected but weak 'Scottish Convention' with 125 members. Its work would be closely tailored to Westminster's; it would not be able to initiate legislation of its own; and it would be able to discuss only those issues that Westminster decided were Scotland-specific ones. There were no suggestions for limiting the number of MPs from Scotland who would carry on travelling south. This was minimalist devolution. The Douglas-Home report was accepted by the 1970 Scottish Tory conference, albeit with some MPs and party officials expressing their distaste, and was included in that year's election manifesto.

But once Heath got into power, two months after the report's publication, he showed no inclination whatsoever to press ahead with it. Conservative devolution was pushed aside by other issues. Heath announced (shades of John Major in 1992) that reform of the structure of local government in Scotland was more important than devolution. He would also have to wait for the continuing Kilbrandon Commission to report. His real reasons, though, seem to have been merely that the SNP were doing less well in the polls and in local elections and that the Scottish Tories had proved disappointingly unenthusiastic. Devolution had been a useful ploy but now seemed less so. Heath folded up his kilt and saltire and shoved them into some dim mental recess. The era of Ted McHeath, Scottish resistance leader, had ended as abruptly as it had started. Just as in the early 1950s, Tory devolution had proved more attractive as a weapon in opposition than as a guiding principle of government. As we shall see, there were compelling parallels with Labour after 1970. In both cases there was a precipitate decision by the London leader, which met with puzzlement and hostility among his Scottish activists and MPs and produced, after a lot of ballyhoo, a rather modest proposal. The difference between the two was what happened next and merely reveals the similarity between their motives. When Heath attained power the Nationalists were rumbling quietly in the glens (they managed only 12 per cent and a single MP in the 1970 election). So nothing happened. By the time Wilson came back in 1974 the Nationalists were streaming down the hillsides, threatening to seize serious numbers of Labour and Tory seats, so devolution was pushed ahead. A Nationalist vote may have been many things – a silly vote, a selfish vote, a brave vote, a patriotic vote. But in the 1970s it was never a wasted vote.

How Labour Remembered Home Rule

In the immediate aftermath of Hamilton Labour had been slower to move than the Conservatives. It is generally easier for oppositions than governments to make dramatic policy U-turns, but Labour also had a particularly profound hatred of the SNP, which meant that any concession to Nationalism was painful. Jim Sillars, who converted later, remembers going to a meeting in Ayr shortly after the by-election at which Winnie Ewing's 'venomous and offensive' onslaught on his beloved Labour Party turned him bitterly against the idea of any move towards self-government: 'The small opening in my centralist mind closed like a trapdoor.' He went away to co-write a popular anti-Nationalist pamphlet, 'Don't Butcher Scotland's Future'. But if anti-SNP feeling was strong among the Labour grass roots, it was equally powerful in the party hierarchy, dominated by the staunchly Unionist Willie Ross. At the March 1968 Scottish conference of the Labour Party he stamped on a pro-Home Rule motion from the Glasgow Hillhead party (then, as now, more Nationalist than most). Ross savaged Nationalism, with the support of young anti-Nats like Tam Dalyell. The devolutionists, including Donald Dewar, regarded as a dangerous young Turk (strange but true), were trounced. The *Economist* concluded at the time that Labour in Scotland was not ready to flirt with anything that might encroach on the Treaty of Union of 1707: it had been victory for Ross and 'the elderly phalanx of machine-run Scottish Labour MPs who have graduated from union branch to town council to safe seat in plodding progression, and who thought no cataclysm could ever touch them'.

But the ageing Rossmen could not hold out for ever. The intellectual mood in Scotland was infecting Labour too. The Scottish Trades Union Congress was asked by the mineworkers in 1968 to campaign for a Scottish parliament (and was rebuked by Ross for listening to Mick McGahey, the communist miners' leader – he warned them not to be 'the Scottish Trades Union Congrouse'). A few months after its conference the party in Scotland proposed that there should be meetings of the Scottish Grand Committee in Edinburgh, a minor concession that, nevertheless, had been suggested by the young David Steel in a Scottish Liberal pamphlet as a stepping-stone to a full Edinburgh parliament. Labour's Scottish council also set up its own committee, which finally reported two years later against the idea of a Scottish parliament. In London the Cabinet left-winger Richard Crossman had been trying to persuade Wilson to go much further. Tam Dalyell, who adored Crossman, believed it was because of his bad relations with Willie Ross. He pins down the day of his conversion to Home Rule to 6 May 1968, when Crossman had wanted to listen to a parliamentary debate on social work in Scotland but was told to keep away because Ross would interpret his arrival as sinister butting-in. Dalyell quotes Crossman as saying:

You and Willie Ross – you're just as bad as he is really, though in a less uncouth, smoother way! Go around shouting about the Scottish Nationalists wanting separation, but what both of you and your friends actually want is to keep your Scottish business absolutely privy from English business. You and Willie Ross want a system which gives you the worst of both worlds, and that's why I'm in favour of a Scottish parliament!

Wilson allowed Crossman to chair a Cabinet committee that produced, from February 1969 to 1972, the first versions of the Scottish select committee (another idea mooted by Steel). All these small moves can best be seen as hairline cracks spreading across the Labour–Unionist dam: unimpressive in themselves but a sign of something bigger about to break.

Wilson himself twisted and turned. Here was a conundrum. The Nationalists might be a serious threat. Ted Heath was posing as a devolutionist, and the Scots might be impressed by that. Something might have to be done to cheer the Scots up. On the other hand, Willie Ross was black-affronted at the very thought of appeasing the Nats. Dick Crossman seemed keen on devolution, but then Dick was always a bit wild, a bit flighty. This was the kind of juggle of personalities and tactics Wilson lived for. He appears to have had no strong views of his own on Scotland, other than a Prime Minister's instinctive preference for retaining as much power as possible within a few hundred yards of London SW1A. In private he talked about the threat of the Nationalists; in public he started to speak in a vaguely modernizing tone of the need to bring government nearer the people. But his public utterances were so bland and generalist that one must assume that his privately expressed fear of nationalism was the dominant motive behind devolution. His fluent vacuities about handing power to the people could have been used by Margaret Thatcher at any stage of the 1980s to justify her attempt to demolish virtually everything Wilson stood for. Devolution was, in short, a Wilsonian wheeze, not a constitutional reform.

Wilson decided that a Royal Commission would be just the thing. Like referenda, Royal Commissions are a way of resolving problems that Cabinets are too split to deal with. They are also a convenient way of delaying decisions. Despite his earlier mockery of them (he once complained that they 'take minutes and waste years'), Royal Commissions became a favoured Wilsonian device. Wilson intended to call an election shortly and knew that the Commission would be unable to report until afterwards. So there would be the invigorating impression of activity without the risk of committing the government to anything. He managed to convey a due sense of personal excitement about the Commission by failing to remember to mention it in his own exceedingly long account of this government. The Crowther Commission (which changed its name to the Kilbrandon Commission, after the Scottish judge who took it over when Crowther died) was seen as a dodge when Wilson unveiled it. Speaking in the Queen's Speech debate in November 1968, that sparkling Labour Home Ruler John P. Mackintosh told the Commons: 'I can only assume that the reason the Government have chosen to set up the Commission is because of a fundamental difficulty in their ranks in deciding on the matter . . . we are rudderless on the matter, and this contributes to people's disillusionment with politicians.' And with one politician in particular.

Still, Wilson's dodge pleased the Labour leadership in Scotland, which duly produced an anti-devolutionist report of its own and submitted it to the Kilbrandon Commission three months before the 1970 election. Since most people who write about these matters are Nationalists or Home Rulers, Labour's 1970 report has had a bad reputation. In fact, the party went to great lengths to argue the economic case against devolution or separation, insisting that the cultural and the economic must be kept apart. Scottishness was important, but 'a separate Scottish economy is only possible if people are willing to accept a dramatic fall in living standards as the price for independence. They are not.' The party approved local-government reform but, on the national question, was more conservative than the Tories: 'we are convinced that most thoughtful Conservatives will reject the shallow thinking behind the Douglas-Home proposal for a Scottish Convention.' The calm and self-confident surface of the Labour Party's prose gave no hint of how quickly its arguments would be overturned.

For now, to almost everyone's surprise, Labour was returning to Opposition. England turned against Labour (more so than Scotland), and Labour won back Hamilton. The sole SNP gain that June was the Western Isles, won by Donald Stewart, the first Nationalist to win a parliamentary seat at a general election. In Scotland the aftermath of the 1970 election was not unlike the aftermath of 1979 or 1987. It seemed, initially, business as usual: back to the familiar Labour-versus-Tory Punch-and-Judy routine. The Scottish question, like Punch's baby, was knocked on the head and thrown out of the window. True, there were oral sessions of evidence to the Crowther/Kilbrandon Commission with Labour and the STUC emphasizing the economic problems of separation, and Labour actually saying it would prefer Tory rule at Westminster to a Labour-dominated Scottish parliament. But this was quiet conversation, a murmur almost, in the background of public life. The foreground was dominated by unemployment, rows over Catholic schooling and council-house rent increases and the Wheatley Commission local-government reforms as the Scottish regions were carved out.

Oil-rich and Jobless:
Scotland in the Seventies

Under the crust of business as usual, bigger forces started to shift the way politicians thought. Three issues in the early 1970s nudged the Scottish debate along – oil, Europe and jobs. In October 1970 BP struck oil 110 miles off Aberdeen, at what was to become the giant Forties field. Further strikes came at Brent and Ninian. The Nationalists were not slow to spot the implications. Gordon Wilson, a lawyer in Dundee and the future leader of the SNP, wrote to Gordon Campbell, the Tory Scottish Secretary, demanding that all the oil revenues should go to a special account for the exclusive use of the Scottish people. He was brushed aside, but the government took the hint: to undermine the use of oil as Nationalist propaganda, revenues would appear only in all-UK accounts. Even so, the public-expenditure implications of the discoveries were clearly dramatic, and for a while everyone struggled to grasp their scale. Five years after BP had brought the first oil ashore the British sector of the North Sea had produced only 1 million tonnes of oil. But in 1976 alone that jumped to 11.5 million tonnes, and by 1979, the year of the devolution referendum, 76.5 million tonnes were being pumped ashore. For a time the devolution debate ran on crude – crude oil, crude arguments.

Oil quickly started affecting politics on the ground, not only in the think-tanks. Labour's Harry Ewing, for instance, had been the candidate in the 1971 Falkirk, Stirling and Grangemouth Burghs by-election, which took place shortly after the North Sea strikes. He faced the veteran SNP supporter, Robert McIntyre, the man who had won the 1945 by-election and who had led the Nationalists through their darkest days in the immediate post-war period. McIntyre used the oil issue skilfully, came close and gave Ewing, who was to become a devolution minister a few years later, a real fight. In the same year the SNP was turning much of its research work on to the issue, with the party chairman William Wolfe declaring that oil should be the most important element in its propaganda. Gordon Wilson linked the fashionable talk about devolution to the North Sea strike by arguing for a step-by-step march to independence. Step one, a devolved Scottish assembly would be set up. Step two, it would take control of the fabulous oil reserves. Step three, Scotland free. In September 1972 the SNP launched its most famous slogan, 'It's Scotland's Oil', followed a year later by 'Rich Scots or Poor Britons?'. The latter, with its undertone of ditch-the-English selfishness, confirmed to Unionists the underlying nastiness of the SNP. In truth, it made quite a few Nationalists queasy. But the Unionists were trying to have it both ways: oil had blown away the central anti-Nationalist argument, made by Labour three years earlier, that Scotland was simply too poor to go it alone. The issue seemed to work for the party: Gordon Wilson came within 2 per cent of seizing yet another Labour stronghold at the Dundee East by-election in January 1973. By that spring, on somewhat spurious grounds, the party was claiming a trebling of support.

The second big change was the European Economic Community. The SNP campaigned fiercely against British membership. In May 1967 it had even sent a gloriously pompous note ('The Scottish

National Party, being the sole political body competent to speak for the Scottish Nation, serves herein due notice . . .') warning that an independent Scotland would not necessarily honour any European treaty obligations entered into by Britain. This missive, with its echoes of *The Mouse That Roared,* was translated carefully into French and dispatched to twenty-seven states, not forgetting the USSR and Albania. Nationalist hostility to Europe was eroded only slowly: in the 1975 referendum senior SNP people shared platforms and motorcars with prominent Tories (Teddy Taylor) and Labourites (Jim Sillars) to campaign against continued British membership of the Community (or the Common Market as it was then called offshore). Wolfe said the Common Market was 'encouraging the exploitation of labour, forcing hundreds of thousands of people to lose their identity and migrate for the sake of a form of so-called progress, which has its roots in inequality and greed'. Throughout the mid-1970s the SNP's policy was for a separate Scottish referendum on Europe after independence, and it was strongly opposed to political and economic union. In 1975 the SNP also believed that the role of the Strasbourg parliament should be 'chiefly consultative'; its general position was rather like that of the English Tory Euro-sceptics of the 1990s. By comparison with the way in which they grasped the oil issue, the Nationalists were extraordinarily slow to spot the political opportunities of Europe: indeed, they did not fully do so until they came under Sillars' influence in the late 1980s. The most forward-looking thinking about Europe came from Labour MPs, who started to wonder whether the development of a centralist European politics might eventually require a balancing system of local parliaments to close the democratic gap.

The third big change in the early 1970s was unemployment. Many thousands of Scottish workers were losing their jobs primarily because of the obsolescence of Scottish heavy industry and the *laissez-faire* attitude of Heath in London. In 1971 came the Upper Clyde Shipbuilders' work-in, led by the charismatic communist shop stewards Jimmy Reid and Jimmy Airlie. The sit-in, though it involved a minority of the workers, caught the Scottish imagination and was supported by Labour, the Nationalists, churchmen and communists. Reid and Airlie led 70,000 protestors in the biggest demonstration in Scotland anyone could remember. Heath's government panicked and partially bailed out two of the bankrupt shipyards (one was sold for oil-rig construction). Along with the nationalization of Rolls-Royce, this spelt the end of Heath's experiment in hard-edged, proto-Thatcherite economics. In Scotland the message seemed to be the heady one that unity and a bit of imagination could make the London ministers jump. This trickled too into the new Home Rule brew. In February 1972 the STUC held a 'Scottish Assembly', bringing employers, trade unionists and politicians together to debate the condition of the Scottish economy. Pro-devolution feeling was strong. James Jack, general secretary of the STUC, announced that he was all for a Scottish parliament, 'which will be a workers' parliament', while the CBI's Scottish Secretary declared that he too was impressed by the enthusiasm for devolution.

These political arguments did not tempt Labour people to defect to Nationalism (though some leading Liberals were tempted). The 1970s were a time of bitter class politics, and many on the left, like the talented journalist and Labour politician Brian Wilson, saw the SNP as the enemy, 'tartan Tories' who could never be trusted. Two small episodes give the flavour of this. The first was a private flirtation between anti-European Scottish Conservatives and the SNP. In his diary (parts of which were published later in the Scottish cultural magazine *Cencrastus*) the journalist Neal Ascherson recorded that friends of Teddy Taylor, the populist Tory right-winger who was later appointed shadow Scottish Secretary by Margaret Thatcher, had made approaches to the SNP in 1973. One prominent Tory councillor from Taylor's Cathcart constituency did defect, though Taylor says he was never involved. The SNP's national executive discussed what to do if 'a certain person' applied to join. The SNP was certainly optimistic, and some members wondered if Taylor would want to be president if he did come over. Given that Taylor was a committed hanger-and-flogger, the fact that the SNP was even talking to his Unionist association – the same one that provided the right-wing Nationalist Scottish Party in the early 1930s – is revealing of its relaxed attitude to left–right politics. Shortly afterwards the Glasgow industrialist Sir Hugh Fraser joined the SNP and promised fellow businessmen they would get 'a fair crack of the whip' in independent Scotland. The SNP itself proudly proclaimed that it had 'broken the conformist barrier' of being left-wing or right-wing and stood for 'New Politics'. In practice, New Politics often tended to mean blaming the English for everything and promising gurgling barrels of oil-rich dosh to smother every problem.

The second episode, which took place at the same time, shows how the left, in turn, regarded the SNP. The socialist 7:84 Theatre Group (so named because 7 per cent of the country owned 84 per cent of the wealth) was touring Scotland with a play called *The Cheviot, the Stag, and the Black, Black Oil*. A polemic about Highland history, landlordism, the Clearances and the role of American companies in the exploitation of North Sea oil, it was easily the decade's most famous piece of theatre in Scotland. Towards the end of the company's first tour around the Highlands, Billy Wolfe asked 7:84 to perform the play to the Scottish National Party's annual conference at the west Highland town Oban. The actors agonized about how to respond: as John McGrath, the director, wrote in a published edition of the play, 'We wrote, pointing out that we were not nationalists, and would attack bourgeois nationalism.' But Wolfe repeated the invitation, and the group went because there were socialists in the SNP and 'It would do no harm for the chauvinists and the tartan Tories to get a dose of what we were saying.' The performance was a success but was followed by fierce confrontations between the actors and the political activists about their rival philosophies.

Towards Dalintober: Labour's Devolutionists

Outside the SNP the Home Rule movement slowly gathered a little momentum. Politics is partly about the living arrangements of the participants. The gang of Labour devolutionists was formed when Harry Ewing, Alex Eadie and Jim Sillars happened to share a flat in London during the early 1970s. They, along with John Robertson, who had been cold-shouldered by the party leadership after calling for a Scottish parliament when he was first elected in 1961, were the small band who relentlessly propagandized and lobbied for Home Rule inside the Labour Party. Mackintosh, the intellectual MP whose death in 1978 robbed the Home Rule movement of its most eloquent advocate, was an ally but more of a loner. As we shall see later, the devolutionist MPs also started to meet with journalists and Labour politicians in Scotland. Sillars dates his conversion from arch Nat-basher to a born-again Home Ruler to the South Ayrshire by-election, which took him into the House in 1970. It was remembered as a particularly savage battle, in which Sillars continually taunted the SNP's Sam Purdie with treachery in turning away from Labour to Nationalism (something Sillars would later do himself). He thrashed Purdie in terms of votes, but Purdie's arguments about Labour's inability to defend Scottish working-class voters had seeped into his mind. Purdie, he says in his autobiography, 'kicked away my confidence ... [by 1972] I was definitely no longer a Unionist.' In London the gang of four initially had a hard time of it. Ewing remembers: 'We took some very, very heavy defeats ... we were virtually ostracized.' But they lobbied and hassled and argued away, and by 1973 smoke signals were emerging from the Westminster lobby writers that other Scottish Labour MPs were starting to agree with them.

In October Kilbrandon's Royal Commission reported – the egg laid by Harold Wilson three years earlier had finally hatched. It contained not one but several chickens. The majority report came home to Labour to roost: it called for a Scottish Senate, or Scottish Convention, of 100 members, elected by proportional representation and with wide-ranging powers. There would be a Scottish Cabinet, headed by a Scottish Prime Minister. To compensate for this, the Scottish Secretaryship would be abolished and the number of Scottish MPs at Westminster would be cut. The Senate, or Convention, would be funded via Westminster, the relationship being overseen by an Exchequer Board. Predictably, Willie Ross, Labour's once and future Scottish Secretary, did not fancy being abolished. Nor was Labour keen on seeing its precious MPs culled. Ross baptized the majority Kilbrandon Report the 'kill devolution' report. There was a small chicken too – a minority report that suggested a much weaker, administrative assembly. Finally, there was a memorandum of dissent, calling for a federal solution, with five English regional governments to balance the Scottish and Welsh assemblies. The first chicken was for Home Rule; the second was Unionist; and the third was federalist. Even after three years the Royal Commission had not managed to produce a unanimous, coherent plan. Far from concluding the debate, the Commission started it off again.

Labour's Scottish council, with brilliant mistiming, had just re-stated its opposition to any devolution in a pamphlet called 'Scotland and the UK'. In his foreword to it the party's new Scottish Sec-retary, Peter Allison, said that new factors, including oil and the EEC, made it essential to update the 1970 anti-devolution case. But the document was a flimsier, less coherent one than the 1970 paper it was supposed to replace. It referred insultingly to an assembly as a 'Scottish Stormont' and advocated instead the kind of legislative tinkering with grand committees and select committees that had been heard from Labour before and would be heard from the Tories later. Allison promised that Labour's position would not be 'merely emotionally attractive'. It certainly wasn't that. Within a couple of weeks of the Labour pamphlet's being completed and the Kilbrandon Report published, the SNP had seized Glasgow Govan in a spectacular by-election victory with uncanny echoes of Hamil-ton. It was then a grim, decaying constituency, with dreadful social problems. It isn't much better now. Jim Sillars was among those canvassing it for Labour and noticed with horror the rats scampering around the stinking housing administered by the Labour council. He was campaigning against the SNP's Margo MacDonald, an abrasive and glamorous young working-class Nationalist. Having been the celebrity by-election winner, MacDonald lost Govan at the subsequent general election, but she became one of the SNP's most popular and recognizable leaders. (Eight years later Sillars and she married. Seven years after that he won Glasgow Govan as the SNP candidate in another November by-election. And lost it in the subsequent general election, when it returned yet again to Labour.)

Four months after the shock of Govan came the February 1974 election, bringing back Wilson in a minority government. Heath had tried to hang on by doing a deal with the Liberal leader, Jeremy Thorpe – and another with the SNP. The discussions with the Nationalists were more tentative and less well known and took place via Teddy Taylor in Scotland. The SNP duly made a series of quite tough devolutionist demands to Heath in Downing Street. But the intriguing prospect of a Tory–Liberal–SNP coalition was quickly ended by the collapse of the Heath–Thorpe talks. The SNP had been worth Heath's interest because it had made its first substantial electoral breakthrough, winning six new seats, two of them from Labour. Its success put Harold Wilson on the spot too. Willie Ross had refused to have devolution discussed in the manifesto, and the party had performed less well in Scotland than Ross and Wilson had hoped, winning forty seats and seeing its share of the vote cut to under 37 per cent. Internal opinion-polling for Labour suggested that if it did not do something about devolution, another thirteen seats could be lost to the SNP at the next election. This, because of the weak position of the Wilson government, was clearly only months away. Faced with a game of political hop-scotch, Wilson was always nimble on his feet and was promising a devolution White Paper by the Queen's Speech debate that opened the new Parliament. By June 1974 his government had published it, listing a series of possible forms of devolution.

Wilson, though, had one obvious problem: the Labour Party leadership in Scotland remained fervently anti-devolutionist. There had been signs that the Scottish party as a whole was slowly shifting ground. At its annual conference, held at Ayr in March 1974, there were more motions in favour of devolution (ten) than against (six). But the debate was bitter, bad-tempered and disfigured by personal attacks, both inside the hall and in the bars. In classic Labour style a statement was cobbled together to disguise the gaping splits in the party. Perhaps more significant than the formal proceedings was the publication of a strongly pro-devolution pamphlet, 'Scottish Labour and Devolution', by the gang of four. Harry Ewing believes it was a turning-point in the argument: 'I think Willie Ross thought it would only sell about twenty copies – with the four of us buying five each. But it sold out immediately and we had to reprint.' Suddenly everyone seemed to want at least to know about devolution – a striking change from the ignominy the devolutionists had suffered a year earlier at the Dunoon conference, one of their low points. The tide was turning.

But three months later came an absurd interlude. The Scottish football team had, for the first time in twenty years, made it to the final stages of the World Cup and on 22 June was playing Yugoslavia in Frankfurt. No patriotic Scottish male would be thinking about anything else, of course. And eighteen of the twenty-nine members of Labour's Scottish executive proved themselves patriotic enough to fail to turn up to its meeting that day – which happened to be when it was discussing devolution. The executive would, it had been assumed in London, agree with the Downing Street line in favour of devolution. But of the eleven who did arrive at the meeting six were anti-devolutionists and voted against all the Home Rule schemes put before them, adding a motion, for good measure, that derided 'constitutional tinkering'. Oops: none of that had been in Harold Wilson's careful script. The Scottish media and the Home Rulers inside the Labour Party erupted in indignation (but only after they too had finished watching Scotland fall out of the World Cup after drawing with Yugoslavia). The *Economist* summed up the situation with brutal frankness: the Scottish executive's decision had been 'acutely embarrassing for Mr Wilson, who is anxious to palm the Scots off with any amount of devolution which will keep them quiet'.

Wilson refused to be deflected, though Cabinet committee meetings through the summer and early autumn of 1974 showed that senior ministers were still worried and divided about his plan. Roy Jenkins, the right-wing, brilliant and rather chilly Home Secretary, and Denis Healey, then the embattled Chancellor, were among those who expressed scepticism, though Healey became converted. Civil servants also seemed dubious to the point of hostility. But the Cabinet majority was behind Wilson. Even Ross, who feared that devolution might lead to the break-up of the UK, believed it was impossible to turn back now. Norman Hunt, a dissenting member of the Kilbrandon Commission who had called for executive devolution, had been brought into the government by Wilson as Lord Crowther Hunt, and he was now asked to work towards legislative devolution.

So, in pursuit of an end intended to cheer up the Scottish electorate, Wilson was now obliged to be nasty to the Labour Party in Scotland. At his instigation a special conference was to be called in Glasgow. And this much was clear: it would reverse the decision taken by the football-shunning Scottish executive. Alex Kitson, the transport workers' union official and a prominent fixer of the day, was ordered to help ensure the vote went the right way. He had been brought up in a political household in Edinburgh and had been a member of the pro-Home Rule (and splendidly named) Scottish Horse and Motormen's Association, which later merged with the transport union. He had inherited the devolutionist strain of thought in Scottish trades unionism that had trickled down from Gladstonian Liberalism and the old Independent Labour Party. He was, in short, a believer as well as a fixer. (Indeed, he is partly responsible for the political views of Sean Connery, the Scottish actor who campaigned for a 'yes' vote in the 1979 devolution referendum and who gave his active support to the SNP in the 1992 general election. Connery, as a boy, lived near Kitson in Edinburgh's Fountainbridge district and hung around the stables of the St Cuthbert's Cooperative Dairy where Kitson worked, taking a job there as a 'van-boy' on the milk round. As they clattered round Fountainbridge Kitson harangued Connery, and his early political lectures left a lasting impression on the actor-to-be.)

'Dalintober Street' has gone down in the mythology of the Labour Party in Scotland. It is generally intoned with a mixture of awe and regret, as if it were the scene of some Chicago gangland massacre. In fact, it was merely the location of the Glasgow Co-operative Hall, where the party met in August 1974 under orders from Wilson. But there Labour set Scotland's agenda for the next five years by agreeing, sceptically but overwhelmingly, that it wanted 'a directly elected assembly with legislative powers within the context of the political and economic unity of the UK'. The straight-forwardly Unionist phase of Labour in Scotland was thus terminated. Kitson had been highly effective in bringing round the big union votes – which were not always surrendered in a mood of fervent enthusiasm. Alex Donnett of the General and Municipal Workers' Union, the first to declare his card vote, was embarrass-ingly honest about his motives: his union wanted no impediment to the return of a Labour government, he told the conference. And if devolution was the price, well, he supposed they would pay it. Other unions, like the miners, were Home Rulers already. Some constituency parties voted for devolution in a mood of alarm about their friendly neighbourhood Nationalists. Dalintober Street was portrayed by the Labour leadership as a return to the party's grand old traditions. But it was a victory for fix and fear, not a triumph of principle. The meeting is remembered, on all sides, without affection. The Home Ruler Sillars recalled it as 'a mixture of sourness, sincerity and cynicism', and the Unionist Dalyell wrote in his diary at the time: 'Yesterday was a bad, bad day.' But Dalintober did the trick for Harold Wilson.

Division in London: Rebellion in Scotland

After Labour turned, the party was not backward in proclaiming its new gospel – one that had been composed, after all, for electoral reasons. The White Paper was published a few weeks before the election. Even at this stage Harold Wilson's cynical attitude towards his own creation was caught by Barbara Castle in her diary: 'Launching is to be next Wednesday. "And God help all who sail in her," said Harold.' A tabloid-style edition of *Labour News*, posted through letterboxes across Scotland during the October 1974 election, hailed the proposed assembly as 'Powerhouse Scotland'; Labour MPs started talking about it as a Scottish parliament; and the party's sole Scottish television broadcast was given over to a discussion featuring keen devolvers like Mackintosh, Sillars and George Foulkes, who made it clear they assumed the proposed assembly would have wide fiscal and economic powers. The election went quite well for Labour in Scotland; indeed, party officials argued that Wilson owed his UK-wide majority, which was only four, to the Scottish result. But with the SNP at their all-time high point, and with a Commons majority that could (and would) melt away, the pressure for devolution was as intense as ever.

Ted Short, Wilson's former chief whip and now the Leader of the Commons, was given the job of translating the vague promises of the election into firm legislative proposals. He had been working with Crowther-Hunt on the earlier plans, but his first White Paper was unpopular with almost everybody, and a second one was promised for the autumn of 1975. The project was centralized in the Cabinet Office, where a Constitution Unit was set up and spawned scores of interdepartmental committees, examining every aspect of policy relating to Scotland. But complexity was the least of the problems. Throughout the year the Cabinet was badly divided: Jim Callaghan and Shirley Williams were among those who were clearly in the sceptical-to-hostile camp, along with Healey and Jenkins. Short had to fight hard to keep any momentum going at all. Three times during 1975 – in January, June and September – special Cabinet think-ins on devolution were held at Chequers. At each one Wilson and Short faced obstruction and verbal ambush by anti-devolution ministers. But Cabinet ministers could be kept in line; more serious was the bubbling anger starting to emerge from some Labour back-benchers, including Neil Kinnock, who attacked Short at a private meeting in April for trying to treat different parts of the UK separately on a 'racial basis'.

There was suspicion of Scottish devolution from two sources inside the Parliamentary Labour Party: the northern English MPs, who were jealous of any special treatment of their traditional re-gional rivals, the Scots; and younger, left-wing MPs like Kinnock, who thought any dabbling with Nationalism was a betrayal of class politics. The Northerners could have been bought off by a promise of similar treatment for their own area. The left-wingers could not have been bought off by anything. A speech made by Kinnock in February 1975 gives the flavour of their argument:

I believe that the emancipation of the class which I came to this House to represent, unapologetically, can best be achieved in a single nation and in a single economic unit, by which I mean a unit where we can have a brotherhood of all nations and have the combined strength of working-class people throughout the whole of the United Kingdom . . .

In his autobiography the late Eric Heffer gave a rather more idiosyn-cratic view of the socialist case against devolution:

My opposition arose out of my understanding of international socialism and the ideas of the German-Polish Socialist Rosa Luxemburg and the Austro-Marxists like Otto Bauer and Max Adler. The Austro-Marxists who led the Austrian Social Democratic Party were in favour of the Austro-Hungarian Empire being transformed into a socialist unified state. It was a pipe dream . . . in the Commons I made speeches drawing attention to what the Austro-Marxists and Luxemburg had argued. They cut little ice.

In Scotland too, the parallels between the Habsburg and Windsor empires were little noticed.

Neil Kinnock, the more substantial anti-devolutionist, was already being gossiped about as a future leader of the Labour Party. Jim Sillars was sometimes mentioned as his obvious rival from the left. The two men shared a lot: both came from working-class communities in Labour heartlands (Tredegar is to Welsh socialism what South Ayrshire is to Scottish socialism); both were excellent orators who arrived in the Commons in 1970; both were on the left; both were short-fused gamblers who nevertheless took their politics seriously. Kinnock and Sillars had been offered junior government jobs within a few months of one another and had both concluded this was an attempt to shut them up, so refused them. Both men had experienced unpleasant confrontations with Nationalists in their respective countries but had reacted in opposite ways politically – Sillars had been slowly attracted, Kinnock for ever repelled. Devolution proved to be a scarring, toughening education for each of them, but it left Kinnock stronger than ever inside the Labour machine and would soon pitch Sillars, bellowing prophetically, into the wilderness.

Neither the true seriousness of the potential Labour rebellion at Westminster nor the deep hostility of important Cabinet ministers was fully understood in Scotland, where things seemed to be going rather well. Harry Ewing, who had impressed Short with his campaigning in Falkirk during the election, had been appointed as minister in charge of devolution in the Scottish Office team, initially without the knowledge or approval of Willie Ross himself. The devolutionists were delighted – they thought they had hit the jackpot. In fact, as we have seen, Ewing was inevitably going to be a minor player in a controversial Cabinet-level operation. As the long debate inside the Cabinet Office about the shape and powers of the proposed assemblies wound on, the Scottish devolutionists became complacent. Sillars and Ewing were still sharing a flat but observed the proprieties by not discussing what was going on inside the machine. Ewing seemed, on the surface, optimistic enough.

Ewing and Sillars had not merely been parliamentary collaborators. From the early 1970s they and other MPs had been meeting regularly in Scotland with journalist sympathizers to talk about Home Rule, including autonomy for the Labour Party in Scotland (though Ewing, of course, dropped out when he became a minister).

Indeed, they had formed that most innocent and dangerous of things, a group. They called it the Watchdog group. They felt the party had become a slave to Transport House in London and was, as a result, stodgily slow in reacting to the new Scottish politics. Bob Brown, a journalist who had worked for *The Times*, *The Economist* and the *Glasgow Herald*, publicized the thinking of this group in two articles in the *Glasgow Herald* in November 1974. These suggested that Scottish socialists might need to create a 'Scottish Labour Party' modelled on the one initiated by Keir Hardie in 1888 but inside the British Labour movement. The articles were later seen as evidence that the 1976 rebellion was the result of a deep-laid plot. But the Watchdogs, as their name suggests, saw themselves first as Labour loyalists, albeit of a local variety. Brown, who wrote the articles under a pseudonym, 'James Alexander' (the first names of his two children), says now: 'When I sat down and wrote those two pieces, I certainly had no notion I was writing some kind of definitive blueprint for a new political party.'

The flirtation between journalists (including prominent Scottish political writers like Jimmy Frame and Chris Baur) and politicians may seem strange today – indeed, incestuous. But Scottish political journalism had been elevated by devolution: before the rise of the SNP and the Home Rule question there had simply not been much to write about. When the story started to look interesting the Scottish reporters' status rose. And they attracted new recruits: in 1975 Neal Ascherson, for instance, who had been reporting on Eastern Europe for the *Observer*, returned to Edinburgh and the *Scotsman*. So it was in the interests of the political journalists to ensure that devolutionist politics got plenty of coverage in the Scottish press. Clearly, political journalists must be numbered among the groups who would have benefited most from a Scottish parliament. I do not mean that they were cynical or insincere, just that their position in the system made them more aware than most of the attractions of Home Rule. The Watchdog group gave the politicians a coterie of clever men off whom they could bounce ideas and against whom they could test arguments and gave the journalists an inside track on the Home Rule story. The situation can be compared with the influence of social-democratic journalists like Peter Jenkins on the founders of the SDP a few years later.

This crossover between politics and journalism was obvious enough to anyone who read the Scottish press closely and became, at times, semi-public. At Labour's Scottish 1975 conference in Aberdeen, for instance, the Watchdog group booked itself a dinner table for an evening of fruitful conspiracy. Its members were aghast to discover they had been placed in the centre of the restaurant, surrounded by glass partitions: as they plotted away in their fish tank Labour Unionists at other tables stared, goggled-eyed, and jotted down their names.

When the White Paper, *Our Changing Democracy*, finally appeared in November 1975 the Watchdogs responded with some sustained barking. The devolutionist Scottish press (allied, of course, to the Watchdogs) was equally alarmed. The *Scotsman* called it 'an assembly in chains', and the mass-circulation *Daily Record* shouted: 'We were promised more. We want more!' The government was offering, it seemed, only a Toytown assembly that could be easily and regularly overruled by Westminster and had only tiny tax-raising powers. To those who had not witnessed the attacks of senior ministers on the very idea of devolution and who had not heard the warnings of the Labour whips about rebellion at Westminster, it seemed a terrible sell-out. Harry Ewing took the full-frontal blast of the irritation and disappointment of his Scottish intimates. Harsh words were exchanged. The flavour of the time is given in an exchange of letters between Brown and Ewing. Bob Brown told his old friend:

Less and less do I find myself able to go along with Labour ... I cannot appreciate why you can express satisfaction publicly, or even privately, with the approach that has been taken and the course being sailed. It's an open question with me at the moment as to my own immediate action, which may or may not depend on what our group decides to do. But I must tell you that there is no chance of my being conned indefinitely ... I'm more sad and distressed by it all than I can say.

Ewing wrote back, sounding tortured. He said he was not prepared to discuss his private feelings, though Brown's letter was 'difficult' to answer:

In taking the decision I eventually arrived at I realize only too well how this must appear to my close friends and particularly to Jim [Sillars] and yourself and it would be an understatement to say that I have not enjoyed the thoughts of the impression my decision may have given.

But he had decided to go along with the White Paper 'in the interests of the Labour Party in Scotland'. In the interests, in other words, of continued unity between Labour Home Rulers and Labour Unionists. Ewing ended his letter by pleading with his fellow devolutionists for understanding.

Whatever the quality of understanding on a personal level, the Watchdog group's political reaction was dramatic. They broke entirely from the Labour Party to found the Scottish Labour Party (SLP) in a great splash of publicity during December 1975–January 1976. Sillars, Bob Brown and Alex Neil, Labour's Scottish research officer, met at Sillars' house in Ayr the day after the White Paper had been launched. Brown recalls that he warned Sillars and Neil of the consequences, for them personally, of breaking with their party – 'You know what the Labour Party does to folk who do this' – but both were determined to try to create a more socialist, more nationalist, successor. Given that this was the first grass-roots split from the mighty Labour movement in its history, it was accomplished in a mood of reckless impetuosity and without a fraction of even the modest preparation that went into the launch of the SDP five years later. Brown says: 'I don't believe Jim and Alex rated the chances of the SLP taking off very highly. I certainly didn't.' Since Sillars' character has been so consistently attacked (and since he has done his own reputation so little good with his various percussive onslaughts on both rivals and voters), it is worth quoting here the Brown assessment: 'My view of Sillars is quite unmisty. He can be very impetuous. That is his worst fault. But I think he is the most considerable politician Scotland has produced in my working lifetime . . . a man of remarkably high principle, great integrity and clear vision.' Many in Scotland would give a horse laugh to all that, but Sillars has great courage and many talents, for all his political failings. The number of times he is quoted in this book shows that even when he is wrong, he can be so with magnificent eloquence. As the charge is sometimes made that Sillars has been an opportunist, even careerist, politician, it is perhaps pertinent to note that he has proved a remarkably incompetent careerist.

The organization with which he will be for ever associated, the SLP, was, as an organization, a brief and spectacular disaster. Its story is complicated but can be boiled down to a few essentials. Formally launched in January 1976 at a packed, excited meeting in Glasgow, it attracted about 900 members but was heavily infiltrated by Trotskyists. That October, during an acrimonious 'first congress' at Stirling, one faction was expelled and marched out to reconvene in the town's Station Hotel. The SLP was badly split, and from then on it started to collapse. It tried to support itself upon those flimsiest of crutches, opinion polls. But the mix of political idealists and journalists that had created the party was never enough to keep it in the highly competitive race of 1970s politics. The SLP had been meant to attract working-class Labour supporters but, as its recorder Henry Drucker has noted, ended up recruiting their up-wardly mobile student offspring instead. Its two MPs were defeated at the 1979 election, after which the SLP ceased to exist.

It had spotted a real gap in the market: there was, and is, a space between 'real' Labour people and 'real' Nationalists that is now inhabited by the left-wing moderates in the SNP and the nationalist faction in the Labour Party. But the SLP was just too inexperienced, too small and too poor to exploit this gap. Some of its former members who stayed in politics returned to Labour, like John Mac-Allion, now Labour MP for Dundee East and a Scotland United supporter after the 1992 election, or Maria Fyfe, the Labour front bencher and MP for Glasgow Maryhill, who was prominent in the Scottish Constitutional Convention. Others, like Sillars and Neil, went into the SNP and rose to its leadership group. Both groups of former pupils affected the parties they joined and, to that extent, maintained the spirit of the SLP. In the SNP Sillars and his friends helped secure the victory of the left: today the old SLP dream of a leftish party that believes in independence in Europe has become reality – albeit in another party, which also includes a more tradition-alist wing. In the Labour Party ex-SLP supporters have been among those who have been active in its quasi-Nationalist group, Scottish Labour Action.

There the arguments in the 1990s about devolution for the Scot-tish Labour Party uncannily echo the thinking of the Watchdog group of the 1970s. Here, for instance, is Sillars, quoted by Bob

Brown in 1974: 'Policy-making in relation to a Scottish parliament must be done in Scotland, not by the National Executive but by the Scottish element of the party; and for that the necessary policy-making machinery will be required. This means, de facto, a Scottish Labour Party.' And here is Ian Smart, a Paisley lawyer and leading light in Scottish Labour Action, addressing a packed meeting at the Edinburgh pub, Jock's Lodge, during Labour's 1992 Scottish conference: 'It is ludicrous that we are talking about Home Rule for Scotland but we do not have it for the party . . . the Labour Party in Scotland has to be sovereign in [Scottish] policy-making . . . We will be talking not about the Scottish Council of the Labour Party but genuinely about the Scottish Labour Party.' Among those applauding through the haze of cigarette smoke were ex-members of the SLP.

A Failure of Leadership:
the SNP and Devolution

The Scottish Nationalists themselves also suffered a severe crisis of identity in the 1970s. Devolution had, as we have seen, been cooked up in London specifically to induce this. It did confuse and divide the Nationalists, who, throughout this period, rowed and agonized about their strategy – even, at times, about their very purpose. Should they go along with devolution, supporting Labour or the Tories in government as a stepping-stone to independence? Or would devolution, as a half-way house, pre-empt the real aim of 'Scottish freedom'? There is no right answer to the choice faced by the SNP; since a Scottish parliament has not been created, we cannot know whether it would be the 'slippery slope' to separation. This is a matter of faith. But devolution offered the Nationalists something real, in the here-and-now. And that was attractive. So, reluctantly and with many hesitations and pullings back, the SNP became entangled with devolution and therefore – just as Callaghan had planned – entangled with Labour's survival at Westminster. When the SNP broke free again, pulling Callaghan down in the process, it was close to cracking up because of the strains imposed by its illicit cohabitation. The devolution years left on the SNP emotional scars that help explain its neurotic behaviour later.

Its oil campaign started to wind down in 1974, as Kilbrandon and the prospects for devolution became the big question in Scotland. After the February 1974 election the seven-strong SNP parliamentary group, led by the moralistic old Islesman Donald Stewart, imposed tough conditions for supporting Labour devolution. But the SNP was not in quite as strong a position as its electoral success suggested. In the hysterical atmosphere of the time it looked like a huge, threatening native army. It was nothing of the kind; its leaders understood that it was being used by Scottish voters partly to frighten the Unionist parties into conceding something less than independence. Full independence was supported by only one Scot in five, and when the government's moderate devolution proposal was published nearly two-thirds of SNP supporters rather liked it. This underlined the fact that the SNP, despite being on an upswing, would have to compromise. In the October 1974 election it won another four seats and pushed its vote to just over 30 per cent (up from 21.9 per cent in February). This was described by Billy Wolfe as 'a decisive step to self-government for Scotland'. But his use of the phrase 'self-government', which hangs uneasily between devolution and independence, was a significant slither.

In May 1975 the SNP's conference agreed that it should participate fully in any directly elected assembly, 'to make a constructive contribution in those limited areas of responsibility likely to be given to the assembly by the present Westminster government, and to work vigorously to extend the assembly powers until it becomes a real Scottish parliament'. This was the high tide of devolutionary feeling inside the SNP. Political nationalism is a fundamentalist creed, and the need to compromise divided the Nationalist membership. It caused serious argument among the leadership in Scotland. It provoked private rows among its MPs. During the next year, as Labour started splitting over devolution, the SNP fundamentalists fought back. In the following May the party's elected ruling body, the National Council, was convulsed by a surge of belligerently pure Nationalism. Although the Council confirmed that it would tolerate an assembly, it emphasized that this could be 'a possible stepping-stone' only and voted for a motion that insisted that 'Nothing short of independence will meet the needs of the Scottish people in whom alone the sovereign power of Scotland resides.'

From then on, skirmishes between devolvers and fundamentalists broke out at every level. Margo MacDonald, the former victor of Govan and now a vice-chair of the party, urged 'a hard-line campaign on the theme of independence' in September 1976 (it duly followed two months later), while Wolfe himself continued to stress the opportunities offered by the Scotland and Wales Bill to spread the message of self-government. The argument was complicated by a second simmering dispute about whether the SNP was left-wing or moderate, and the two disputes tended to merge. Although the match was never exact, the fundamentalists on independence tended to be moderate or even right-wing when it came to conventional politics, while the devolutionists were more often left-wingers. In the mid-1970s most Nationalists would have abided by the answer given later that the party was a 'moderate, left-of-centre' one, but after the 1979 defeat this dispute ripped the party asunder.

The argument was also about style, echoing the SNP's search for respectability in the 1930s. The party leadership seemed almost obsessive about the need to be calm, downbeat, pro-royal, loyal to the Commonwealth and so on. This was a sign of the times. The mid-1970s were a nervy era when questions about the rule of law were seriously asked and when the mainland started to come to terms with the fact that Northern Ireland was in a state of perpetual, if contained, warfare. It was then too that various would-be 'tartan terrorist' organizations started to gather headlines in Scotland. They were small, ineffectual and composed mainly of fantasists and incompetents, but they damaged the SNP's image, to the extent that some party members believed that the attacks on pylons and oil pipelines had been carried out by government agents. A novel, *Scotch on the Rocks*, co-authored by the Tory politician Douglas Hurd and televised by the BBC in 1973, infuriated the SNP by linking left-wing extremism, violence and Scottish nationalism. In 1977 the Queen used her Silver Jubilee to swipe at nationalism and devolution, recalling the 'benefits which Union has conferred'. Neal Ascherson noted in his diary in March of that year that at the *Scotsman* 'Few days go by without a reader's letter or political speech which accuses the SNP of either fascism or the intention to use the bomb and the Kalashnikov.' In the Commons the Nationalists suffered similar attacks: the anti-apartheid campaigner and

Labour MP Bob Hughes, for instance, told its MPs they were 'the kind of people who remind me of Afrikaaner Nationalists'. It was against this background of guilt by association that Wolfe, believing self-government to be imminent, repeatedly warned his party to avoid an aggressive image: 'Reassurance is the essence of what we must project.' Keep calm, stay moderate, he kept telling the SNP, and they would come into their inheritance. In December 1977 he felt able to tell the party's National Council: 'It is 270 years since we last had a parliament in Scotland. We may have the foundations of one, with the first provincial assembly elections, in eighteen months' time.'

In fact, what the SNP would have in eighteen months' time was disaster: the loss of all but two of its parliamentary seats, the installation of an anti-devolution Conservative government and internal warfare that highlighted the very traits Wolfe had been warning against – republicanism, leftism, schism and what he called 'vulgarian capers'. After 1979 the SNP blamed its misfortunes on Labour's incompetence and unpopularity. The truth is that the SNP itself, by failing to be either strongly in favour of devolution or strongly against it, completely confused its supporters and eroded its own political position. By the autumn of 1978, when the party was doing badly in by-elections and was back down to 20 per cent in the opinion polls, Wolfe was arguing that hostility to all-out independence was to blame. Others said just the opposite. Still others wanted the party to lurch left, to take on Labour directly. The period was marked by a breakdown of trust between the SNP MPs and the party's leading figures in Scotland. There was tension between parliamentarians, who felt they were the natural leaders, and the SNP's formal leadership in Scotland, which considered the MPs its pawns. The party had never before had a big Westminster presence and found the dilemma of 'who leads?' a novel and knotty one. Inevitably some of the MPs became more embroiled in and interested by devolution, as they debated it in the House, just at the same moment as some SNP activists in Scotland wanted to withdraw from the whole devolution business.

There were deeply unpleasant meetings, including, on one occasion, a punch being thrown at Winnie Ewing, the SNP's *grande dame* and current Euro-MP. In July 1977 a meeting was held between Donald Stewart, the parliamentary leader, and Wolfe to try to resolve differences, and the MPs started to make greater efforts to keep the Scottish leadership and membership in touch with what they were doing. Not everything they were doing, of course: some of the antics of Nationalist politicians were a problem in themselves. The best of the SNP group were decent patriots who distinguished themselves. But for a few, as for a few MPs from other parties, Westminster proved an inglorious and best-forgotten interlude.

The Revolution Deferendum: the Parliamentary Road to Thatcherism

The 1976 Scottish Labour Party rebellion against the party nationally had had an impact at Westminster that was too little noticed by the Home Rule movement in Scotland: the defection of Sillars and John Robertson, plus the decision of John Stonehouse to sit as an independent and Reg Prentice's later defection to the Conservatives in October 1977, slowly stripped away the Labour government's tiny majority. Its undignified wriggling as it tried to get devolution through the Commons has to be seen in the light of its awkward parliamentary situation. Threats came from the Nationalists and Home Rulers on the one side and from the anti-devolution Labour rebels on the other.

Wilson continued to make a clever and negative case for devolution until his resignation. A few weeks before he went he was claiming proudly that devolution 'directs itself to the problems of strengthening the overall unity and cohesion of the United Kingdom itself'. He reserved most of his scorn for the Nationalists and argued, with a fine streak of perversity, that Scotland's economic failure under successive London governments was the prime reason for its staying British. In an independent Scotland, he asked the Commons, what would be the future of the high-cost Scottish coalmines? Or the expensive rail network, which was condemned to heavy losses? Or the Linwood car plant? Or the Bathgate truck plant? Or Clyde shipbuilding? (Most of the coalmines, part of the rail network, Linwood, Bathgate and most of the shipbuilding have since, of course, disappeared. But no doubt it seemed like a good argument at the time.) Wilson also attacked Liberal federalism in wearily cynical terms: 'We all know what happens when legalistic and judicial processes are inserted into human affairs.'

In March came his sensational, unexpected and never fully explained resignation. He was replaced by Jim Callaghan, and Michael Foot was appointed Leader of the Commons with special responsibility for devolution, along with a new deputy, a sharp young lawyer, John Smith. Civil servants observing the Whitehall and parliamentary negotiations at the time concluded that Smith was not emotionally committed to Home Rule as such but was an extremely astute lieutenant to Foot, who even at the height of his influence in government was no details man. Jim Ross, then Under-Secretary in charge of the devolution unit at the Scottish Office, says that Smith was 'an up-and-coming junior minister and did damned well; he was an absolute master of the complex and enormously wide-ranging subject'.

But, yet again, the mood in Scotland and the mood at Westminster were opposed. Labour in Scotland, by now hypnotized by the breakaway SLP and the continuing threat of the SNP, had committed itself to tougher devolution, including economic powers for the assembly, at its conference. In London the rebel MPs were stepping up their campaign against any form of Home Rule. Had anyone cared to look, disaster was just along the Commons corridor. In November Kinnock tabled a Commons resolution calling for a referendum on devolution and attracted seventy-six signatures. It seemed a natural idea at the time; Labour had, after all, settled its internal problems over continued membership of the Common Market only eighteen months earlier with another referendum. Callaghan conceded the second referendum. Later he was to complain bitterly about the wrecking antics of the anti-devolutionists. But he had been well warned. Dalyell recalls going to him to talk about devolution and finding that Callaghan wanted to know only Dalyell's feelings about Cyprus. As chairman of the Labour back-bench foreign affairs committee, Dalyell did have feelings about Cyprus but insisted on trying to discuss the more immediate Scottish crisis. He was told, in typically avuncular Callaghanese: 'Don't worry about this devolution thing, Tam, you just go chuntering on.' (Tam did – and eventually helped chunter Callaghan back to his farm.)

There was only one mildly cheering sign for Labour: the Conservatives were also split over devolution. Broadly speaking, the Tory left, including the shadow Scottish Secretary Alick Buchanan-Smith, the shadow minister Malcolm Rifkind, the Scottish party chairman Russell Fairgrieve and, indeed, the young Ian Lang, were strongly in favour of devolution. Their arguments tended to be that devolution would bring government nearer the people and was anyway demanded by Scots (something the polls seemed to show). The right, led by Iain Sproat, a controversial Aberdeen South MP who helped found the 'Keep Britain United' and 'Scotland is British' campaigns, and by Teddy Taylor, by now the leading bare-knuckle anti-devolutionist, were mostly opposed. The right argued that an assembly would be merely another bureaucratic tier and would be dominated by socialists. When Margaret Thatcher seized the party leadership from Heath she inherited his proposals and his Scottish team. To begin with she stuck by both. In November 1975 she had told a meeting in Glasgow that devolution mattered to ensure that more decisions affecting Scotland were taken in Scotland, and in the same month she explained to the Commons her view of the difference between Scotland and Wales: 'Scotland has had its own legal system and separate legislation for some years ... also, there is much more demand for such an assembly in Scotland than there is in Wales. Therefore, although we are pledged to a Scottish assembly, we have made no similar pledge about a Welsh assembly.'

The following January she went further, telling the Commons that a Scottish assembly should have its relationship with Westminster subjected to judicial control, not the 'arbitrary political veto' suggested by Labour: this would get rid of the 'terrible idea ... that because one does not like what the assembly does with the powers one gives it, one can say "no". That is not devolution at all.' Intriguingly Mrs Thatcher argued for 'Bill of Rights' clauses in a devolution Bill to protect fundamental freedoms: 'It would not be a Bill of Rights but clauses tantamount to it ... it would be a new constitutional venture, but the whole exercise is a new constitutional venture.'

But her party in Scotland was as divided as ever. A few days before the debate the Tories' Scottish Central Council had been split on whether or not to support a directly elected assembly, though it decided to do so. Her natural allies on the right were campaigning ever more loudly against devolution. Indeed, her support for Bill of Rights clauses reflected their fear of a hard-line socialist regime in Scotland. The pro-devolutionists, by contrast, were not her sort of Tory. And to those listening closely to her tone it was obvious that she was changing her position. In that same debate, for instance, Buchanan-Smith told the Commons, 'The Conservative Party is the party of devolution,' while she told MPs 'Let it be remembered that we are the Unionist party.' Her choice of pronoun was significant. She insisted, more and more strongly, that 'Devolution should march hand in hand with a conscious and deliberate attempt to scale down the size of government.' Back-bench Tory radicals like Nigel Lawson had been arguing that the withdrawal of government from much of the economy and public life *was* the best form of devolution – the real way to hand power back to the people. That became Mrs Thatcher's view too. As Labour became more and more entangled with its own complex and compromising proposals, she pulled her party back. Eventually she retreated to a position of de facto hostility to devolution, covered with the figleaf of some better, weaker and (always) vaguer scheme. By the end of the year her U-turn had been accomplished. She whipped her party into the 'no' lobby against the Scotland and Wales Bill, causing Buchanan-Smith and Rifkind to resign from the Conservative front-bench team. From the back-benches they urged continued support for an assembly. Teddy Taylor was appointed in Buchanan-Smith's place.

But Conservative loyalty to the party leader meant that the division of Tory opinion never really helped Labour. The Scotland and Wales Bill, which received its second reading against Tory opposition in December 1976, chugged forward agonizingly slowly. It was being attacked by Tory right-wingers, Labour left-wingers, constitutionalist theorists, die-hard Unionists, English nationalists. And always, always, at inordinate length. It became obvious to Callaghan that it would be necessary to cut short the debate with a guillotine motion or lose the Bill and that a Labour rebellion would probably mean that the government would lose the guillotine motion anyway. There was no way out. As Callaghan said in his memoirs, had he simply withdrawn the devolution Bill without a vote, 'The Scottish National Party would have had an electoral field day: the demand for independence might begin to grow and even reach dangerous proportions if no effort was made to accommodate the middle ground.' In February 1977 the inevitable happened: the guillotine motion and the Bill were defeated with the help of twenty-two Labour rebels. There was despair among the devolutionists. In Edinburgh the *Scotsman*'s editorial team gloomily decided that if the choice was now the Union or independence, the paper (which had once been staunchly Unionist) would opt for independence. Gordon Wilson, the SNP MP, reported back to his party's National Council that the government was 'in utter confusion about what to do next'. The Unionists, though, were jubilant. In his introduction to a book by Tam Dalyell published that year the English historian Hugh Trevor-Roper, now Lord Dacre jubilated away about the courage of the rebels. Indeed, he got a little carried away: 'I can think of no parallel to the action of those twenty-two MPs on 22 February 1977 since the debate, on 7 May 1940, which persuaded Neville Chamberlain to resign.'

Perhaps it was time to give up the whole devolution business? But however difficult the parliamentary situation, the performance of the SNP in the May 1977 district council elections reminded Labour of the dangers of shrinking back to straightforward Unionism. The Nationalists made huge gains, seizing 131 seats from Labour and leaving the party of government without control of a single important Scottish district council. Two months later Michael Foot duly told the Commons that the government had finally decided to split the Scotland and Wales measures and bring in a new Scotland Bill, which would give extra powers to a Scottish assembly, including the ability to dissolve itself and hold a Scottish election after a two-thirds majority vote. The Scottish political leader would be called the First Secretary, and the other members of the Edinburgh administration would be called Secretaries. For the Tories Francis Pym dismissed the Labour solution as 'a minor operation instead of major surgery'.

This new Scotland Bill received its second reading on 14 November 1977. It was one of the key debates in the devolution saga. Reading it now, one is struck by how much more forceful and vivid were the opponents of devolution compared with its weary and ground-down sponsors. Bruce Millan, appointed Scottish Secretary in succession to Willie Ross, warned MPs that Scotland demanded an assembly and that the Conservatives' counter-proposals for a near-powerless one would be 'a recipe for conflict'. But his half-hearted attempt to chill the blood got nowhere. Norman Buchan, the left-wing sceptic, spoke for many when he said:

The last time I spoke on this matter, on 22 February, I said that if the Bill was defeated there would be a strong reaction in Scotland. I was wrong. There was no march or demonstration and not one window was broken in St Andrew's House. Even the SNP knew that it could not mount a demonstration.

Robin Cook, then an Edinburgh Labour MP, agreed. He had been unable to find any interest in the Bill in Scotland. Not a single letter had been sent to him. Although he was later to change his mind about devolution, Cook's prophecy about the coming referendum campaign in Scotland was remarkable for its accuracy:

I want to kill not the Bill but this issue . . . If we are to kill the issue, it can be done only in the referendum to follow the Bill. I have a lively expectation that it will be done. If I am right in reading the mood of my constituents, it will be defeated, not by the majority vote against it, but by the fact that we shall have such an unimpressive proportion voting that no government in their senses will be able to claim that they have a mandate for such major constitutional change.

And so it was.

Although there were eloquently pro-devolution speeches from Buchanan-Smith and John Smith, Millan had to concede that the government had failed to come up with any watertight taxation proposals for the Scottish assembly and then found much of the debate centring on that old poser about the powers and numbers of Scottish MPs at Westminster. It was the same question that had obsessed Unionist MPs all through the century: in 1914 the then Tory leader, Arthur Balfour, had asked: 'Are you going to leave the whole of these seventy-two Scottish Members here to manage English education? . . . It is an irresponsible scheme.' John Major made the same point in June 1992, telling Ayr Tories that, with devolution, 'The future status and number of Scotland's MPs at Westminster would inevitably be diminished.' In the late 1970s the problem of the Westminster status of Scottish MPs and English MPs (a problem that had already existed in the case of the Northern Irish Members, to nobody's great discomfiture) was universally referred to as 'the West Lothian question' in honour of Tam Dalyell, the West Lothian MP who posed it with characteristic doggedness.

That November evening Dalyell was in much more than dogged form, seizing on SNP descriptions of the Bill as a first step on the road to self-government. He argued that the contradictions inherent in devolution would mean the new assembly could not endure but 'will have the life of a butterfly'. Within weeks of a Scottish assembly being established in Edinburgh it would be clamouring for more powers and more money. If the Bill were passed, the devolutionary coach would be 'on a motorway without exit roads to a separate Scottish state'. There was much scribbling and nodding on both sides of the chamber. The Conservative shadow Commons leader, Francis Pym, derided the idea that 'Something has to be done; this is something; therefore we must do it'. Even though his own counter-proposals for yet another talking-shop in Scotland were pitifully weak and were shredded by John Smith, Pym had struck home. Although the Scotland Bill passed its second reading with a majority of forty-two, there seemed a palpable lack of enthusiasm for it.

Throughout the rest of that winter the government, now temporarily sustained by the Lib–Lab pact, battled on with the Scotland Bill. The SNP MPs varied in their feelings but were still under pressure from fundamentalists at home and were far from enthusiastic about the legislation. Gordon Wilson accepted that it was stronger and simpler than the earlier Bill but noted that it still lacked the economic dimension the SNP had always wanted: therefore 'The Government cannot rely on the SNP keeping them in office.' More ominous still, the government was forced to concede an amendment successfully moved by the rebel MP George Cunningham (a Scot, sitting for the Islington consitutency in London) that required the devolution Act to be repealed if it were not supported by at least 40 per cent of the Scottish electorate in the forthcoming referendum. This hurdle, unique in British political history, was justified on the ground that a change of such constitutional magnitude required a more than usual degree of public support. Privately some of the Labour ministers believed it meant the game was up. On 31 July 1978 the Scotland Bill received the Royal Assent; as with the Welsh devolution scheme that passed into law on the same day, all that was required was the referendum.

In Parliament the issue of devolution had been an exhausting, complex and wearisome affair, with moments of high drama and some fine speeches but many more hours of grinding and barely comprehensible procedural warfare. Yet it had, by keeping the Scottish Nationalists and the Liberals precariously on board, allowed Callaghan's leaky ship to stay afloat. As he said later, somewhat cheekily, devolution 'helped to distract parliamentary attention from a morbid preoccupation with the state of the economy'.

In the last lap before the referendum itself Labour had a run of three good by-election results in Scotland. Even the famous Margo MacDonald could do little for the Nationalist cause at the hustings; she failed to emulate Winnie Ewing at Hamilton, where the seat was held by the Labour Unionist George Robertson. At Glasgow Garscadden, Donald Dewar, a devolutionist and future party leader in Scotland, held a Labour seat that had been represented at local level by six Nationalist councillors. After his victory furious Nationalists flung beer cans and covered the coats of Labour supporters with spittle: Dewar's distaste for the SNP was doubtless influenced by that night. The third by-election was caused by the death of John P. Mackintosh in July 1978. Had he lived, some Labour MPs believe he would have swayed the result of the referendum campaign. The SNP failed to make much impact in his Berwick and East Lothian seat against another Labour Home Ruler, John Home-Robertson, partly because of a bitter internal fight between their candidate, Isobel Lindsay, and the former SNP candidate – an affair that took up an inordinate amount of time and emotional energy at SNP headquarters. It started to look as if Labour was, after all, turning the corner. Then came the 'winter of discontent'.

On the day of the referendum it snowed. The February 1979 campaign had occurred against a backdrop of foul weather and a perpetual stream of stories about strikes in schools, hospitals and other public services. Callaghan's prestige and influence were already crumbling. The Labour message in Scotland was a divided one, with well-known figures like Cook, Dalyell and Brian Wilson campaigning vigorously against devolution. Local parties were sometimes split. About a third of constituency Labour parties declined to campaign at all, and many others had members working in the 'no' camp as well as in the 'yes' one. Indeed, neither camp existed as a single entity, since both the pro- and the anti-devolutionists were split into rival campaigns, largely because of Labour distaste for working alongside other parties. On the 'yes' side Labour set up its own 'Labour Movement Yes' campaign rather than joining 'Yes for Scotland', which included the SNP, the rebel Scottish Labour Party, a string of prominent clergymen, trade unionists, writers and public figures such as Lord Kilbrandon, Sean Connery, the actor Andrew Cruikshank and the banker Angus Grossart.

The Conservatives campaigned mainly on the 'no' side, though there were some prominent exceptions, such as Malcolm Rifkind. The Tories were on a high in Scotland, as elsewhere; one opinion poll in February 1979 put them on 35 per cent north of the border, up ten points on their October 1974 performance. On 14 February Lord Home of the Hirsel, the former Tory Prime Minister, made a notorious plea for Scots to 'vote no for a better Bill', suggesting that a Conservative government under Mrs Thatcher would produce a better scheme. This was echoed by George Younger after the election when, as the new Scottish Secretary, he promised the Commons all-party talks, and by Mr Rifkind, a new Scottish minister, who spoke of a new phase of devolution. The long stretch of Conservative government that followed never gave any indication that the promises were seriously meant. Later, in private conversation, Margaret Thatcher tended to terminate discussion of the Scottish constitutional question by announcing firmly: 'I am a Unionist.'

During the referendum campaign itself, although the canvassers on door steps seeking a 'yes' vote started to become first alarmed and then despondent about the response, there was little official sign that the main parties thought anything other than that overwhelming victory was likely. Indeed, they allowed their over-confidence about the result to inflame their natural mutual hostility. Labour's Scottish Secretary, Helen Liddell, explained in a letter to local Labour parties that 'The achievement of an Assembly for Scotland will be ours and it would be wrong to allow our consistent opponents ... to claim credit for this constitutional advance.' If that seemed complacent, her statement later, that 'We will not be soiling our hands by joining any umbrella "Yes" group,' revealed the sectarian and partisan attitude of Scottish politics just ahead of the general election. She has been rightly chastised for this; but critics of Labour should remember that the SNP was little better: Gordon Wilson had told the party's National Council meeting in March at Paisley that SNP members should not 'speak on the same platform as people who are normally our opponents'. Labour campaigners on the 'no' side also judged it wiser not be publicly associated with their ideological enemies. In the event the two main anti-devolution campaigns were 'Scotland Says No', dominated by businessmen and lawyers and heavily backed by the Scottish Conservatives, and the separate 'Labour Vote No' committee, working alongside it. Both included Labour MPs, but the Labour campaign also brought in trade unionists and younger Labour activists like Brian Wilson and Adam Ingram, later the MP for East Kilbride and Neil Kinnock's parliamentary aide.

The failure by politicians to submerge their party differences in a common cause hardly helped to inspire voters. But although both Labour and the SNP had shown weak leadership, there was more to it than that. The devolution referendum result cannot be isolated from the general unpopularity of the Callaghan government during that winter of closed schools, piled rubbish, furious public-sector workers, unburied dead and general sense of drift. It has been argued, unconvincingly, that Scotland's World Cup football humiliation in Argentina in 1978 had helped to cause a national failure of self-confidence. This may have played a tiny part, but economics and politics were more important by far. In 1979 devolution carried the stigma of a failing government. It had been imposed on a doubtful party by a London leadership for purely electoral reasons. It had been legislated for in a fog of internal dissent and confusion. It was campaigned for by divided parties at a time of economic chaos. In some ways it is surprising that so many Scots voted for it.

Slightly more than 1.23 million Scots did so on 1 March 1979. Some 1.15 million voted against an assembly. Though higher than the European referendum, the turn-out was modest – 63.8 per cent – and the majority was slim. The 'yes' vote represented 32.9 per cent of the overall electorate, far below the 40 per cent required by the Cunningham amendment. Indeed, none of the Scottish regions cleared the hurdle. Dumfries and Galloway, the Borders, Grampian and Tayside, as well as the Orkney and Shetland islands, all voted against devolution, perhaps reflecting the mistrust of rural areas for Edinburgh and Glasgow politics. The result was a devastating blow for Labour and for the SNP, which immediately launched a 'Scotland Said Yes' campaign to try to persuade Callaghan to ignore the 40 per cent rule and press ahead with devolution anyway. Electoral manoeuvring aside, did they have a case? It is quite clear that the 40 per cent hurdle was, in the context of a country that regularly elects Westminster governments on a minority of votes actually cast, an unusual stratagem advocated by people who wanted to destroy devolution. But, given the actual result, it is hard to feel a sense of outrage that an assembly was not established because less than a third of the electorate wanted it. The argument that big constitutional changes should have widespread popular support is hardly an undemocratic one. Part of the bitterness and disillusion with which the Scottish political and journalistic world greeted the result (lots of references to 'bottling out', just as in 1992) reflected the amazement of Scotland's urban, leftish-leaning establishment that their assumptions were not shared more widely throughout the country.

After the referendum there followed frenzied negotiations at Westminster to try to keep the Act alive. There was much talk about a 'Frankenstein' solution, keeping the Act in suspended animation until after an election and then reviving it again. The SNP MPs, who had been badly split the previous autumn over an earlier debate on whether to vote down the government, were divided about tactics yet again. Among those trying hardest to save the government were John Smith, by then in the Cabinet, and Jim Sillars of the SLP. Among those prepared to kill off devolution and risk the election was Neil Kinnock. But the SNP, though some of its parliamentarians twisted and turned, was fed up with Callaghan and devolution and felt that it might as well go for a quick election. After the party's March National Council meeting in Dundee decided, in a mood of near hysteria to issue an ultimatum to Labour. Callaghan was probably doomed. Michael Foot did everything he could to claw back votes in support of Callaghan, who wanted to cling on for a few more weeks. But he failed to make it, and when he announced a further delay the SNP put down a motion of censure, which was seized upon by Margaret Thatcher. One SNP MP, George Reid, had privately described its determination to pull down Labour as the act of 'suicide pilots'. During an evening of high drama two SNP MPs abstained, and Callaghan famously mocked the majority of the Nationalists who were voting against him as the first recorded case of turkeys voting for Christmas. At first the Labour front bench thought it had held on, by a single vote. But no: it lost by the same significant margin; the election followed; and Thatcherism was born.

Even as a word 'devolution' has never regained its popularity in Scotland. Home Rule, which does not carry the implication that something has been graciously handed down by Westminster, is now used by those who want change that stops short of full independence. Devolution reeks of failure – failure of leadership, failure of nerve. But the most potent messages from the 1970s are more complicated. Devolution failed because it was imposed from above; the kind of Scottish Home Rule movement that started to emerge in Scotland in the 1980s and will be discussed in the next chapter was simply not there in the 1970s. Had devolution been a demand from the people, the Callaghan government's loss of authority would not, presumably, have discredited it so badly. Perhaps, therefore, something else was needed. Not a new party. Not another schism. Not a takeover. A new kind of politics.

5

New Politics, Old Parties: Scotland After 1979

'The best Party is but a kind of Conspiracy against the rest of the Nation.'

George Savile, Lord Halifax, London, 1750

When Strathgawkers or Strathgowkers
blether aboot jinin thegither
an a tourist hinks baith
waant thi wan hing

then Strathgowkers mean
victory o Strathgowkery
an Strathgawkers waant
Total Strathgawkinization

Robert Crawford, 'Talkies', 1992

Civil Politics

Much of the political history of Scotland during the Thatcher years is similar to the English and Welsh experience: newly confident Conservative ministers; Labour faction-fighting and reform; the firework of the Liberal-Social Democrat Alliance. But the constitutional question provided a context that was lacking in England. By the later 1980s its influence had produced the first possible signs of a new kind of politics. This new style, a crumbling on the edges of the established parties and a greater readiness to try cross-party cooperation, is in its early stages and may disappear again. But it also seems to be offering lessons for the conduct of politics south of the border during the mid-1990s that are already being taken up by Opposition politicians and constitutional reformers. For want of a better shorthand term, and to distinguish it from ordinary party politics (politics with uniforms, for the mind if not the body), it can be called civil politics.

Civil politics may be defined as politics that involves significant numbers of people outside the parties, well-meaning amateurs, and/or requires significant cross-party cooperation. It happens only rarely in a developed democracy, where the aggressive competition of parties is essential to the system. Civil politics occurs when voters, including party members, think that the party system is failing to answer a specific demand. When effective, it is so only over a relatively short period and if directed at a particular objective. Civil politics does not, of course, happen only in Scotland. The 'peace people' in Northern Ireland unsuccessfully attempted a kind of civil politics. The opposition to the poll tax, violent in England though not Scotland, was a sort of uncivil civil politics. The 'Live Aid' fund-raising for the Ethiopian famine, led by Geldof at a time when the government was failing to raise the level of aid to the Third World significantly, was civil politics. So are the constitutional reform movement Charter 88 and the rise of the influential environmental pressure groups. If, as seems entirely plausible, the Conservatives' rule at Westminster is a long-term fact of life, civil politics in Britain as a whole can only become more important, not less. The most dramatic recent example of the phenomenon happened far beyond Britain. The popular uprising against communism in Eastern Europe, the Baltics and the old Soviet Union was accomplished by amateurs and civilians. The rattling keys and lit candles of the East have been much cited by Scottish Home Rulers. And they have a kind of blood-thrilling, romantic resonance. But the comparison is impertinent. Scotland's difficulty in rediscovering its nationhood within a centralized, multinational democracy is not remotely akin to the oppression suffered by Hungarians, Czechs or Poles in the early 1980s.

By the end of the 1980s some Scottish Opposition politicians had begun, tentatively, to work with one another, and with non-party figures, towards a common aim. Why? Above all, because of their common failure to influence Westminster government, even marginally. The cynical interpretation might be that Scotland had produced a political class, the would-be rulers of the Labour and Nationalist and Liberal establishment, who were unable to find a role and engaged in a series of desperate manoeuvres to keep themselves in business. Yet, taken together, these people do represent a substantial majority of the Scottish electorate, and their campaigning for a Scottish parliament has consistently been supported by the Scottish people in every way opinion can reasonably be measured – or, rather, every way but one. In an otherwise astute and interesting book on the growth of Scottish nationalism Keith Webb wrote in 1977: 'If devolution were to be shelved by an impotent Labour government or permanently killed by a resurgent Conservative administration, the consequences could well be civil violence . . . a guerrilla campaign could well be the result.' I do not quote this to mock Mr Webb; and, as we shall see, there were fringe groups who were prepared to try violence during the 1980s, and no one knows what lies ahead. But it cannot be emphasized enough that the Scots have little enthusiasm and less talent for insurrection or even for the milder forms of civil disobedience. Civil politics has thrown up rather dignified, even somewhat pompous, bodies like the Constitutional Convention and the Campaign for a Scottish Assembly. Unionists who deride them, and use the absence of smashed glass or intimidating crowds to question how much Scots want constitutional change, are deploying an immature and ultimately perilous argument that mistakes the character of Scottish public life.

It also ignores the persistence of a Home Rule tradition that has not always been nationalist – indeed, has sometimes been anti-nationalist. It emerged in modern form in the Liberals' Young Scots Society and the Scottish Home Rule Association, in the early Scottish Labour Party and in the various patriotic groups that preceded the formation of the National Party of Scotland in the 1920s. It was embodied by the National Party faction that during the 1930s believed in dual membership with other parties, broad coalitions and moderate demands. It was given voice by the Scottish Covenant Association in the 1940s and 1950s. It was submerged during the high tide of Unionism in the later 1950s and 1960s, but it broke surface again, during the devolution years, inside Labour, the SNP itself and the SLP and then in cross-party groups like Scotland Says Yes. In the 1980s, as we shall see, it produced the Campaign for a Scottish Assembly and, through that, the Scottish Constitutional Convention. In the immediate aftermath of the 1992 election other groups – Scotland United, Democracy for Scotland and Common Cause – emerged. In almost every form it argued that self-government would produce better government; that the beter demo-cracy was the near-at-hand one, and that Home Rule for Scotland need not mean the splitting apart of Britain. The continuous presence of Home Rule opinion and its persistent, cyclical appear-ance in politics suggest it is pretty deeply rooted.

Scottish politics and British politics are, meanwhile, interwoven: policies promulgated from London, such as privatization, the Citi-zen's Charter and the levels of tax rates, often dominate day-to-day politics in Scotland. By the same token, Scottish political experi-ments, may influence the way politics is conducted in London and Birmingham and Cardiff – and there were tentative signs by the summer of 1992 that cross-party working on the Scottish model was coming into fashion in England. But if the Scottish way of doing politics is exportable, its particular atmosphere is not. Small countries do things differently. Politicians of opposite parties and viewpoints have been to the same state schools, worship in the same churches (a remarkable number of Scottish politicians are elders, or at least members, of the Church of Scotland) and live in the same parts of Glasgow and Edinburgh. They cram together into taxis to and from airports, ask after one another's wives and children and share the same hesitant attitude when it comes to London. Civil politics is made easier where public servants, bankers, lawyers, university professors, journalists and party *apparatchiks* move in one another's little circles. It can be a claustrophobic and clique-ridden world as well as a warm and sustaining one. It can nourish, and has nourished, personal vendettas of extraordinary (verbal) savagery as well as fruitful cross-party friendships. But, for good or ill, it is the world where the Scottish debate continues.

Thatcherism in Scotland

The Thatcher years started in Scotland with conventional left–right debate, virtually excluding the constitutional issue. It was only after two successive defeats, in 1983 and 1987, that the Scottish Opposi-tion parties began seriously to think about cooperation. It became clear not only that Scotland was voting for left-of-centre parties and getting a right-wing government but also that the right-wing gov-ernment was intent on changing the nature of Scottish society itself.

What became known as Thatcherism was viscerally and intellectually opposed to the post-war Scottish consensus, characterized by the domination of the public sector and a quasi-socialist tone in urban public life generally. With its mass public housing, high union membership and struggling heavy industries, Scotland was like a lot of England, only more so. But its subtly different intellectual and political climate made it much more resistant to the politics, if not the policies, of Thatcherism. As the 1980s wore on, the disparity between the politics of England and of Scotland became more glaring. And people started to wonder about Home Rule again.

Mrs Thatcher herself could not understand why the pure milk of Adam Smith was not imbibed with more enthusiasm in his own country. She did not possess a deep understanding of Smith's thought in all its social richness (something also true, Scottish partisans of the economic philosopher would say, of the free-market Adam Smith Institute). Nor was she, perhaps, well informed about contemporary Scotland. Still, Mrs Thatcher had a point. It was curious that free-marketry, once the core of Scottish economic thinking, was now considered a shameful perversion, in roughly the same category as cricket or cross-dressing. The great symbolic non-meeting of minds occurred on a Sunday, 21 May 1988, at the Church of Scotland's Assembly Hall on the Edinburgh Mound. There Mrs Thatcher, the Methodist free-marketeer, came to sermonize to the Kirk. She spoke eloquently about the need for wealth creation, quoting St Paul to the effect that the man who refused to work should not eat. One of her endearing characteristics has always been her inability to disguise her embarrassing but honest views. So she said to the Kirk Assembled, all hodden-grey with caring: 'I confess that I always had difficulty with interpreting the biblical precept to love our neighbours "as ourselves" until I read some of the words of C. S. Lewis. He pointed out that we don't exactly love *ourselves* when we fall below the standards and beliefs we have accepted. Indeed, we might even *hate* ourselves for some unworthy deed.' Hail the neighbour-hating strain of suburban Christianity! Her seed fell on stony ground. Ministers rushed to describe her address as un-Christian and a travesty of the Gospel, while the Moderator (the elected head of the Kirk for that year) presented her with a book about 'fair shares' in economic distribution.

There was one small but fertile Thatcherite plot in Scotland. Farther up the coast St Andrews University had had a neo-liberal tradition in economics since the early 1950s, thanks largely to a young lecturer called Ralph Harris, who later founded the Institute of Economic Affairs and was ennobled by Mrs Thatcher as Lord Harris of High Cross in 1979. By the 1970s St Andrews had become a seminary of the 'new right'. The salt-soaked and decrepit former capital of Scottish Christianity turned out many of the radical young clerks of Thatcherism. Many were English, and they moved to London to create, in a score of pamphlets, the Thatcherite theology as it unfolded messily and pragmatically behind the decisions of Cabinet sub-committees and legislative sub-clauses. Among the students who arrived at St Andrews as a teenage socialist and was converted to Hayek and Friedman was Michael Forsyth, the influential Scottish Thatcherite minister and early champion of the poll tax. There was a cold intensity about the St Andrews new-rightists that seems, on reflection, terribly Scottish. It has been argued here and elsewhere that the intellectual earnestness and schismatic tendencies of Scottish socialism owed something to Calvin. Is it just possible that the Thatcher reformation did too?

The link between Thatcherism and British Unionism was taken for granted but ought, perhaps, to have provoked more curiosity. There was little that was logical about it. Mrs Thatcher's Unionism came from her old-fashioned English monarchical heart, not her radical American head. On many questions (the constitution, law and order, the family) she was no libertarian but an orthodox, solidly conservative thinker. The Scottish question was one such — something that Mrs Thatcher would not talk about in the conventional sense but would merely assert about. Discussing the Union with her was not a rewarding experience: she would talk about the glories of the Empire and Commonwealth and the British mission to save the soul of Europe. To that extent Mrs Thatcher's Unionism was instinctive and not what would normally be called Thatcherite.

There was a further contradiction in all this. One of the reasons why Thatcherism failed to put down political roots in Scotland was that the disappearance of the Tory populists north of the border (Teddy Taylor, who lost Glasgow Cathcart in 1979, was the last substantial one) left the party sounding rather anglicized and aristocratic. Mrs

Thatcher herself was widely loathed, even by some traditional Tories. The idea of the Tories leading a fightback against the state, and vested interests, on behalf of the small people – which had some resonance for English working-class voters and certainly motivated radical Thatcherites like Forsyth – seemed ludicrous on Scottish housing estates. The state was far away; it was 'them down there'; it was, in some indefinable way, English. Even the most local expressions of its failure, the filthy social security offices or incompetent local housing authorities, could be blamed on a cold-hearted regime too far away for imagination to reach or anger to affect. Even for better-off Scots the notion that higher public spending in Scotland meant higher taxes seemed far from obvious. Public spending rumbled north on ox carts from a basement in Whitehall. It was determined by negotiations between the provincial ministers and the capital's ministers, not by the decision of Scottish electors. The same was true of taxes. Putting 'getting' and 'spending' together in an immediate and direct fashion, as would have happened had there been a tax-raising Scottish parliament, was probably the only way 'Thatcherite' politics might have been spread. But the lady's constitutional and economic messages were scrambled. What was that about standing on your own two feet?

In the event Thatcherism failed even to win the wholehearted affection of the Scottish Conservative Party. At successive conferences in Perth or Aberdeen young Thatcherites formed a dark rectangle of waving, pin-striped conviction amid the dun moorlands of tolerant tweeds and the outcrops of pink-faced old ladies. But they were always a minority – as were the only Scottish ministers who ever really embraced the Thatcher message, Michael Forsyth and Allan Stewart. The party was more rural-paternalist than suburban-radical in 1979, and it ended the 1980s the same way. When Forsyth was made chairman of the Scottish party in July 1989 and brought in a series of young Thatcherites to shake it up, the traditionalists fought back. Malcolm Rifkind, then Scottish Secretary, disliked Forsyth's abrasive style and revolutionary agenda. Perhaps he was affected by the drip-drip of rumour and innuendo to the effect that Mrs Thatcher was privily intent on dispatching Rifkind ('Malcolm, we need someone of your calibre to take charge of office-furniture procurement') and replacing him with Forsyth.

Perhaps temperament came into it. Rifkind's air of effortless mastery contrasted with Forsyth's tense chippiness. In private Forsyth's friends find him engaging company and genuinely, self-deprecatingly funny. But perhaps being Thatcherism's lonely missionary among the Painted People got to him after a while. Rifkind confronted Mrs Thatcher, and after a nasty battle Forsyth was forced to resign suddenly as chairman the following September, getting a promotion at the Scottish Office in recompense. And that was the beginning and the end of Scotto-Thatcherism in the Conservative Party.

Which did not mean that Thatcherism as a set of government policies, rather than as a philosophy, was repulsed at the border. In George Younger and Malcolm Rifkind, neither of them soulmates, she had two effective managers of change. Younger was sympathetic to the anti-spending-cut 'wets' in Cabinet in the early 1980s and, while tolerating the central thrust of Thatcherite policy, tried hard to cloak it in the consensual language of the Macmillan era. He did more. He prevented the closure of Ravenscraig steelworks in the autumn and winter of 1982, when his resignation (never actually threatened) hung in the air; he saved the Locate in Scotland inward-investment bureau; and he won a fight with the Treasury over rates revaluations in spring 1985. Without him the interventionist Scottish Development Agency might have been dismantled in the early 1980s. But Younger proved an adroit enemy of Labour councils, such as Lothian, which wanted to confront Westminster. His 'Gentleman George' persona helped disarm angry opponents, and the few but high-profile occasions when he rebelled persuaded some that he was a passionate anti-Thatcherite. He was not. The idea of Younger as a tartan-clad resistance leader is grossly overdone: the odd threat and a softer style did not add up to sustained rebellion. He effectively bypassed Labour with measures such as the council house right-to-buy scheme and the 1980-81 'parental choice' education Bill. He gave polite but hard political leadership during the miners' and teachers' strikes of 1984-5. He was lucky, as his successors were not, in being able to dismiss the constitutional issue airily as being no longer of interest to Scottish voters. He modified Thatcherism rather than deflecting it and was regarded highly enough by that tough lady to be asked to run her leadership campaigns in 1989 and 1990 (a decision that proved a mistake).

Similarly, Rifkind could fight back over the Forsyth style at Scottish Conservative headquarters, or over poll-tax rebates, and could speculate daringly about still being in politics after Mrs Thatcher had gone. But he pushed through the poll tax, derided the Scottish dependency culture and oversaw privatization of the Scottish electricity industry. Rifkind inherited the party in the run-up to the 1987 election and took the view that a genteel, behind-my-palm repudiation of Thatcherism would not save the Scottish Conservatives. So, although a wet and untrustworthy creature in the unforgiving eyes of true believers, he pushed the Thatcher agenda with some vigour in the later 1980s. Thatcherism might have progressed faster, and spoken more vividly, had Teddy Taylor and then Michael Forsyth been running the show, but Thatcherism did happen in Scotland. George Younger and Malcolm Rifkind, displaying skill, good humour and loyalty, were the men who made it happen.

The changes they initiated through Scottish legislation, combined with the UK-wide trade-union reforms, public-spending restraint, income-tax cuts and the curbing of local authorities, added up to a substantial shift in the mood and structure of Scottish public life. Scottish parents used Thatcherite legislation to switch their children from the schools chosen for them by their education authorities. By 1984–5, 20,800 a year were applying to do so, including 15 per cent of parents of children going to state schools in Tayside and nearly 13 per cent of Glasgow parents (the applications came from right across the social spectrum, and parents often gave their children's wishes and poor discipline as the reasons). Scottish families bought their council houses. In December 1979 more than 1.07 million Scottish households, 54 per cent of the total, lived in council or state housing – a bigger proportion than in some communist-bloc states at the same time, as Tory ministers were fond of pointing out. By September 1991, 243,000 had moved out of state or council tenancies, and the proportion had fallen to 38.8 per cent. That is a huge change by anyone's standards. Scottish trades unions found their status and power diminished, particularly in the wake of the miners' strike, which had a devastating effect in Scotland, though it was relatively peaceable and disciplined there, compared with Yorkshire, Kent and South Wales. Even as Labour councillors picked up control of the cities and most regions in the mid-1980s, they found themselves forced to act as local agents for Thatcherism, introducing competitive tendering and spending cuts.

So the Tory disappointments of the 1983 and 1987 elections in Scotland did not halt Thatcherism there – indeed, barely diverted it. Because of this, Thatcherism became the central factor in the rebirth of Nationalism and Home Rulery. In the 1983 election, for the first time for many years, the difference in voting north and south of the border was much remarked on. In Scotland Labour had a lead over the Conservatives of 6.7 per cent, while in England and Wales the Tory lead over Labour was 17.5 per cent. Some of the sting was taken out of this by the very poor showing of the SNP (for reasons we shall come to). The Nationalists retained their two seats but only came second in seven others and lost fifty-three of their seventy-one deposits. In Scotland, as elsewhere, the real breakthrough seemed to come from the Liberal–SDP Alliance, which won five more seats than the Liberals had managed in 1979. Since this was as much an English phenomenon as a Scottish one (though both the 1983 Alliance leaders, David Steel and Roy Jenkins, were sitting for Scottish seats), it helped to blur the emerging Scottish–English divide. Labour was the party most affronted, and its activists started to mutter about Tory-dominated Westminster's 'right' to rule Scotland. The muttering grew much louder in 1987, when the Scottish Conservatives suffered their worst defeat since 1910 and saw three seats fall directly to the SNP. They ended that election with only ten Scottish MPs, a fifth of the Labour total.

This mismatch between the way Scots swallowed some tenets of Thatcherism while voting against them caused grave concern and much internal debate inside the Scottish Conservative Party (as it did, for opposite reasons, inside the Labour Party). The Thatcherite solution was to keep dousing the natives with radical legislation and wait for them to convert. It was singularly ineffective. Scottish Thatcherites had argued that their policies would have a useful political side-effect. They would free 'Labour's serfs' from their dependency on Labour-run councils, Labour-run education authorities and Labourite union bosses and therefore, in time, destroy the very basis of Labour's huge Scottish vote. In fact, a long period of radical right-wing reform, which helped to make England more strongly Tory, had the opposite effect in Scotland and failed to make the Scots more Unionist (see p. 175). Why did Scotland not follow its socio-economic profile, which is not dissimilar to that of the English Midlands, and vote like the Midlands, where the Tories routed Labour again and again (winning a ten-point lead and twenty-eight more seats, for instance, in 1992)? In Scotland, Labour and the SNP routed the Tories, even though Scotland had become a relatively prosperous part of the UK. This can be explained only by the Scottish question – Scotland's different political culture and aspirations, in the widest sense – and gives the lie to those who argue that Scottishness is a fetish of the political classes that does not much interest Scottish voters.

But Scotland's status in the UK was a subject considered taboo throughout the Thatcher period and, apparently, virtually so under John Major. There had been occasional appeasing squeaks. At the Scottish Conservatives' 1984 conference Younger waxed eloquent on the Scottish style of government and claimed that Scotland was run from Edinburgh, not London. This was a little cheeky and also inaccurate: the officials may have been clustered in New St Andrew's House, but the orders and the general direction of policy came from Downing Street. After Rifkind had taken over, this one-time devolutionist made occasional comments about Home Rule being logical if there were a UK-wide federal solution. There was a 'one day, some day' lilt to his words. His successor, Ian Lang, called for a national debate on the constitutional future of Scotland, while Major spoke of 'taking stock' after the 1992 election.

Intriguing words, all of them, and much chewed on by the Scottish media (which, like mountain goats, have had to learn to get by on thin fare for long periods). But no action ever followed. In 1979 the all-party talks on the constitution produced only the window-dressing reform that the Scottish Grand Committee would meet periodically in the former Royal High School building at Edinburgh's Calton Hill, which had been gutted and refitted to house the Scottish Assembly. The Grand Committee had been a legislative instrument throughout the century, but since it was limited to Scottish MPs after 1979 and therefore did not have a Tory majority, its law-making role was destroyed. It became only a grand name for all the Scottish MPs slumped side by side without power to agree or amend legislation. Many talented politicians

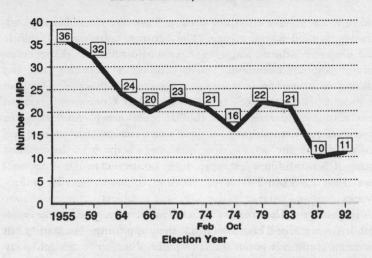

Tory MPs in Scotland, from 1955 to 1992

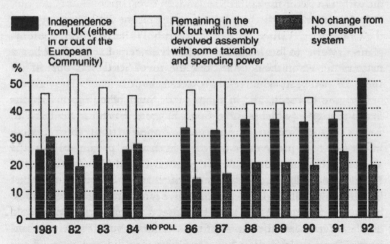

Source: ICM Research; the Scotsman. Based on 1,000 face-to-face interviews in 52 randomly selected constituencies in Scotland; results of first survey conducted in each year. (Questions slightly modified from 1988.)

Who wants what for Scotland

resented the touring company because it seemed like tokenism and, frankly, something of a bore. The Scottish press showed a little more interest in the meetings that have continued to be held periodically in Edinburgh ever since but to little effect. A talking-shop is a talking-shop whether it meets on a Thames mudbank or a Lothian hillside. In the Commons the Scottish Select Committee inquired into this and that but failed (unlike some other committees) to overcome partisan sniping. It was never much of a success and collapsed after the 1987 election, thanks to a boycott by the depleted band of Scottish Tory back-benchers. Its revival in the 1990s will not cause the Plain People of Scotland to invest heavily in fireworks.

The one great opportunity which Thatcherism gifted to the Scottish left was the poll tax. This is not the place for the fascinating but tortuous arguments about the tax's political paternity, except to say that assorted St Andrews intellectuals were seen in the vicinity of Downing Street in a state of undress nine months before the unhappy event. What is clear is that relatively small numbers of outraged Scottish householders and businessfolk can be blamed for the early arrival of the tax in Scotland.

Promises to abolish the rates had been being made regularly by the Conservatives since 1974, but Scottish Tories had been contemplating reform of local taxation seriously since 1982. Scotland had a strict rating-revaluation cycle, but the revaluation was put off, in 1983, for two years while reforms were being discussed. The reforms never came to much, and in 1984–5 (the Scots being more virtuous in this matter than the sensible English) the revaluation went ahead. As the figures started to emerge, it appeared that some people might face four- or fivefold increases in their bills. Some of this was alarmism, but lurid headlines frightened ratepayers. An academic Strathclyde study concluded afterwards that 'The pressure was confined to a small but vociferous and active number of pressure groups, both of the ratepayer and business variety.' Such vociferous people did, however, scare the pants off the Conservative MPs. As one said later: 'I have never had as big a postbag. And when I checked the names and addresses, they all came from areas which were solid blue on the canvass cards.' Another believed that his seat would be lost because of revaluation (it was, though perhaps for other reasons).

Michael Ancram, the minister in charge of local government in Scotland, had his ears chewed off. The situation was made worse because the concurrent shuffling around of central-government grant actually hurt Tory councils and helped Labour and Liberal ones. Councils of all hues used the ballyhoo to raise spending, and real bills really rose. The places hit hardest, when they finally arrived, were the richer parts of Edinburgh, the Borders, Perthshire and the north-east, all traditionally Tory. The party of the grouse moor had blown a hideous hole in its brogue.

It howled and it hopped. The then Scottish Tory chairman, Lord Goold, had an urgent meeting with Mr Younger and Mrs Thatcher. He tried, and failed, to get the revaluation postponed or abandoned. He warned publicly that it would be a huge vote-loser. Tory local-government leaders agreed that it was proving massively unpopular. They too predicted a terrible electoral backlash. Perhaps surprisingly for a debate conducted largely between Conservatives and business-men, there was a distinct quasi-Nationalist tinge to it: Scottish enterprises would be hurt, while English ones, with no revaluations, would not. In fact, business ratepayers overall were not much af-fected by the revaluation. But there were many moving laments about Scottish football clubs being squeezed while English ones prospered, Scottish high-street stores suffering while Harrods rubbed its hands and so on. Lord Goold said revaluation demonstrated that 'Scotland suffers, while England does not,' and the 1985 Scottish Tory conference left the party leaders in no doubt about what the party workers felt and how strongly they felt it.

A mood of something like panic among Scottish Tories certainly helped to crystallize opinion in favour of a swift abolition of the rates. The poll tax was, simultaneously but coincidentally, emerging from an Environment Department committee headed by William Waldegrave as the favoured way of doing so. Forsyth was among the right-wing Thatcherites campaigning for it. At a meeting at Chequers on 29 March 1985, as the furore in Scotland was reaching boiling point, the Local Government minister, Kenneth Baker, per-suaded Mrs Thatcher of its merits. At the Conservative conference at Blackpool that October Younger told Baker, who had just been promoted to Environment Secretary, that he wanted separate Scot-tish legislation a year ahead of England. He got his way. One MP who was prominent in the discussions said later that the party's view in Scotland was that nothing mattered except that the Tories were able to go into the next election saying they would get rid of the rates. There was too little close examination of the alternative. So while Baker wanted the poll tax phased in slowly, over a ten-year period, the Scottish ministerial team wanted the new tax implemented quickly, as a 'big bang'.

It certainly went bang. The Nationalist mythology has it that the poll tax was an example of Scotland being used for political vivisection by the cold-hearted English. In fact, it was the Scottish Tories who fought to have the tax quickly (a rare example of self-assertion by the party in Scotland that does not reflect favourably on its collective wisdom). The English ministries tried again to prevent a separate Scottish Bill, but Younger insisted, and work went ahead in the winter of 1985–6 to bring in Scotland's 'community charge'. Younger was discussing the Green Paper, *Paying for Local Government*, at the fateful Cabinet meeting on 9 January when Michael Heseltine walked out over the Westland affair. Younger had been presented with a silver model of a bed of nails by ironical colleagues the previous summer, and he was keen to leave the Scottish Office. When Heseltine slammed the door he was, to his pleasure, offered the defence portfolio.

Rifkind, prostrated by flu in his Edinburgh house, was telephoned within a few minutes of Heseltine's walk-out by Mrs Thatcher and appointed Scottish Secretary. He forged ahead quickly with the new tax, despite derisive Opposition attacks on its 'medieval' and unpractical nature. The Scottish Bill was published in November 1986, a centrepiece of the relatively light pre-election Queen's Speech. During a gruelling Westminster tussle that winter, it was rushed and guillotined through the Commons. Attempted filibusters were brushed aside, complex Opposition arguments ignored. It went through, of course, on the votes of English Conservative MPs like Heseltine and his followers who would later revolt against the tax when it was applied to their own constituents. In May 1987 Mrs Thatcher announced to an ecstatic Scottish Conservative conference that the new tax had received the Royal Assent. Registration started in April 1988, to the sound of a furious Labour Party debate about the merits of a non-payment campaign, and the tax itself arrived the following year.

It caused mayhem. By 1991–2, in the third year of the tax, local authorities were raising only 76.5 per cent of the community-charge money they needed to fund their budgets. Tens of thousands of people had dropped off the electoral roll (some reports say Mrs Thatcher has privately attributed the 1992 Tory victory to this). Glasgow voters, shortly after the general election, elected the militant poll-tax opponent Tommy Sheridan as a district councillor . . . from his prison cell. A wild success it wasn't.

The poll tax sums up a great deal about Scottish politics in the 1980s. It was introduced in the teeth of criticism and warnings from the vast majority of Scottish MPs, local government evaluators and chairmen of finance committees. It was proof against all forms of opposition. At Westminster the line-by-line criticisms of Labour, Liberal, SDP and Nationalist MPs had virtually no impact on the final, guillotined Bill. Neither did the confrontational antics of Scottish MPs who tried disruptive tactics. When the Bill for the English and Welsh version came in a year later, it had to be used to plug gaps in the Scottish legislation, and the biggest concessions wrung from the Treasury came because of pressure from English Conservatives, not Scottish MPs. The disastrous results of the 1987 election for the Scottish Conservatives caused no second thoughts. In Scotland, Labour tried legal but populist opposition. That got nowhere – nor, by the rules of the Westminster game, could it ever have.

There was also a law-flouting campaign of non-payment led by the SNP and the Trotskyist Militant Tendency. Its effect was to deprive councils of money they needed for urgent purposes. But did it change the government's mind? It is said in every golf-club bar, about once every five minutes, that nothing is certain in this life bar death and taxes. Strike off taxes: 700,000 summary warrants for non-payment of the poll tax had been issued in Scotland by the end of its first year, and the total over three years reached 2.5 million. Many of the non-payers were opportunistic. Even so, this was defiance on an extraordinary scale. It certainly made the job of local authorities much harder. But non-payment did not kill off the poll tax. The decisive things that did so were the outbreak of violence in England and the opinion-polling evidence for English Conservatives that they would lose their seats if the tax stayed. The poll tax was a bad tax in every corner of the United Kingdom. But at least in England it was a bad tax brought in by the party with the most seats and the most support. In Scotland it was a bad tax brought in by a minority party with minimal support beyond its own ranks. Such, at least, were the quasi-nationalist arguments proposed by Labour and the Liberal Democrats during the poll-tax saga. If they can do that with just ten MPs, ran the sad refrain, what can't they do?

The Polite Party

The poll tax was also the ultimate expression of Labour impotence during the Thatcher years. There had been others: the failure of so many campaigns to save factories, smelters, pulpmills, shipyards and steelworks; the failure to prevent the closure of the Gartcosh steelmill despite a famous march on London; the failure to turn aside housing, educational and health reforms. But nothing hurt so much as the poll tax. In 1983 and then in 1987, with fifty MPs that time, Labour promised that its Scottish strength would be used to 'defend Scottish voters'. The ordinary politics of taxes, housing grants and privatization became Scottified. As Donald Dewar noted in a Fabian pamphlet published shortly after the 1987 defeat, the Nationalist challenge was strong: 'Can Labour deliver? Can the fifty MPs protect Scotland from Mrs Thatcher? Can the poll tax be stopped? Can Labour set up the assembly?' (No, no, no, no.) Dewar went on: 'If the answers are in the negative the Nationalists will be there to draw some very uncomfortable conclusions . . . Scotland went over-whelmingly for Labour and the reward, or so the argument runs, is a continuing dominating Tory majority.' Dewar's logic, which he was lucky not to have quoted back at him, was inescapable. Feelings started to harden inside the STUC, which is sometimes described as the political wing of the Labour Party in Scotland, and among some Labour activists. The split Labour Party of the devolutionist 1970s was evolving into the Home Rule party of the 1990s. But it was taking a long, miserable decade to do it.

Labour had actually done rather well in the 1979 election. It won three extra seats, forty-four in all, as good a total as it had achieved since the balmy, pre-Hamilton days of 1966. With the collapse of the SNP, the Conservatives had done even better, reclaiming six seats, mainly in the north-east. Still, Labour considered that it would be well placed to harry the Scottish representatives of Thatcherism. 'Harry' is a word much beloved of Opposition politicians trying to explain what they can(not) achieve against a strong Commons majority. It is a good word: it has connotations of men on horseback waving their swords and shouting ruderies, from a safe distance, at a larger army they cannot hope to defeat. Occasionally a sickly straggler is knifed or a baggage cart seized. Labour's Scottish team, faced with a radical legislative programme, similar in its range to that of 1945, stabbed a few ministerial reputations and helped to seize the very rare extra cartload of loot for some specific purpose. But it proved wholly unable to stop the Thatcher army in Scotland. Nor was there any constitutional reason why it should. As a party that supported the Union, it was obliged to accept Westminster rules, however much it disliked them. So Labour accepted the rules. And harried.

The 1980s saw some formidable Scottish Labour talent making its mark in the Commons: Donald Dewar, Robin Cook, Gordon Brown and, of course, John Smith provided much of the backbone of the Kinnockite party. Small victories were won – Younger's determination to prevent the closure of the Ravenscraig steelworks owed something to effective Commons opposition, and Cook achieved reform of the law on homosexuality. During the passage of half a dozen complex pieces of legislation Dewar and others showed a grasp of detail and a feeling for the views of their constituents that ministers seemed sometimes to lack. But, faced with a big English majority, there was little the forty-four, then fifty, Scottish Labour MPs could do, and they rarely rattled the Scottish Office team. This was partly because of the nature of politics at Westminster, where, as family-starved weekly commuters, Scottish MPs form a club within a club. Labour front-benchers were, and are, able to point out the flaws in ministerial arguments, brandish embarrassing quotes from their earlier speeches, get air time from Scottish broadcasters to attack Tory arguments. But they had not the will to disrupt Parliament or get into a knife fight with Scottish Tory ministers. The various attempts by smaller groups to bring Parliament to a halt petered out. After 1987 the SNP, helpful as ever, referred to them as 'the feeble fifty'.

If Westminster was to prove an unlikely forum for national dissent, what about Scotland itself? There too Labour retained the instincts and composure of a natural party of government that had found itself, by some unfortunate misunderstanding, temporarily on the wrong side of the green-baize door. In the years when Labour's British conferences featured whey-faced trainee Leninists and tousled Trots from suburbia, its annual Scottish gatherings were douce affairs where, when the sun went down, ruddy-faced working men in dark suits would waltz stiffly with smartly dressed female councillors. This was a party keener to avoid shameful daftness than to take to the streets.

Inside its executive, to be sure, a war of attrition rumbled on between the old guard and the left-wing Labour Coordinating Committee (LCC) from 1978 to 1983. Young politicians like George Galloway, who flew the Palestinian flag from Dundee City Chambers, Bill Speirs (now deputy general secretary of the STUC), Bill Gilby of the public-sector union NUPE and Michael Connarty, later the controversial left-wing leader of Stirling district council, challenged and eventually ousted some of the silver-heads of the 1970s. But the Scottish party did not swing violently leftwards as a result. This was partly for a reason that non-aficionados of Scottish Labour politics will find bizarre: the communists helped to keep the lefties out. The Scottish Labour movement has long had a communist tinge: the Communist Party had been strong in Fife and part of Glasgow and was still influential in some unions, such as the mineworkers and the transport and general workers, well into the 1980s. One of Labour's nicest and most able MPs, Norman Buchan, was a former communist (he left over Hungary) and a witty, gentle man who embodied the intellectual hunger and work ethic of the Party at its best.

He and his wife Janey Buchan, the MEP, had offered hospitality and political argument to a generation of Scottish Labour youngsters. After he died in 1990 the sight of crowds of Paisley people and politicians, including the aristocratic Tory minister Lord James Douglas-Hamilton, lustily singing socialist anthems in his honour was an unforgettable one. The Communist Party was bitterly hostile to Trotskyism and the kind of ultra-leftism that was infecting Labour in the south: it was sober, and disciplined, and somewhat cautious. Members of Labour's executive believe its influence was essential in keeping the Scottish party on an even keel.

The rise of the left in Scotland in the 1980s proved to be as much a generational change, as one Labour establishment gradually replaced another, as a hardening of Labour ideology. The new generation was not particularly 'tartan'. A lot of people had been bruised or plain bored by devolution and were keener to address other, more immediate, issues. The party did not reverse its devolution policy. Indeed, at Labour's 1981 Scottish conference the executive published a policy statement on devolution that went a bit further than the 1970s position, suggesting a toughened-up assembly, able to vary income-tax rates and with some powers of economic intervention. The policy paper lamented that such an assembly might have stopped council-house sales and the assisted places scheme.

But that was all it was – a lament. There was little sign of a Home Rule movement either at Westminster or among party activists. Until the aftermath of the 1987 election it was strictly for the hobbyists. Granted, the stronger devolutionists, such as Alex Kitson, Dennis Canavan and George Foulkes, had been busy enough in the Labour Campaign for a Scottish Assembly that by now saw the Home Rule argument through the prism of Thatcherism. George Foulkes spoke in one of its pamphlets of 'the remoteness and alienation from the centre of power . . . and the consciousness that Thatcher has no mandate in Scotland'. This was an early (1981) use of the 'no mandate' argument – the notion that election results in Scotland should be regarded as somehow separate from English ones and that a party that failed to gain a majority in Scotland had no moral right to rule there. In the early 1980s it was rightly regarded by Labour as a quasi-Nationalist argument, fit to be muttered in moments of intense personal frustration over a large whisky but never to be publicly proclaimed. Only when Mrs Thatcher won in 1983, with a crushing UK majority of 143, did it start to surface more openly.

By then the most nationalist of Scottish Labour activists were worrying away at the discrepancy between how Scots voted and how they were ruled. No-mandatery really is the fault line between conventional Labourism and nationalism. Even before the 1983 election George Galloway had suggested, in the magazine *Radical*

Scotland, that Scots might have to organize a 'representative Scottish Convention' to challenge Mrs Thatcher if she won again. He also wanted demonstrations and strikes and even talked of a 'march on London'. Galloway has never been in the Labour mainstream; he is a bright man and can be charismatic, but he has a weakness for military metaphors and is loathed by some of his Westminster colleagues. Others, though, were also talking tough. George Foulkes wrote a notorious memorandum suggesting that the Labour movement should organize a referendum on Home Rule and explaining how Scottish Labour MPs could disrupt Parliament in an orchestrated, months-long campaign. This proved unpopular with the MPs being volunteered as Home Rule shock troops. Gordon Brown and Norman Godman, strongly backed by John Smith, outflanked Foulkes, John Maxton and Dennis Canavan with an alternative strategy to argue English Labour MPs around to devolution and create a 'broad-based movement for change' in Scotland. Once the vote had been won little was seen of the broad-based movement. Rather more dramatically, Robin Cook, a leader of the 'no' campaign in the devolution referendum, announced to a meeting of the Scottish Socialist Society in July 1983: 'I have not been an extravagant supporter of the Scottish dimension. but I have changed my mind. I don't give a bugger if Thatcher has a mandate or not – I will simply do all I can to stop her.' These sentiments were still considered mildly eccentric from 1983 to 1987, but after the second defeat of the 1980s they became almost commonplace.

What, meanwhile, of Neil Kinnock? How had the antidevolutionist Welshman of the 1970s reacted to the slow change of mood in Scotland? Through the mid-1980s there was little controversy about devolution: it was a second-order issue. From manifesto to manifesto and policy document to policy document, it was hardened up slightly as Dewar responded to the Thatcher revolution and the slow re-emergence of the Nationalists. Kinnock had had to make bigger sacrifices than swallowing Scottish Home Rule as he sought to unite the party and shape it into a credible challenger for power. He trusted and liked Dewar, finding the lanky and cautious Scotsman both endearing and funny, and allowed him a large amount of leeway in handling the Scottish party. In March 1986, on his way to the Scottish Labour conference, Kinnock promised for the first time that a Scottish parliament would be legislated for the first year of a Labour government. But the mask occasionally slipped. At the 1988 Scottish Labour conference Kinnock gave a somewhat uninspiring speech, which failed even to mention devolution or Scotland's constitutional position. Taxed about this on television later, he made an irritated, throw-away remark. There were lots of things he hadn't discussed, he said, such as 'environmental conditions in the Himalayas'.

Stunts and Schism: the SNP in Torment

The Scottish National Party, meanwhile, had seemed at times about as relevant to the debate as those Asian snowscapes. Its search for a new direction after 1979 led to a long and bitter fight between left and right. There were campaigns of civil disobedience, expulsions, mutual denunciations of irreconcilable factions, stormings out and breakings in. At times it seemed about to disappear up its own fundamentalism. At other times it seemed like the Labour Party of the early 1980s. The left–right divide had been evident during the 1970s but as a minor theme. It was the trauma of the 1979 election result, when the SNP's parliamentary representation fell from eleven to two, that set the scene for civil war. By that summer the SNP's standing in the polls had crashed from percentages in the mid-30s to just 12 per cent. And some of its best and brightest concluded that a new start was needed: the SNP had to become a leftist republican party.

Since it had tended to win most of its seats in the Highlands and the relatively prosperous north-east, it may seem strange that the SNP was in any way attracted to the socialist creed of the central belt. But it was precisely there, in Glasgow and the Labour-held industrial towns (as anyone who could count up to thirty-five and read a map could see), that the SNP had one day to achieve its electoral breakthrough. The SNP's base was not socialist (indeed, it had many right-wing supporters). But to advance beyond its base it had to attract socialists. This conundrum had produced the fence-sitting answer that the SNP was 'a broad centre party', as Andrew Welsh, the chief whip, put it in 1978. Yet its only MEP, Winnie Ewing, sat in a right-of-centre group in the European Parliament, and before the SDP was formed in London the party leadership had occasionally talked about the attractions of renaming the SNP the Scottish Social Democratic Party. The truth was that, in the conventional left–right spectrum, the SNP had no primary colour at all.

In June 1979, after the SNP's National Council had met to brood over the election results, a group of leftish members, including Margo MacDonald, decided to form an internal SNP Socialist Group. In August this became the 79 Group, committed to trying to shift the SNP's centre of gravity to the left. This was an audacious aim and a risky one. Jim Sillars, who was shortly to join the SNP (and, indeed, marry Margo MacDonald), had warned only two years earlier, 'A positive attempt to carry the SNP to socialism would smash the party to pieces, and when its forward momentum was gone, the Unionists would have a field day.' He changed his mind about that, but Sillars in 1980–82 nearly proved Sillars in 1977 absolutely right.

The 79 Group lived only two years and had about 200 active members. Its newsletter, which was published through 1981–2, carried the masthead 'For a Scottish Socialist Republic'. Much of its activity was centred on supporting workers at the Corpach pulpmill, British Leyland's Bathgate truck plant and the Invergordon aluminium smelter. It believed in cooperation with kindred spirits on the left, and its style was not dissimilar to that of other leftists of the same period: when the Prime Minister met a small demonstration at the Scottish Conservative conference at Perth in May 1981, *79 Group News* announced: 'A rather shaken Mrs Thatcher was hustled into the hall as missiles were thrown and anti-Tory slogans rained down on her ears.' It mourned the death of the Irish republican hunger-striker Bobby Sands and earned a rebuke from the party leadership for inviting a Sinn Fein speaker to one of its meetings. (This youthful republicanism was later seen by one of its most active members, Alex Salmond, as its worst mistake.) But, like so many leftist groups, the 79-ers were happiest and most successful when they flung themselves into internal party politics. At that they were briefly but astonishingly successful. At its high point, the SNP's May 1981 annual conference at Aberdeen, the group won a clutch of places on the SNP National Council and among the office-bearers – Jim Sillars was elected vice-chairman for policy – and committed the party to 'civil disobedience on a mass scale'.

Despite the frequent use of a tough-looking logo bearing the words 'Join the Scottish Resistance', the 79 Group-inspired civil-disobedience campaign did not get very far. The most widely publicized event came when Sillars and five followers attempted to occupy the Royal High School building at Calton Hill, Edinburgh, and to hold a debate on Scottish unemployment in the empty Scottish Assembly chamber on 10 October 1981. This was intended, as Sillars told the SNP's National Council beforehand, to 'drag our opponents into the constitutional argument, during which we could lay bare that the renewed talk of "devolution" from Labour and the Social Democrats is a time-wasting trap'. In the event security men impeded them, and although Sillars managed to get in and read a statement, it was all rather less than heroic. An account of the 'occupation' by one of the team suggests eloquently enough how the visions of resistance leaders collide with hard facts: 'It proved impossible to open any of the windows and so we decided to break one . . . This turned out to be difficult because the window was double-glazed with security glass. However, when a large enough hole had been made, Jim Sillars tumbled through . . .' He was arrested and later fined £100 for vandalism. A week after the assembly stunt a crowd of SNP supporters, including the party president, Billy Wolfe, turned up on Calton Hill for an official demonstration with flags representing the Scottish constituencies. There had been more talk of civil disobedience, but there were police. And they had dogs. Big ones. So nothing much happened.

SNP traditionalists, who had lost the vote at the Aberdeen conference, shunned such demonstrations and made little secret of their contempt for the 79 Group and civil disobedience. The party was virtually in a state of civil war. Attacks on the 79 Group had started the previous year, though they had been repulsed. The Group was helped by the fact that another internal organization, Siol Nan Gaidheal (Seed of the Gael), had also been founded in 1979 but was approved of by some of the 'fundamentalists' who detested the 79-ers' socialism. Siol Nan Gaidheal was a bizarre organization whose popularity among some mainstream Nationalists reflected the mood of deep depression about orthodox politics in the early 1980s. It was militaristic in image and sufficiently right-wing in ideology to be accused of 'fascistic tendencies' by 79-ers. It was certainly hardline, romantic, even fantasist, and obsessed with Celtic culture. Its members liked to parade about in Highland dress, with dirks and swords, in front of a black-hooded drum corps. It obstructed attempts to survey the Western Highlands for nuclear dumping. It also had a penchant for burning Union Jacks and attracted SNP veterans like Billy Wolfe and Willie McRae (later found shot dead, some Nationalists think by the British secret service). But Siol's operations were not always as revolutionary or awe-inspiring as the group liked to think: *Radical Scotland* reported mockingly in 1983 the arrival of some of its members on a day trip to Arbroath Abbey (scene of the famous declaration in 1320). The Gael Seeds had intended to burn a Union Jack but were refused entry by the aged ticket collector, one Harry McNulty, an old soldier who did not like the cut of their jib. The nationalist revolutionaries then repaired to the other side of the road to burn their flag there, but found they had run out of lighter fluid. And gave up.

It is one of the more cheering aspects of Scottish public life that (so far) even militant nationalists have shown little inclination for violence of any sort. And the very few who have have shown even less aptitude: a recent account of 'tartan terrorism' is mainly a record of minor explosions at remote sites, failed letter bombs and captured bank robbers. One incident can stand for many others. An attempt to blow up the Scottish Assembly building was made by the so-called Army of the Scottish People in June 1980. The ASP was apparently well armed but had to abort this, its first serious mission, because of the arrival of some tourists and 'an amorous homosexual' who kept peering into the would-be terrorists' Ford Cortina. The ASP carried the bomb back to Glasgow, where it went off on the kitchen table in one of its members' flats, leading to the arrival of Nemesis in a panda car. Although the various fringe nationalist groups who have been mentioned in previous chapters were followed in the 1970s and 1980s by a number of tiny republican extremist organizations, none of them managed to do much damage. After Siol Nan Gaidheal was finally banned by the SNP, it too spawned a would-be terrorist offshoot, Arm Nan Gaidheal, which carried out some petrol bombings in Dundee, Edinburgh and Glasgow. Property owned by Labour and the Conservatives was damaged, but nobody was injured.

Siol Nan Gaidheal was linked by both its enemies and its supporters to the general problem of 'factions' (normally code for the 79
Group) within the SNP. Thus Gordon Wilson spoke severely of
Siol Nan Gaidheal's 'silly antics' in his December 1980 report to the
SNP's National Council before swiping at 79 Group strategy and
warning the party of the danger of following Labour's practice of
having wings and factions, which led only to 'bitterness and internal
strife'. And, at the same meeting, the Bothwell branch of the SNP
linked Siol Nan Gaidheal with the 79 Group as 'strands of opinion'
within the nationalist movement that should be tolerated. There
was a sort of bitter comedy in the fact that such mutually hostile
wings of the nationalist movement should rely on one another for a
tacit alliance against the leadership. But, like most political jokes, it
was a sour one, best appreciated by the SNP's enemies. Because
both groups sounded extreme and both advocated civil disobedience and extra-parliamentary action, they probably became
loosely associated in the minds of some voters.

The leadership's fight against the factions and their extra-
parliamentary posturing took a long time but was finally successful.
Both the two main factions attracted furious hostility from other
SNP members. In December 1980 the Tayport branch of the SNP
declared that the 79 Group's socialist republicanism was 'repugnant
to the majority of the people of Scotland'; the following autumn the
Cumbernauld East branch attacked it for acting 'in a subversive
manner' inside the party. An internal inquiry was launched into Siol
Nan Gaidheal and concluded in March 1982 that it should give an
undertaking to stop marching under its own banners and with its
own drum corps at SNP rallies, to accept SNP discipline and to
stop heckling or disrupting other political parties. Throughout the
period, with SNP support at derisory levels, Gordon Wilson was
ramming home the danger of factionalism by talking in the bleakest
possible language about the party's future. In his March 1981 report
he wrote that if the party went too far left, 'we could find ourselves
on the fringe of politics'. This view was derided by the 79 Group,
which criticized his 'soggy centralist ideals'. But that December
Wilson struck again in even clearer language, saying that the party's
campaigning (including the civil-disobedience antics) had been
negative and that the SNP 'just does not attract enough general

credibility . . . In the turmoil of British politics, the SNP, filled with frustration from the events of 1979 and public bickering, has appeared as a spent force.'

The confrontation could not be long delayed, and it came on 3 and 4 June 1982 at Ayr, where the SNP held its most traumatic conference since the wartime split in Glasgow forty years earlier. The traditionalists, led by Winnie Ewing, had by then formed the Campaign for Nationalism. This was as an act of deliberate provocation, intended to force a ban of the other groups. The 79 Group had a nasty feeling about what was coming. Sillars, who was a close ally, though never expelled as a member, used the Ayr conference edition of *79 Group News* to attack 'the old myth that the Scots can be led to independence in some sort of tartan trance, which makes them conveniently blind to economic and social realities'. He warned that at the conference 'the Merchants of Despair will be seeking to paralyse the mind of the party.' On the second day of the conference Gordon Wilson put his own political future on the line by making it clear that either the internal groups would have to go or he would. Deep down, he was ready to quit. But his motion, 'That this conference demands the immediate disbandment of all organized political groups within the party and declares that membership of the party is incompatible with membership of any [such] group . . .' was passed by 308 votes to 188. Afterwards Sillars complained in an internal SNP paper: 'At Ayr, we had a chairman who held a gun to his head and dared the conference to make him pull the trigger. Moral blackmail . . .'

Maybe. But it worked. Wilson declared that he had been given authority to 'end the civil war raging since 1979 by ordering the disbandment of groups'. The Campaign for Nationalism, its purpose completed, quickly obeyed the order to disband. Siol Nan Gaidheal was expelled and crumbled, though a successor of the same name is reappearing in the 1990s. The 79 Group met in Edinburgh in August and formally agreed to disband but immediately reconstituted itself as the Scottish Socialist Society, which (to avoid the terms of the Ayr motion) would be cross-party, not simply an internal SNP group. The stratagem failed: on 21 September 1982, two weeks after taking part in the party's National Council at Dunfermline, Alex Salmond, Stephen Maxwell, Kenny MacAskill and four other

79-ers were ejected from the SNP. A long and wearisome appeal, involving forty hours of hearings in front of a party tribunal, with a lawyer appearing for the seven, ended when their expulsion was commuted to suspension, and they were allowed back into the party at the end of April 1983. Salmond says now that the experience was traumatic enough to give him a strong desire to expel no one from the modern SNP. As the dislike of the 79 Group was as much about its readiness to work with Labour Home Rulers, its story, and Salmond's involvement, is not a wholly negative one.

But the affair had sapped the SNP's strength. Although Gordon Wilson was reporting 'a great improvement in spirit and morale' by March 1983, Sillars moved a vote of no confidence in him (and lost it by 136 votes to forty). Sillars, who has never been a happy loser, was said to be contemplating quitting politics, and he left Scotland to work in the Middle East for a year. His wife, Margo MacDonald, still strongly associated with the 79 Group, resigned from the SNP and developed a career as a television presenter. Around and in front of the SNP's internal knife fight British politics had been moving on: the emergence of the SDP in alliance with the Liberals, and the Falklands war, helped to push nationalism to the fringe of the political debate. At the 1983 election the SNP scored less than 12 per cent of the vote and, though it held its two 1979 seats, failed to make a single gain.

The party revived – but slowly. A truce developed between the fundamentalists and the devolutionists. Meanwhile the SNP defined itself more clearly on the political spectrum as a left-of-centre party, and it gradually reversed its traditional hostility to the European Community, to the point where it became an actively enthusiastic proponent of what it called 'independence in Europe'. Sillars and his friends from the Scottish Labour Party had been quick to realize that an irreversible shift had occurred that gave a new perspective to the need for Scottish self-representation at Brussels as well as at home. Was the SNP changed by the socialist SLP members? 'Independence in Europe' provides the clearest evidence that it was. But other Nationalists had also been slowly coming round to the idea that the EC could provide new opportunities.

As with the old British Empire, the new Europe offered the prospects of a self-governed Scotland that was also securely inside a bigger entity. So, even if independence no longer meant quite what it used to mean, it did not mean isolation either. The rarely mentioned but pervasive fears of a tariff wall running from the Tweed to the Solway Firth would not be realized. In the context of the EC there would be less chance of an ill-tempered rupture with England, while oil and fishing grounds would make Scotland welcome in the Community generally. The country would, in addition, rediscover its old Europeanism from the pre-Union centuries. From the mid-1980s onwards Sillars started to produce a stream of papers and speeches firming up this strategy. Europe also enabled the SNP to produce that mysterious mixture, an internationalist nationalism. As Sillars said in a pamphlet he produced in 1991: 'Those narrow minds that weep for lost sovereignty should remember the vale of tears that narrow nationalism dragged Europe's people through in two wars. No nation with a modicum of self-respect and sense of responsibility to others can stand aside ...' And this, remember, from the deputy leader of a party that described itself first and foremost as nationalist! In the 1980s this new Europeanism certainly helped to spread the SNP's appeal to people who would have been uneasy about old-style separatist nationalism.

How practical a policy was it? The constitutional question about whether an independent Scotland would have to reapply for membership of the Community hinges on the status of the two 'successor states' to the UK and is complex. Senior European legal authorities think Scotland would have a right to remain in the Community; politically, the thing might hinge on how secure Berlin, Madrid and Paris were feeling about their own territorial dissidents. There are other drawbacks. A small but clear minority of Scottish voters have always told opinion pollsters that they want independence of the EC as well as of the UK. Eventually a tiny group of hard-line Nationalists, calling themselves Sovereignty '90, broke away from the SNP over this issue. If Scottish Nationalists had been arguing that British monetary policy was out of kilter with Scotland's economic cycle, why should they believe a German monetary policy would be better? And Scotland's supposed influence in Europe can be easily exaggerated: as Isobel Lindsay, a Nationalist critic of the EC, put it, the policy was projected as 'an escape into a Utopia in which strong influence could be wielded and generous regional grants received, where great changes could be achieved without much being changed'. In fact, under current arrangements, an independent Scotland would have 1.5 per cent or less of the total EC population, just three of the seventy-nine weighted votes in the Council of Ministers and 3 per cent of the seats (though sixteen rather than the current eight) at the Strasbourg parliament. Even so, the idea of some independent status in Europe seemed attractive to the vast majority of Nationalists: at its 1988 conference the SNP voted for 'independence in Europe' as its main election theme by a majority of eight to one.

The move to the left was symbolized by the return of figures like Salmond, MacAskill and Sillars to the party leadership, but the SNP still had to keep its feet firmly planted in the rural areas, which still offered its best parliamentary prospects. Salmond, for instance, who now describes himself as 'the socialist leader of a social-democratic party', was returned in the 1987 election for Banff and Buchan. This is a relatively prosperous fishing constituency on the north-east coast that was represented by the Tory populist Sir Albert McQuarrie and remains traditional in outlook. But the SNP continued to manage to change its image in different parts of the country. In the urban areas its leftism was underlined by the endorsement of the 'Can Pay, Won't Pay' campaign against the poll tax, agreed at the 1988 conference by a large majority. The SNP committed itself to recruiting 100,000 non-payers. As we have seen already, many more people than that did not pay the tax, but identifying the proportion of political refuseniks is impossible. At the same time the party started to win growing support from young, left-wing, working-class voters in the council estates. Labour canvassers noted a harder, more aggressive edge to the Nationalists.

If 'independence in Europe' was a good slogan and a plausible route for modern nationalism, and if the leftish stance of the SNP made it better placed to worry Labour, there were still some obvious gaps in the jigsaw. How would the SNP reconcile its nationalism with the apparent preference of Scottish voters for something more moderate? And how would the party react if asked to join a more general anti-Thatcher campaign? One answer – or, rather, one way of avoiding the answer – was to support an elected Scottish

Convention, which would meet to agree a new constitutional settlement for Scotland. That would allow the SNP to campaign with other parties for a convention without compromising its ultimate ambition (since the SNP could then argue for independence *inside* the convention). This idea surfaced at the first meeting of the SNP's National Council after the 1979 election, when Isobel Lindsay submitted a paper suggesting that the disastrous experience of devolution might mean that Scottish politicians would have to work together for change inside Scotland. Gordon Wilson was also an early proponent, provided the Convention was a directly elected one – indeed, he submitted a Private Member's Bill to the Commons the following March calling for a Convention that would bring 'the issue of Scottish government back home where it belongs'. The party's left wing, including Salmond and Sillars, was, at that stage, also in favour.

The traditionalists, led by Maggie Ewing and Jim Fairlie, were strongly against. The issue was fought through many meetings of the SNP leadership during the early 1980s. In 1982 it provided a rare issue that linked Sillars and Gordon Wilson: when the latter's proposal for an elected Convention was voted down by the party's national executive, Sillars complained about the 'serious error . . . unless the party backs Gordon Wilson's initiative, we are in danger of seeing a first-class idea stolen and used effectively by others'. At the 1983 conference at Rothesay a motion calling for 'the establishment of a Scottish Convention which will be empowered to produce a system of self-government acceptable to the people of Scotland' was defeated by 173 votes to 141. Gordon Wilson had intended to speak in favour but decided the mood was so hostile that it would be awkward for him, as leader, to do so. One critic called this 'a lunchtime conversion'.

In March the SNP decided not to participate in a day of action being held by the cross-party Campaign for a Scottish Assembly (CSA), though (unlike Labour) it did join a CSA working party on the remit of a future Scottish parliament. The mood was summed up at about the same time by Jim Fairlie, the SNP's senior vice-chairman, who rhetorically challenged its national council: 'Is there any way we can continue to participate in these meetings held under the auspices of the CSA without compromising our integrity as Nationalists and completely demoralizing our own party members? I don't think so.' Later that year, though, the moderates hit back: at the SNP's 1984 Inverness conference a motion calling for 'an elected Scottish Constitutional Convention' was narrowly passed, by 246 votes to 238. The next day the SNP voted by the same narrow margin to support the CSA. Fairlie resigned as senior vice-chairman, declaring: 'This party has to declare once and for all whether it is going for independence or some form of gradualism . . . The gradualists have knocked the guts out of the constituencies.' The SNP was in danger of withdrawing to 'the fringe of Scottish politics . . . part of an anti-Tory coalition', he added. But Sillars, by now back from the Middle East, and Alex Salmond were jubilant.

From then on the SNP was committed, at least in principle, to working with the other parties on Home Rule inside an elected Convention. In a policy paper produced in 1987 the party even suggested that the elected aspect was negotiable. A Constitutional Convention could 'still be done with widespread support from institutions', including all Scottish MPs, local authorities, trade unions, the Churches and voluntary bodies. Now, as it happened, this was an idea whose time had come.

Wheedling and Knocking Heads: Towards the Convention

At this point, and with a short sigh of relief, it is time to turn from party history to civil politics. Both Labour and the Nationalists had tried extremely hard to avoid any suggestion of a broad Home Rule movement. But their strategies had ended at dusty dead-ends. Stocked with talent and bulging with votes, MPs, policy documents and cocky assertiveness, neither had been able to satisfy the widely held aspiration for a Scottish parliament. For voters who wanted either a leftish government or a Scottish government (that is, most Scottish voters) the parties had been, in Westminster terms, quite useless. And there things might have ended.

But the idea of cross-party action, which flickered briefly and unsuccessfully during the final phase of devolution, had been kept going by the Campaign for a Scottish Assembly. Isobel Lindsay, who broke with the party, was a founder-member. She explains the thinking behind the CSA thus: 'The lessons of 1979 were that the people on the "yes" side had spent more time fighting among themselves than for devolution. So the intention was to try to establish a body that, while its immediate objectives might be quite modest, simply kept the debate alive.'

The CSA's preliminary meeting was held a few months after the 1979 election, in the Clyde Street, Glasgow, offices of the Iona Community. (There are no plaques – it is now a disco.) That meeting swiftly reminded everyone of the difficulties of cooperation. Labour's Home Ruler George Foulkes arrived early, fresh from his bitter South Ayrshire contest with Jim Sillars, then of the SLP, whom he had put out of Parliament. He sat down. Footsteps echoed down the corridor. Sillars peered around the door, stiffened and came in. He sat through the meeting but said very little and, a few months later, joined the SNP. The other founders of the CSA were a kenspeckle lot. They included Jim Boyack, who had been a Labour councillor and, as a young man, was involved in the Covenant Association of the 1950s; Dougie Bain, the brother of the golden-fingered Shetland fiddler Aly Bain and a Communist Party member; Isobel Lindsay herself, who had been heavily involved in the Campaign for Nuclear Disarmament and the Committee of 100 before joining the SNP in its year of reawakening, 1967; Nigel Grant, Professor of Education at Glasgow University; George Foulkes and Dennis Canavan, the Labour MPs. Jim Ross, the Under-Secretary at the Scottish Office in the 1970s devolution unit, was a recruit from the Labour campaign and became a central influence. Jimmy Milne, general secretary of the STUC, was an early supporter, as was his successor, Campbell Christie, and Hugh Wyper of Glasgow Trades Council. The convener for the first few years was Jack Brand, an eminent Nationalist historian from Strathclyde University. Although there were some Conservatives and more Liberals, the CSA were clearly a mingling of Nationalist and Labour Home Rule traditions.

It formally established itself in the spring of 1980 at a big meeting in the Assembly Rooms (no relation) in George Street, Edinburgh. Although several hundreds of people turned up, the campaign was unambitious through the first half of the 1980s. Lindsay says of it, 'Those who kept it going were not high-profile people in the political parties, but that wasn't necessarily a bad thing. What it managed to do was modest; it kept the idea of cross-party co-operation going . . . it was reasonably well respected as being well-meaning and genuinely trying to build some consensus.' But there were no illusions: this was the new Ice Age for Home Rulers. In the Winter 1980–81 edition of the radical Aberdeen-based magazine *Crann Tara* Jack Brand was advertising the merits of the CSA but admitting 'We shall have to dig in for a long fight.' It held conferences (some of them well attended), published leaflets and issued badges, organized the occasional demonstration, lobbied delegates and arranged fringe meetings at party conferences, obtained some press coverage. Alongside the CSA was the magazine *Radical Scotland*, the successor to *Crann Tara*, which provided a printed forum in which leftish, nationalist politics could be debated – a space between the SNP and the Labour Party. But the CSA was, for its first seven or eight years, a minor player in the wings of Scottish public life. Its true historical significance is that, without it, the Scottish Constitutional Convention would never have happened.

The CSA believed that, to get Home Rule back to centre stage, it would be necessary to bring together Labour, the Liberal Democrats, the SNP and all other Home Rulers and nationalists in Scottish public life. It wanted to unite the majority who were opposed to the status quo. But why should anyone listen to the CSA? To get around this obstacle, the organization hit upon a clever political wheeze. Sitting in a coffee house in Edinburgh's Grassmarket, Jim Ross, the former civil servant who often describes himself as an 'ancient troublemaker', and Alan Lawson, editor of *Radical Scotland*, decided to try to gather a group of eminent Scots to act as a bridgehead between the CSA and the parties. This was agreed at the CSA's annual conference, and shortly before Christmas 1987 Jim Ross announced in one of a series of articles in *Radical Scotland*: 'We can't merely hold the line and wait for better times. We either advance or retreat.' He suggested that a Constitutional Convention should draw up a 'practicable blueprint' for an assembly. To explain what the Convention was for, and to rally support for it, there needed to be a report 'by a representative group of people who are not enslaved to political parties but who carry political weight' – or, in other words, the leadership-in-waiting of a civil political movement.

The people chosen for what became known as the constitutiona steering committee give an insight into Scotland's anti-establishmen establishment. It was chaired by Sir Robert Grieve, Emeritu: Professor at Glasgow University and a Scottish super-mandarin. He had been chief planner at the Scottish Office, had been chosen by Willie Ross to chair the Highlands and Islands Development Board, had chaired the Royal Fine Art Commission for Scotland and had held a bewildering number of academic and public-service posts. Working with him were William Anderson, Scottish secretary of the National Federation of Self-Employed and Small Businesses; Ian Barr, then chairman of the Scottish Postal Board; the Revd Maxwell Craig, then chairman of the Kirk's Church and Nation Committee; Canon Kenyon Wright, general secretary of the umbrella group, the Scottish Council of Churches; Joseph Devine, the Roman Catholic Bishop of Motherwell; Judy Steel, wife of the Liberal leader and a festival organizer; Neil Mac-Cormick, son of the SNP founder and Covenant leader of the 1950s and a Professor of Jurisprudence at Edinburgh University; and other academics, writers and women's aid workers. There was at least some attempt to balance the huge male bias that is all too traditional in Scottish politics.

The committee represented some of the great and the good of Scottish life, a fact that certainly helped to draw the parties into talks about the Convention. There was, however, an element of deception in all this. The main author of the document they pro-duced, the 'Claim of Right', was the 'ancient troublemaker' Jim Ross, who was secretary to the committee and who had jointly suggested the idea in the first place. The CSA, lacking its own national organization and a large membership list, was using a certain amount of ventriloquism to persuade the big parties to take its ideas seriously. But it worked. The editors of the *Scotsman* and the *Glasgow Herald* were dined and prepared. In the words of Hilaire Belloc, 'The stocks were sold: the Press was squared: The Middle Class was quite prepared.' 'The Claim of Right' was launched in Edinburgh in July 1988, a mix of cogent historical analysis and proposals for a Convention – 'constitutional machinery' that the Scots must create themselves.

It reads more impressively than the famous Covenant of the

1950s and is still an essential document for anyone wanting to understand modern Scottish politics fully. It contains the odd hint of menace:

We have described a situation in which the spirit underlying the Treaty of Union has been eroded almost to the point of extinction; in which the letter of approved Scottish parliamentary procedures is no longer being honoured; in which the wishes of the massive majority of the Scottish electorate are being disregarded . . . In such a situation one would expect to see signs of a breakdown of respect for law. They [wrote the committee, with an eye on the poll tax] are beginning to appear.

The 'Claim of Right' concluded by arguing:

There is a profound hypocrisy in saying that the Scots should stand on their own two feet while simultaneously denying them management of their own political affairs . . Scots can stand on their own feet only by refusing to accept the constitution which denies them the power to do so.

With that, the grand-sounding committee tossed the ball at the feet of the Scottish MPs, local authorities, unions and other institutions. And, of course, the party leaders.

None of them, bar the Liberal Democrats' Scottish leader, Malcolm Bruce, was immediately enthusiastic. The SNP's national executive voted in August 1988 to agree to meet other parties to talk about the Convention idea, but this should not be taken too seriously. It would have been hard for the Nationalists to explain away an outright rejection of the plan – particularly as Gordon Wilson himself had called for a Convention, albeit an elected one, back in June 1983. Then he envisaged it as 'a mechanism to take the debate on Scotland's constitutional structure away from London's in-built inflexibility. Its purpose is to allow representatives of the Scottish people, whether MPs or separately elected, to direct Scotland's future within Scotland'. This was precisely what the CSA had in mind. But the mood of the SNP meeting that August was sceptical, though rather dismissive. Jim Fairlie argued that any talks with other parties would end up with concessions and a dilution of the independence ideal, but he was told, in effect, 'It's quite safe to vote for that because Donald Dewar will never agree.'

Donald Dewar proved cleverer than that. The Labour cauldron

had been bubbling. The nationalist Labour argument lurched forward, predictably, after the defeat-in-England, victory-in-Scotland election of 1987. The first signs were modest. The Labour Coordinating Committee organized a conference on the question of whether Mrs Thatcher had a mandate to govern Scotland. The general secretary of the STUC, Campbell Christie, who had been a powerful backer of the Home Rule movement since he had returned to Scotland to take up the job in 1986, organized a 'Festival of Scottish Democracy' in Glasgow. Neither the SNP nor the Liberals turned up, but a downpour did. The following January Labour published its new Scotland Bill, with plans for a 144-seat assembly that could vary the rate of income tax. It was the thirty-first such Bill in the previous 100 years but was described merely as a 'campaigning tool'.

In March 1988, at Labour's annual Scottish conference, a new ginger group was formed by the nationalist tendency in the Labour Party. It was called Scottish Labour Action (SLA) and took over from the dying Labour Coordinating Committee as the main Labour pressure group. It was critical of Neil Kinnock and of Donald Dewar's leadership: its founding statement noted bitterly that, after the inevitable defeat of January's Scotland Bill in the Commons, 'A deathly silence has fallen, punctuated only by the occasional observation that the next election is only four years away.' The SLA, led by an Edinburgh Home Ruler called Bob McLean and a Paisley lawyer, Ian Smart, called for civil disobedience and non-payment as weapons against the poll tax, required the disruption of Parliament and asserted 'Scotland's right to self-determination on such a basis as the people of Scotland themselves decide'. On the poll tax, as we have seen, the wilder spirits were defeated. But the SLA gathered some 200 activists and went up and down Scotland's constituency Labour parties, lecturing them on non-payment and on the national question. They used the poll-tax issue, which greatly excited Labour activists, as the excuse for the invitations, and then turned to the constitutional matter when safely inside the door. The appearance of this unfamiliar group, which attracted the support of five MPs, alongside an STUC that was already deeply committed to the Convention was an uncomfortable signal for the Labour leadership.

Dewar himself, though he disliked the anti-Westminster rhetoric of the 'Claim of Right', had been a long-time devolutionist. He had been one of the Labour MPs who had actually campaigned for a 'yes' vote in the 1979 referendum. He has often suffered criticism from more urgent comrades, but he proved an astute and clever leader. Under a more demanding or self-indulgent man, Labour in Scotland might well have broken apart. Dewar, though, moved his party into the Convention so gently and so slowly that barely anyone noticed until it had been accomplished. He knew Jim Ross quite well from work they had done together in the early 1980s and was aware that the STUC and prominent regional council leaders favoured the Convention. In September he crossed a personal Rubicon and decided to take Labour into cross-party talks on the Constitutional Convention. Given the divisions in his own party and the dangers of being dragged into a quasi-Nationalist forum, it was a decision that took some courage. Labour's Scottish executive decided to take soundings inside the party. At a speech to students at St Andrews University on 21 October Dewar signalled that, as far as he and the Labour Party were concerned, the era of ordinary party politics in Scotland, which had lasted for the past nine years, was over: 'Scots are going to have to live a little dangerously for a while.'

A month later, back came Govan. The second SNP seizure at a by-election of this heartland Labour seat sent shock waves across Scotland's political community. Labour lost a majority of 19,000-plus to Jim Sillars, the one-time 'hammer of the Nats' and now the SNP's most charismatic, adored – and hated – individual. Govan was almost as grim a place as it had been when Sillars canvassed it for Labour in 1973. Labour's choice of candidate, an identikit trade-union career man, hardly helped. A mixture of frustration with Tory rule and Labour's inability to do anything about it was clear across the constituency. Labour had brought in trendy young Kinnockite workers from London who looked as though they had been marooned on Mars – albeit on a part of the planet whose incomprehensible creatures were said to be Labour supporters. The SNP leadership, which privately reckoned that Sillars was the only candidate who could win the seat, flooded it with supporters from across Scotland. And, for Sillars, the victory was sweet.

Immediately after Govan he seemed keen to bury the hatchet with Labour and to find ways of cooperating. He had had Labour instincts from his youth, and he still had an ambiguous attitude to his old party. When he formed the SLP Sillars had naïvely insisted on dual membership with the real Labour Party – he seemed to hope his rebellion would be forgiven and that he could remain friendly with his former comrades. His behaviour after Govan was similar: although he was quick to take offence, part of him probably hoped that the SNP left-wingers and Labour would join hands. He was quickly and brutally disabused. Sillars was regarded as the ultimate traitor by Labour, which did its best to offend him. A party supporter, for instance, spotted him shopping in Glasgow's Sauchiehall Street during a Scottish debate in the Commons and phoned George Robertson, the Labour front-bencher. Robertson popped into the chamber to announce mockingly the behaviour of the Scottish Nationalist saviour. Even closer to home, another Labour front-bencher, George Foulkes, complained strongly to STV about pro-Nationalist bias from its political presenter, Margo MacDonald, Sillars' wife. His mood darkened.

Even before the by-election result there had been a chilling in the air among the SNP executive. Govan tilted the mood further. The party had agreed to take part in the formal cross-party talks on 27 January 1989 in Edinburgh, where minimum preconditions could be put. These were to be exploratory talks only, and no final decision about 'in or out' would be taken until the SNP's next executive meeting in February. Sillars and Gordon Wilson, both early proponents of an elected Convention, and Maggie Ewing arrived in Edinburgh to talk with Labour and the Liberal Democrats. Every side had problems with the 'Claim of Right' proposal. Dewar still disliked the nationalist imagery and wanted it toned down. Malcolm Bruce was worried that his party would be dragged into something that compromised its commitment to voting reform. The SNP thought that the distribution of membership was grossly unfair to it. As it was based on the 1987 election results, and as the party had shot upwards in the polls and won Govan in the interim, the SNP was right. Labour agreed that some extra SNP presence might be accommodated and that anyway there should be no votes in the Convention. It would progress only by consensus, and so Labour would be unable to steamroller the smaller parties.

The SNP also wanted an assertion of the sovereignty of the Scottish people and a multi-option referendum (including independence, devolution and the status quo) as the legitimating final stage in the process. Had that been agreed, which it was not, the Convention's story after the 1992 election might have been rather different. The SNP did not get all its demands, but the Convention's terms of reference were changed to include an assertion of 'the right of the Scottish people to secure the implementation of [that] scheme'. Not all the issues were resolved, but after three hours of talking it seemed that the basis was set for the first meeting of the full Convention, with its other parties, councillors, clerics and so on, two months later. Gordon Wilson said at the packed press conference that followed the Friday talks that they had been 'very successful'. Privately, though, Sillars was warning journalists that the party would not go into a 'rigged Convention'.

That weekend the SNP negotiators received a stream of phone calls from fundamentalist Nationalists who were outraged at the coverage of the negotiations. Gordon Wilson had wanted to put off any decision about the SNP's next move until the forthcoming executive meeting, but the obvious split in the party and the huge press interest persuaded him to contact all the SNP's office-bearers. He reached everyone except Alex Salmond. His informal poll convinced him that he should pull the SNP out of the Convention project immediately, despite (or, rather, because of) the 'successful' talks with Dewar and Bruce. At the end of the day, as one senior Nationalist put it, 'We simply couldn't sit down with the Labour Party.' On Sunday night Sillars announced that the SNP would not take part. The radio news the following morning was the first many Nationalists knew of the abrupt change. Among those who was stunned was Alex Salmond. He had impressed friends earlier as being genuinely in favour of cross-party politics. He believed that even if the SNP was unable to go into the next election on the same Home Rule platform as Labour, the announcement was grossly premature and should have been delayed until after the European elections. That was the moment when the trust between him and Sillars disappeared.

The newspapers were scathing, the other parties unforgiving. Had the Nationalists stayed in the Convention, life would have been much harder for Labour and the Liberal Democrats. Perhaps it would all have ended in acrimony. But it might have delivered a wider consensus for change that would have produced the momentum for a Scottish parliament by the mid-1990s. The Home Rulers in the media and throughout Scottish life thought the SNP had made a catastrophic mistake, taking the ball away at just the moment the game might have livened up. After the high hopes of the meeting and the painstaking effort to bring the parties together, there was much bitterness. Across the country SNP branches were badly split. The party's patriarch, Robert McIntyre (victor of the 1945 by-election), wrote to Gordon Wilson privately to protest about the sudden announcement of the boycott:

We will not get true independence in a oner. People want to see how a parliament or assembly works before going for what we want for Scotland. I fear that by opting out at this stage we confirm the suspicion which has been put about sedulously over the years that the Scots cannot agree amongst themselves. This is surely a time for achieving maximum agreements possible. If the SNP takes that line it will be seen as statesmanlike and cooperative. Of course, the Tories are very cock-a-hoop . . .

McIntyre ended by attacking the 'note of triumphalism' in the SNP after Govan, reminding Wilson of the Battle of Dunbar, when the Scots had Oliver Cromwell at their mercy but, urged on by fanatical preachers, left their impregnable position (to be slaughtered). He pleaded with Wilson to return to the talks. The party started dipping downwards in the opinion polls and lost its post-Govan momentum.

The SNP executive met to discuss its boycott and heard from Isobel Lindsay an eleventh-hour appeal to reconsider. Wilson had sent a lengthy letter to all the party branches explaining his decision, and the stream of letters from Nationalists complaining about it gradually trickled away, then started to be replaced by anti-Convention letters. At the executive meeting Lindsay could not even find a seconder. And at the party's National Council in March at Port Glasgow she was heckled and attacked venomously as a traitor. This was not so much a fundamentalist victory (though it was that) as a rallying of the party against a tempest of hostility from outside. But too many Nationalists were naïvely convinced that their position was unbeatable: they could charge through the next election campaign by themselves and seize large numbers of Unionist seats. Conservatives with a sense of history might have muttered that spring, as Cromwell did at the Battle of Dunbar, 'The Lord has delivered them into my hands.'

The Convention at Work

Nationalist-less, the Convention went ahead anyway. Its first meeting, at the Kirk's Assembly Halls in Edinburgh, on 30 March 1989, was a rather grand occasion. As with the signing of the Covenant in the same room forty years earlier, and even the Church's own Claim of Right there in 1842, columns of soberly dressed public representatives (most of them male, many of them past middle age) queued up to sign a patriotic declaration. This time it read:

We, gathered as the Scottish Constitutional Convention, do hereby acknowledge the sovereign right of the Scottish people to determine the form of Government best suited to their needs, and do hereby declare and pledge that in all our actions and deliberations their interests shall be paramount. We further declare and pledge that our actions and deliberations shall be directed to the following ends: To agree a scheme for an Assembly or Parliament for Scotland; To mobilize Scottish opinion and ensure the approval of the Scottish people for that scheme; and To assert the right of the Scottish people to secure implementation of that scheme.

The joint chairmen were Sir David Steel, the last Liberal leader and a lifelong Home Ruler, and Harry Ewing, the former devolution minister, later to become a Labour peer. Among those who signed up for this semi-nationalist declaration were fifty-eight Labour and Liberal Democrat MPs; seven of the eight Scottish MEPs; fifty-nine of Scotland's sixty-five regional, island and district councils; seven political parties, including the Orkney and Shetland Movement, the Scottish Greens, the communists and the mainstream Opposition parties; the Scottish Convention of Women; the STUC; Gaelic organizations; and representatives of the ethnic minorities and of the Scottish Churches. The only obvious absentees were the Conservatives and the Nationalists (though some dissident SNP members did attend). The insurgent atmosphere was summed up by

Canon Kenyon Wright, who asked the Convention, referring to Mrs Thatcher: 'What if that other single voice we all know so well responds by saying, "We say no, and we are the state"? Well, we say yes – and we are the people.' His rhetorical defiance made front pages and was highlighted by television bulletins as far away as the United States.

The dreary work then started. There were seven full meetings of the Convention, in Edinburgh, Glasgow, Dundee and Inverness, plus about fifty meetings of its executive and various working groups at which the tough talking took place. The administrative back-up came from the Convention of Scottish Local Authorities, whose senior depute secretary, Bruce Black, a former local government official from the Highlands, acted as the spider at the centre of the web of negotiations and compromises. As a decision-making body, the Convention was odd. It had no legal identity nor formal agenda. Its work was done by about thirty people who took no votes. Its large number of unfamiliar partners meant that it worked slowly, but it managed to sketch out the intellectual architecture for a kind of parliament. This would be significantly different from the one at Westminster. It would have a system of super-committees that would combine legislative scrutiny with general research and public sessions of taking of evidence, all in the same area of policy. The parliament's executive would have less than absolute power; patronage would be the responsibility of the Scottish parliament, not the Scottish prime minister.

Much time was spent talking about the representation of women. Scotland has one of the worst records in Europe for electing women MPs; its political culture, like those smoke-hazed drinkeries that used to line every main street with curt 'No women' signs Sellotaped to the door, remains deeply male. In local government women like Glasgow district council's leader Jean McFadden and Edinburgh's former provost Eleanor McLaughlin had recently been making an impact. But of the seventy-two Scottish MPs elected in 1992 only four were women, and there have been no female Scottish Office ministers since Lady Tweedsmuir in the early 1970s (and she had had only two predecessors, Peggy Herbison in 1950–51 and Judith Hart in the mid-1960s). The Convention itself paid tribute to the nation's male-chauvinist traditions; 90 per cent of its members were men. This provoked the formation of a Women's Claim of Right group, and the Labour MP Maria Fyfe lobbied for a voting system that would give each Scottish constituency one male and one female MSP. The same idea was also being canvassed at Westminster, in the face of widespread derision, by the redoubtable right-wing Essex Tory MP Teresa Gorman. Fyfe's plan was quickly blocked as being far too radical. Perhaps so – but those inclined to laugh it off might reflect that the 1914 Scottish Home Rule Bill, which passed its second reading before the war intervened, was derided in the Commons for its ludicrous insistence on votes for women, generally held to be wholly impracticable and undesirable. The Convention agreed 'the principle of equal representation of women within the Scottish parliament' but gave little clue as to how this might be achieved. There was some talk of the parties committing themselves to putting up an equal number of candidates. But if such a parliament does arrive in the formidably male world of Scottish politics, seeing will be believing.

Even so, the seriousness with which this and other parliamentary heresies were discussed may provide early-warning signals for a more general dissatisfaction with the Westminster way. The Convention wanted to open most of the Scottish parliament to members of the public, to give its government only limited and tightly defined powers and to base its position on a Scottish Bill of Rights (as Mrs Thatcher had proposed fifteen years earlier). The Home Rule movement has always had this Janus-faced approach to modernity, both gazing back at Scotland's ancient independence and looking forward to a more up-to-date parliament and political system than Westminster currently provides. Between 1908 and 1914 this modernity meant temperance legislation, votes for women and a more efficient system for dispatching business; in the 1990s it means proportional representation, a Bill of Rights and . . . a more efficient system for dispatching business.

Of these proportional representation had been the hardest problem for the Convention negotiators. It was, naturally, a bottom-line demand for the Liberal Democrat team. At times they were close to giving up, but their position was strong. Without them the Convention really would have been, in the words of one Tory critic, 'the Labour Party at prayer'. Sir David Steel played an important role in encouraging the Scottish Lib–Dem leader, Malcolm Bruce, to plug on. The Labour Party's Scottish secretary, Murray Elder, a protégé of John Smith who later moved to London to run the new Labour leader's office, was influential on the other side. But big changes (as Labour's conversion to voting reform may prove to be throughout Britain) can hang on tiny things.

At Labour's 1990 Scottish conference in the Clyde town of Dunoon the party had to confront the question of whether it would give up the first-past-the-post system that had granted it such over-whelming dominance in Scotland but had hastened Labour's decline in the English south. This was a moment of truth. It suddenly looked, to the cannier souls wandering about the conference floor and indulging in some mental arithmetic, that the decision would go against voting reform. Had it done so, the Convention process would have been brought crashing to a halt. Bill Speirs, deputy general secretary of the STUC, and Bill Gilby of the public-sector union NUPE were alerted and identified the swing votes. These rested with the right-wing engineers' union, the EETPU, which was committed to a system of voting called the alternative vote (disliked by most advocates of proportional representation). Pat O'Hanlon, leading its delegation, agreed to switch sides, provided his union's policy was acknowledged in the motion. This saved the day. O'Hanlon, whose members were virtual pariahs in the Scottish Labour movement, enabled the Scottish Constitutional Convention to carry on because he felt he owed Speirs a special personal debt of loyalty. Back in 1982 the two men had been lonely voices raised against the Falklands task force on Labour's Scottish executive.

No General Galtieri, no Constitutional Convention? At any rate, Dewar was able to agree the principle of a proportional voting system with Bruce. This was a compromise that involved most Scottish parliamentarians being elected from constituencies, with a regional top-up of extra members. It was finally agreed by Labour's national executive in London at the end of January 1992 and con-firmed as the new system by the Convention just before the 1992 election. Long before that, the rest of the Convention package had been presented to the Scottish people. On St Andrew's Day, 30 November 1990, with great civic pomp and ceremony, its central proposals had been unveiled after a parade of all the Scottish lord provosts (or mayors). The report skated over some of the most difficult questions, such as the future numbers and status of Scottish MPs at Westminster. It was in parts a 'lowest common denominator' document, which, trying to reconcile Scottish sovereignty and the Westminster system, contained some contradictions.

But what was its status? It was clearly intended as some sort of threat to Westminster and not one dependent solely on the assumption of a Labour or Liberal Democrat–Labour victory at the election: by purporting to speak for Scotland rather than for individual parties, it had issued a challenge more serious than the usual party-political stuff. Yet, as the SNP put it, 'There is no such thing as a unilateral declaration of devolution.' After the election there was little the Convention could do to push its hard work on to the Westminster agenda without using anti-parliamentary tactics. And this the parliamentarians who had led it were unwilling to contemplate. They were skewered on the contradictions of their own status – the Queen's loyal parliamentarians or quasi-Nationalist rebels? But the Convention had moved the argument on. Its achievement, Bruce Black said later, had been to 'crystallize the middle ground'. It produced a Home Rule proposal for a parliament that was ahead of conventional British thinking about how a legislature should function and was backed by most of Scotland's MPs and many of its most important institutions. It took Labour firmly into the middle of the Home Rule movement. It created an expectation, almost an assumption, that the Scottish parliament would be formed eventually. And it was held up afterwards by Opposition leaders as a possible model for the development of a new politics in England in the 1990s. Not bad for something dreamed up in an Edinburgh coffee shop by two little-known political amateurs.

6

Changed, Changed Utterly:
1992 and After

The sovereignty of the UK Parliament has to be paramount.
It rules out any separate body with entrenched powers that are
not retrievable by Westminster.

Ian Lang, Scottish Secretary, *Financial Times*, 18 May 1992

The Thistle like a rocket soared
And cam' doon like the stick.

Hugh MacDiarmid, from
'A Drunk Man'

Everything was changed, changed utterly. After the 1992 election
Scottish politics, like British politics generally, functioned in a new
world that may have looked like the old one but in which genial
assumptions about 'our turn' and 'it's only a question of time' had
been rudely upended. Plausible new assumptions were that single-
party rule at Westminster had become *the* rule and that the rule
book of Britain was in the hands of an organization totally opposed
to constitutional change for Scotland. Labour, after years of promising this and that and delivering neither, had proved unable to win
even in the trough of a recession. In England, which returns more
than eight in ten of the MPs, Labour had managed to get just under
34 per cent of the popular vote. Swiftly proposed changes in the
parliamentary boundaries, combined with demographic shifts and
an astutely consensual style from Downing Street, all suggested that
Labour would have a hard slog to get near power in 1996–7. So the
most obvious road for Scottish Home Rule since the 1920s, the
election of a Labour majority government committed to it, seemed
blocked. Short of a pact at the next election to reject all the Scottish
Conservatives, there was no parliamentary way for the Home Rule
argument to progress with a reasonable assumption of success –

even though fifty-eight of the seventy-two Scottish MPs were elected on a Home Rule manifesto.

And did Scotland's Labour MPs have the heart to carry on the fight? Like the Liberal Democrats, Labour partially recoiled from constitutional questions after the election, returning to bread-and-butter politics. Many Opposition MPs concluded that Scotland did not really want Home Rule, that the whole thing had been a giant charade in which they would in future decline to involve themselves. Others took the opposite view. Either way, 1992 represented a decisive break in Scottish politics – just conceivably, the end of Scottish politics as a tale in its own right. The implications should give anyone interested in Scotland, or in the future direction of British politics, pause for serious thought. We shall return to these implications at the end of this chapter. But first it seems sensible to assess what really happened in Scotland when Britain as a whole returned its fourth consecutive anti-Home Rule Tory government.

Pop!

The election came at a time of nationalist optimism that made its result genuinely shocking. The Kincardine and Deeside by-election in November 1991 was called after the death of the popular and devolutionist Tory Alick Buchanan-Smith, a man whose party had left him a decade earlier. It confirmed a strongly anti-Conservative mood in Scotland. It is a wealthy constituency, which stretches from Royal Deeside to the outskirts of suburban Aberdeen and rich, red-soiled farms in the south. Anywhere else in Britain it would have been unshakeably Conservative. It fell, predictably, to the main Opposition party in the area, the Liberal Democrats. There was clear evidence of substantial tactical voting by Labour and SNP supporters to stop the Tory candidate, a leftish local laird. Funeral prayers were duly read over the corpse of that tough old biddy, Scottish Conservatism. The by-election was widely held to demonstrate a surge of Home Rulery, even though the previous year a Lib–Dem candidate had seized the equally Tory seat of Eastbourne on the English south coast (and there is no discernible tide of Home Rule fever in Eastbourne). Like Eastbourne, Kincardine and Deeside returned to its 1987 allegiance decisively in the general election itself. The lesson is a familiar one: constitutionally, by-elections are simply a protest event, a higher form of irate gesture.

So Kincardine and Deeside, which blew the first puff of air into the pre-election bubble, offered a wider message about the 1992 election in Scotland: when it came to the real ballot, Scottish voters were concerned about taxes, Neil Kinnock, unemployment and social issues, just as much as English voters. Their hostility to the Conservative economic record and the widespread desire for Home Rule (both good potential by-election issues) did not necessarily mean that they wanted a Labour government or a hung Parliament at Westminster. Scotland is a more plural, contradictory and politically complex nation than is sometimes assumed: much of the busy, bonny north-east is part of a staunchly anti-Labour landscape.

But if by-elections are bad predictors, opinion polls can be equally misleading, and they contributed their bit during the first months of 1992. Throughout the previous year the polls had shown support for independence at percentages around the mid-30s, with a support for a 'devolved assembly' slightly higher. No change was favoured by between a quarter and a fifth of Scots questioned. Then on 28 January 1992, the Scotsman's Scottish political editor, Peter Jones, was shocked to receive the results of his paper's latest polling, carried out by ICM Research and jointly commissioned with Independent Television News. He immediately told ICM: 'This can't be right. This is wrong. Run the program again and check.' But the same result came back: support for independence, either outside both the UK and the EC or inside the EC, had reached 50 per cent, a jump of thirteen points on the previous September. Support for the lesser option of devolution had crashed to 27 per cent. Alex Salmond, by now the SNP leader, toot-tooted: 'This will be Scotland's independence election.' Labour's Dewar was surprised and worried. He blamed the Tory strategy of hardening the choice between the unchanged Union and independence: 'They are playing fast and loose with the Union, driving people to extreme positions.' The poll was widely criticized, and later opinion sampling marked support for independence sharply down again – to 26 per cent by early March. But the polling company had asked the same questions as always, in the same order, and with no new prompt questions.

Something really did seem to be happening. The last people who should have been surprised were the *Scotsman*'s journalists, however: the country had just gone through a roller-coaster few weeks with the media in the driving seat. To explain the *Scotsman*'s poll we must go back and look in some detail at an extraordinary month.

Why had the SNP, which had taken such a knock during the formation of the Scottish Constitutional Convention, been able to bounce back at just the time when Labour confidence was at its highest? First, the Nationalists had had some useful opportunities to exploit. After the Convention had finished and had published its main report in November 1990, coinciding with the Conservative *putsch* against Margaret Thatcher, Labour and the Liberal Democrats had relatively little to do. Labour in Scotland, as elsewhere, was on a taut, pre-election rein: relatively unbelligerent, maintaining a grave sobriety of mien. The Conservatives had a new leader to promote whose views on Scotland were unformed and therefore unknown.

This left a sizeable political space on the left, where the SNP had already tried to squat with its poll-tax non-payment campaign. Since the Govan by-election, the party had been recruiting hard on the council estates and among the crumbling sandstone terraces of west-central Scotland. It was promoting itself as the trendy, exciting alternative to the cautious, old-before-their-time style favoured by the Labour leadership. Sillars' populist oratory (he derided Dewar, at one point, as a Scottish 'Uncle Tom') attracted belligerent young supporters, and the SNP exploited assiduously the backing of pop stars like the Proclaimers and Pat Kane of Hue and Cry. And for the more wrinkled couch-potatoes there was always Sean Connery, who voiced a television broadcast for the party. All in all, the SNP seemed to be recapturing the fizz and self-confidence of its earlier surges. In the late 1960s and the mid-1970s it had had a large youth membership: by 1991 it again boasted a younger age profile, more youth and student branches and younger candidates than any rival. Among its recruits were idealistic, if aggressive, activists who would automatically have joined Labour in previous times, a trend noted gloomily by some alert Scottish Labour MPs. It became, in short, cool to be a Nationalist.

But, without the Scottish media's interest, none of that would have mattered much. The most dramatic example of journonationalism, and certainly the most bizarre, was the conversion of the Scottish edition of Rupert Murdoch's *Sun* to the cause of the SNP. It had moved to Kinning Park in Glasgow to try to take on the Mirror Group-owned *Daily Record*, Scotland's biggest-selling newspaper by far. The *Sun* was not slow to spot that the working-class youngsters who seemed to be moving to the SNP were exactly the sort of people it wanted as readers. Jim Sillars was a friend of Andy Collier, the *Scottish Sun*'s political editor, and had been signed up to write a column for the paper after his Govan by-election victory. This opportunism was much derided by Labour MPs, but the phenomenon of a left-winger being given space for a provoca-tive column in the *Sun* was not unique; Labour's Ken Livingstone was doing the same thing in London. Sillars took to calling himself 'Sunny Jim' and used the money to pay for advice workers in his inner-city constituency. Bob Bird, the *Scottish Sun*'s editor, had been moved north from the paper's Wapping headquarters in October 1990 and says (sounding more anthropologist than hack): 'It only took me about six months to be convinced that there was something very interesting happening out there among the local population.' Urged on by Collier, he decided to back the SNP and started lobbying the *Sun*'s editor in London, Kelvin MacKenzie, for permission. That took another six months and a blizzard of internal memos.

Finally, during the week before Christmas 1991, Murdoch ar-ranged a board meeting at Wapping where his editors were to discuss their plans for the following six months. The night before MacKenzie warned a slightly nervous Bird about his tone when he came to address Murdoch: 'No jokes. You've got to be deadly serious. Give him a straight presentation.' By the following morn-ing, when Bird arrived, MacKenzie seemed to have changed his mind; there were two bagpipers, in full Highland rig, blowing up in the *Sun* editor's office. MacKenzie told Bird: 'Remember – if he laughs, it was my idea.' Inside the board meeting only four or five News International men knew of the stunt and kept, vainly, trying to turn the discussion around to circulation in Scotland. Finally, a slightly perplexed Murdoch agreed and, on cue, the pipers burst in, followed by Bird. Small pause. Murdoch smiled and tapped his foot. He seemed easily convinced and was probably little bothered by the idea. Murdoch is generally happy to subordinate his papers' political profiles to their commercial interests: simultaneously with this decision his new German tabloid, *Super*, was using an aggressively anti-Western line to tempt the same kind of working-class readers in East Berlin as the *Scottish Sun* was going for in Easterhouse and East Kilbride.

On 23 January, with characteristic panache, the *Scottish Sun* flashed its new thistle at a bemused country. Its front page carried a huge saltire and the words 'Arise and be a Nation again' and was followed by five pages of finger-stabbing argument and tabloid analysis. Since the paper sells around 300,000 copies in Scotland, it was an event of some significance. Labour treated the *Sun*'s conversion as proof positive of a Conservative Party-directed strategy to use Nationalism to split the Opposition and retain Scottish Tory seats. There is no evidence that the *Sun*'s thinking was politically motivated. It was commercial but not necessarily Machiavellian. The rest of the Scottish press reacted with splutters of mixed amusement and outrage. Most hurtful of all was the remark from the then editor of the *Sunday Times*'s Scottish edition (a stablemate of the *Sun* at Kinning Park) who wrote from along the corridor that the voice of a 'bar-room cretin' had intruded into the constitutional debate. That editor, Gerry Malone, had been a Scottish Tory MP and is now the Conservative Member for Winchester, and he still feels the remark was one of his finest moments. The *Scottish Sun* persisted, devoting considerable space to SNP propaganda and flying the front-page slogan 'Fighting for Independence'. The *Daily Record*, which had always been a staunch supporter of Labour's devolutionist line, hit back angrily, and a comic, vitriolic newspaper war started. It all echoed the war in the 1930s between the *Record* and the *Scottish Daily Express*. The latter was also an intruder from the south, which had also prefixed the word 'Scottish' to its title and opened Glasgow offices, was also owned by an uncommonly wealthy Commonwealther of Scottish descent (though Beaverbrook was a Canadian and Murdoch an Australian) and was also won over partly thanks to personal contacts with the Nationalist leader.

The 1990s leader, Alex Salmond, had been heavily involved in trying to bring the *Sun* over. He rode the 1992 Nationalist bandwagon with some skill, and, although it crashed spectacularly, is young and determined. He will be around for a while, and he deserves to detain us for a few paragraphs. Salmond had been elected leader in May 1990, aged only 35, in a fight with Margaret Ewing, the Moray MP and daughter-in-law of Winnie Ewing, victor of Hamilton and the only SNP Euro-MP. The margin of Salmond's victory over the younger Ewing – 486 votes to 186 – surprised everyone who had not paid attention to the contest but caused little shock inside the party. The non-Texan Ewings represented an ideologically moderate but constitutionally hardline strain of Nationalism, which had been the core of the party since its foundation. By rejecting the experienced and likeable Margaret Ewing in 1990 the party was in a sense attempting to defeat its own past.

If so, who did it think was its future? Salmond can infuriate his political enemies by his bouncy assertiveness but is probably the most talented leader the SNP has had. He is a black bitch. A compliment: it means he and his family on both sides are Linlithgow-born, in the boundaries of the romantic old town with its fine Stuart palace. His father was a working-class Labour supporter, known jocularly to his Naval shipmates as 'Uncle Joe' for his left-wing views, who later converted to Nationalism and became a civil servant. His mother is a 'Winston Churchill Conservative'. Salmond himself became involved in Nationalist politics at St Andrews University after an argument in December 1973 with his then girlfriend, Debbie Horton from Hackney, who was secretary of the student Labour club. 'If you feel like that, go and join the bloody SNP,' she told him. The next day he did. And the day after that Salmond and a friend turned up at the thinly attended AGM of the university branch of the Federation of Student Nationalists. As the only two members actually paid up to the SNP, they were promptly elected president and treasurer.

Salmond has been in the SNP ever since, except for his suspension in 1982–3 for left-wing deviationism, an episode discussed already. He went on to work for the Government Economic Service in Scotland – considered a bizarre thing to want to do, since most of his fellow-entrants dreamed of the Treasury in London. Then he hopped over the fence, to the Royal Bank of Scotland, where he became chief oil economist. His attractive Georgian office in the Edinburgh New Town was adorned with a poster from the maga-

zine *Radical Scotland*, with an ironical quote by the Marxist thinker
Tom Nairn to the effect that Scotland would be free only when the
last Presbyterian minister was strangled with the last *Sunday Post*, a
mawkish, popular tabloid paper. (When the current writer publicized this, many years later, Salmond was attacked by Conservatives
in his traditionally minded constituency as a bloodthirsty enthusiast
for the garrotting of Kirk ministers! He was, in fact, brought up in
the Church of Scotland, was named after the local minister and is
still an occasional attender in the pews.)

In a party with a terrible weakness for culture Salmond stood out
as a hard-headed man of numbers. His enthusiasm for the 79 Group
told its own story, but as an economist who understood figures,
dressed like a well-doing businessman and was interested in the
party's administrative problems, he was hard to pigeonhole. He was
young, obviously, and bright, it seemed, and swam with a shoal of
equally fresh-faced, assertive left-wingers, most of whom looked to
Sillars as their natural leader. Underneath, Salmond is as romantic
an idealist as anyone in the SNP. But his public image became
steadily more composed and businesslike. He won Banff and Buchan
from the Tory populist McQuarrie at the 1987 election and was
elected SNP deputy leader shortly afterwards in a victory for the
party's pragmatists. Before he made it to the top Salmond was
already a dominant figure in the moderate group of the SNP's
ruling councils. He was less antagonistic to Labour and to cross-
party politics than most. Probably because he seemed too
moderate on the national question, Sillars backed Margaret Ewing
against him in the leadership election. Once he became leader,
though, Salmond worked extremely hard to make the most of
the SNP's 'ourselves alone' strategy about which he had had
personal misgivings.

The hopes and fears of Nationalists in the 1990s rest heavily on
his youthful shoulders. In the new politics of the 1990s the key
question about Salmond is the extent to which he is prepared to
work with other parties to push Home Rule. Is the old sectarianism
as alive and well as ever? The evidence suggests that Salmond, while
playing a careful game, wants to reach out. In 1984, when the SNP
was rowing about devolution versus independence, he said: 'It is my
opinion that when the SNP is about to make a leap forward and

grow it takes a relaxed attitude to self-government, but when it is on the defensive it adopts a tight, narrow attitude.' Significantly, it was Sillars' involvement in breaking off the Constitutional Convention talks with Labour and the Liberal Democrats that destroyed the earlier closeness between himself and Salmond. After that the SNP's national executive contained three identifiable groupings – the traditionalists, led by the Ewings, the Sillars group and the Salmond pool. Salmond, in his early days as leader, could not command a majority with his own supporters – he had to compromise with the fundamentalists or Sillars. With Sillars spending less time in politics, Salmond's position on the SNP executive is likely to become stronger. An early sign of this came in an interview towards the end of May 1992 with the *Dundee Courier*, in which he said: 'The SNP have been seen to be rather confrontational when a softer approach might have paid more dividends. But in looking at these new organizations, like Scotland United [which included Labour MPs], we have to be extremely friendly in our approach . . . I am anxious not to force people into a corner.' He was pushing for a three-way referendum, to be organized jointly with Labour and the Liberal Democrats – something supported by many Labourites but eventually rejected by the party's Scottish leadership. Salmond rejected the Sillars line that anyone who wanted Home Rule was obliged to join the SNP ('It's difficult for people to abandon past allegiances'). And he said his party needed a more user-friendly approach. 'It is possible to maintain the integrity of your own position and argue for it without looking as if you are going to stick the heid on anybody that disagrees with you.' ('Sticking the heid' is a native custom, employed when one is uncertain about the veracity or logic of one's interlocutor.)

So by the beginning of 1992 the SNP, which had been battered by the Convention affair, had a clear strategy, 'Scotland in Europe'; a fresh and impressive leader; and a political gap on the left–right spectrum to exploit. It even had a mass-readership newspaper preparing to support and promote it. Its next boost came courtesy of Sir Robert Scholey, the scowling, pendulously jowled chairman of British Steel – 'Black Bob' to his enemies (of whom, in Scotland, there were several million). On 8 January 1992, the management of British Steel confirmed that the 29-year-old Lanarkshire steel plant,

Ravenscraig, was to be closed. As we have seen, a succession of Scottish Conservative politicians made it clear to Mrs Thatcher that 'Big Blue' was more than a steel plant its company didn't want – it was a vast, brooding symbol of Scotland's industrial potency. Any politician who wanted a future in Scotland was obliged to show some respect. Apart from George Younger's resignation hint in 1982, a promise had been wrung from British Steel by Malcolm Rifkind in 1987 that it would be kept open until 1994, 'subject to market conditions'. This was an obvious, gaping let-out clause, and British Steel was now a free, privatized agent in a difficult market-place, impervious to whinging ministers. Scholey, who had always been hostile to the plant, authorized the brusque closure announcement and then – compounding the blasphemy – made himself unavailable for interview. Poor Ian Lang was judged by his predecessors' success in staving off closure and found wanting. Reports of his anger impressed no one. An opinion poll published in the *Glasgow Herald* on 15 January suggested that if Scots were given a hard choice between independence and the status quo, as some ministers were privately saying should now happen, 48 per cent would vote for the former and only 40 per cent for the latter.

The other man who took the argument forward was Magnus Linklater, editor of the *Scotsman*, who delighted the SNP and the Conservatives by persuading Scotland's four main party leaders to take part in a public debate on the country's constitutional future on Saturday, 8 January. To start with, the Scottish Office was clear that Mr Lang would not take part. To the officials' surprise, he did: he had decided to call for 'a great debate' on the future of Scotland as a way of bringing home the costs and drawbacks of independence or Home Rule. The Tory strategy developed after the Kincardine by-election was to highlight the constitutional question and, in particular, to try to make the SNP and the Home Rule parties seem allies against the Union: Mr Lang wanted to demonstrate that the Conservatives stood alone and was pleased to get a platform on which to do so. Of the four Scottish leaders, Labour's Donald Dewar was the least enthusiastic about the idea of a debate; almost up to the last minute he was telling friends and journalists that he thought it most unlikely many people would turn up on a Saturday night. Even when he heard that the event was sold out, he suggested that many of those who had acquired tickets would not bother to use them. Labour made little effort to press its supporters to turn up. In stark contrast, the SNP made sure its people did apply for tickets. Unlike the others, Salmond practised carefully, using SNP leaders to play the rival politicians and rehearsing his retorts and quips.

Ten days after the death of Ravenscraig had been announced and with the words 'Scotland − A Time to Choose' on a banner behind them, Lang, Salmond, Dewar and the Liberal Democrats' Malcolm Bruce faced 2,500 people crowded into Edinburgh's biggest venue, the baroque Usher Hall. Linklater (the son of the novelist quoted in chapter 2) had caught the popular imagination − another 6,500 people had asked for tickets. For two and a half hours the four leaders spoke, cross-questioned one another and answered questions from the hall. Radio Scotland broadcast the event live, and television showed a shortened version. It is impossible to tell how deeply it affected voters but it certainly set alight the political classes. Full transcripts were taken by government officials and passed around Whitehall. London-based journalists found their pulses racing at the rare spectacle of a lively and crowded hustings.

Salmond, putting the Nationalist case vividly and simply, dominated the debate. Afterwards there were complaints from Labour politicians that the SNP had massed its supporters and encouraged them to behave loutishly and heckle the other speakers. These complaints were backed up in the letters columns of the Scottish papers by accounts from 'Disgusted, Morningside'. Dewar umm-ed and aah-ed and looked physically uncomfortable as he became lost in lengthy subordinate clauses. He was jeered by Nationalist supporters. A cerebral and sophisticated politician, this semi-hustings proved a mistake. Unfortunately for him, television cut his best moment, when he spoke movingly about what being a Scot meant for him. Afterwards he was gloomy and remorseful about his performance. He learned from the experience and, in a re-run of the debate organized by BBC Television's *Panorama* a month later, performed far more effectively. That programme, however, did not have the impact of the Edinburgh debate.

Ian Lang did rather better, despite the unpopularity of his Unionist position. At times he reached flights of eloquence, as when arguing that Home Rule would lead to independence: 'The SNP would be chanting in the wings [chants and cheers from SNP supporters in the Usher Hall wings] like the chorus of some Greek tragedy, ready to bounce us further on against a background of rancour and disunity into the abyss of complete separation.' But Lang, despite saying vaguely that he had some ideas about constitutional change, refused to specify them. In a BBC programme a few weeks later he disappointed Tory devolutionists by virtually ruling out a Scottish assembly and making it clear he was thinking mainly in terms of minor administrative tinkering – something confirmed the following summer. Malcolm Bruce, the Scottish Liberal Democrat leader, a convinced Home Ruler alongside Labour in the Constitutional Convention, also did well. His best line came when he challenged the Tory suggestion that Scots should be forced to choose between independence or the unaltered Union: 'If Scotland votes for separation, it can have it. But if it votes for reform, it can't. Where's the democracy in that?' A good question, still unanswered. The debate showed the rest of Britain that Scots seemed excited about their country's constitutional future again. London newspapers gave it wide coverage and editorialized seriously about the possibility of an independent Scotland. Partly they were excited to find, glistening through the muddy and stale-seeming pre-election debate, an issue that was both important and relatively fresh for their readers. The *Guardian*, for instance, concluded that the Union was not working and added approvingly, in a long editorial, that in Scotland politics was being fought with passion, 'and the sense of great issues being determined was not yet dead'.

Between the debate and polling day all the parties in Scotland acted on the basis that a hung Parliament or Labour victory, and therefore Home Rule, was a likely outcome. Salmond announced to the *Glasgow Herald*, 'I can well foresee circumstances in which the SNP would vote for something less than Scottish independence.' He reckoned his party would take three or four key Tory marginals and be well placed to keep the pressure on at Westminster. If, however, Labour started to fall back in the national opinion polls, the SNP would be waiting to swoop on some of their seats too. Unwiser colleagues burbled endlessly about the huge number of seats the SNP was poised to take. Labour, seeking to hold its Home Rule line, went strongly on the offensive against the economics of independence, attacking the SNP's 'Toytown economics'. John Smith, then shadow chancellor, announced that an independent Scottish government would run up a £7 billion deficit in its first year. Salmond responded: 'Labour's Scottish leadership are in a state of near-hysteria because the SNP are crawling all over them.'

He was right to this extent only: Labour was worried about the SNP. Worried not that it was about to seize a clutch of Labour seats but that its popularity might hand marginal seats to the Conservatives or, at the very least, enable vulnerable-looking Tories like Michael Forsyth to survive. Labour was fighting on two flanks and found this a testing experience. But, overall, it was the confident assumption that a Scottish parliament was only a year or so away that was the most striking aspect of Labour's thinking. While Smith and Gordon Brown were evidently concentrating all their hopes on top jobs in a Westminster administration, Labour's then health spokesman, Robin Cook, annoyed Kinnock by speculating that he would not be able (as a Scot) to oversee the English health service after the establishment of a Scottish parliament. Cook regarded this as a statement of the obvious but, under pressure from Kinnock, retracted the statement: 'In a future Westminster Parliament, elected after the creation of a Scottish parliament, it will be for Neil Kinnock to decide whom it would be appropriate to appoint as Secretary of State for Health.' Tory ministers spotted Cook's point, however, and used it relentlessly to tease other Scottish spokesmen. Where would they serve? Westminster? Or Edinburgh?

The point was not as childish as it might appear. Home Rule had always attracted people for opposite reasons – as a stepping-stone to independence or as a roadblock to preserve the Union. Short of splitting Britain into a federation, something dreamed of by Liberals for a century but as far removed from practical politics as ever, it had to be one or the other. So which kind of Home Rule was Labour offering? The blunt truth was that most Scottish Labour MPs still saw Westminster as the exciting place to be and assumed only second-raters would go to Scotland, while a small minority accepted that Home Rule would indeed lead to semi-independence and were starting to think about careers as Scottish ministers in Edinburgh. Labour was, and is, a Unionist party, which uses quasi-Nationalist rhetoric and tolerates a quasi-

Nationalist faction inside it. That faction is much more popular among the activists in Scotland than among the Westminster MPs. To Labour constituency parties a stream of inquiries was coming from people who wanted to be Members of the Scottish Parliament (MSPs) – including some sitting MPs. This division between quasi-Nationalists and Unionists was also noticeable among the Liberal Democrats, whose then Scottish vice-president, Bob McCreadie, announced that although he did not support the SNP, 'I want the Scottish Liberal Democrats and the Scottish Labour Party to move from a position of passive acceptance of independence to active encouragement of it.' For a member of a party that was formally in favour of the Union, it was an astonishing statement and was immediately jumped on by Malcolm Bruce, who called McCreadie 'wrong, dangerously wrong'. In the 1970s the pressure for devolution had come mostly from the party leadership. In the 1990s the Home Rule faction was strongest among Scottish activists.

Labour's Scottish manifesto, launched at the beginning of March, had dropped all talk of devolution and firmly promised 'a Scottish parliament'. It hailed the Convention as reflecting 'a national consensus for change', which was 'a real breakthrough. For the first time political parties came together to make common cause in the interests of Scotland.' In a bland repudiation of British constitutional doctrine hitherto, Labour said, 'We intend to make it unacceptable to alter the powers of the Scottish parliament without the consent of that parliament.' Did Labour really mean this? That statement suggested that, despite its doubts and division, Labour in Scotland had finally shed its Unionist armour. Some scepticism is in order, but even so the Labour manifesto was a remarkable tribute to the Home Rulers and the Constitutional Convention. At Labour's opening election rally in Edinburgh, Donald Dewar used the kind of quasi-Nationalist argument about the Tories' Scottish mandate he had generally avoided before: 'The status quo is, I believe, untenable. No matter what the Tories say, the great problem for the Scottish political system is why someone like Ian Lang is Secretary of State, calling the shots . . . when almost no one votes for him.'

And what of the Convention? Even its anti-Unionist members felt the hot breath of the Nationalists on them and tried to respond: Isobel Lindsay, convener of the Campaign for a Scottish Assembly, warned vaguely that if the Tories won again, the Convention might respond with some form of 'resistance', including civil disobedience. The Convention held its nerve when its Home Rule blueprint seemed to be losing ground to outright Nationalism. In its final pre-election meeting before the election, held in Edinburgh's Assembly Rooms, it agreed final proposals for the hours, method of business and voting system for its parliament-to-be. All were notable mainly for being different from Westminster ways. The Scottish parliament would not sit late into the evenings, would do most of its work by committees and would be elected by the additional-member system of proportional representation. The Convention's distaste for the Thatcher era was underlined by the fact a Scottish prime minister would not control public appointments; the parliament would oversee all patronage itself. For all the Convention's lack of clarity about other issues, particularly financial, the Labour and Liberal Democrat politicians and their trade union, council and clerical friends had a lot to be proud of. Nor did the SNP escape a final blast from those of its members who believed its boycott of the Convention had been disastrous. Provost Alec Murray, the SNP leader of Perth and Kinross council, asked bitterly: 'Who would want to be in a Scotland governed by Jim Sillars?'

The Conservatives and their business allies were divided and hesitant in the quasi-Nationalist mood, but eventually most of them rallied behind unabashed Unionism. This clear line took a little while to emerge. At Westminster some Cabinet ministers favoured a Tory version of Home Rule; others wanted to tell the Scots to 'shut up or go'. Inside government generally the debate seemed nervy and incoherent. The Tories in Scotland were equally unsure. At least one Scottish Conservative official expected his party to end up with as few as two seats and a major constitutional crisis. Ministers were talking about their prospects of alternative employment outside politics. Some business leaders talked with resignation of finding an accommodation with the Home Rule parliament that was to come.

The Conservative councillors' leader, John Young, called for a commitment to a referendum on Scotland's future to be included in the Tory manifesto. A poll of Tory constituency chairmen by the *Scotsman* found that out of the fifty contacted twenty-nine said the government should consider such a referendum. Lord Sanderson, the Conservatives' Scottish chairman, responded that, correctly worded, this might be possible after the election. Might, not would. Ian Lang, his back to the wall, kept cool. On 3 February he wrote to 50,000 Scottish businessmen warning of the dangers of independence. Pressure was put on the chairmen and chief executives of life-assurance companies, banks, investment houses and industrial companies to come out publicly and warn their workers against the consequences of Home Rule. Some, like the Bank of Scotland's Bruce Patullo, refused at the time but made their hostility to change clear later. Others, above all the life-assurance companies, were more up-front. Michael Forsyth, Lang's deputy, said that there were only eleven Tory advocates of devolution, adding, with a hint of menace, 'and we know who they are'. And on 9 February, in what was widely regarded as a punishment for his views, a prominent Tory devolutionist and old friend of Mr Rifkind, Brian Meek, was voted out of his post as a vice-president of the Scottish Conservatives. The counter-attack was on.

After detailed discussions with Lang and Rifkind, John Major went north to speechify for the Union. His most important such speech was shoe-horned into his crammed pre-election agenda and based on intensive discussions with Lang. Major made it on 22 February, a foul, chill Saturday, when he arrived at a Glasgow hotel and addressed 400 loyal Tory workers. He and a string of other prominent English Tories repeated the central points made then, in only slightly different words, right up to polling day and afterwards. The Union provided most of Major's memorable imagery that spring. And what was striking was the nostalgic, post-imperial rhetoric this deadpan, unrhetorical politician chose to deploy. 'If the Union of our four countries had never been founded, our history would have been entirely different, our destiny far less great. Are we, in our generation, to throw all that away?' he asked, in words that Margaret Thatcher might easily have used – though they would have grated more on Scottish ears had she uttered them. Although Scotland could not be held irrevocably in a Union against its will, 'a solitary Scotland means a solitary England. Two proud nations. Divorced. Marginalized. Diminished. In place of Great Britain, a little Scotland and a lesser Union, each striving, and not always succeeding, to be heard.' After winning the election Major returned to the theme, arguing that Scottish self-government would weaken British influence in Europe and beyond: 'Britain's special authority in the United Nations would end. Britain's influence in the Commonwealth would be weakened. Britain's voice in the great world debates on the environment, trade and debt would be stilled.' There was the Unionist view from Westminster put with rare candour: Scotland was needed as the extra inch on the heels of the British Prime Minister when he or she was standing on the international stage – whether or not the Scots had actually voted for his or her policies and attitude.

Mr Major had thought relatively little about Scottish politics before becoming Prime Minister (though his spell as the Treasury chief secretary had given him a clear understanding of the complex economics of the Scottish Office–Whitehall link). But he had drunk in his party's almost mystical belief in the continuity and success of Westminster and found it natural to play the unadorned conservative: as Lucius Carey, Viscount Falkland, had told the Commons in 1641: 'When it is not necessary to change, it is necessary not to change.' After his pre-election Glasgow speech Mr Major told BBC Radio Scotland that he had painted a 'whole canvas so that we can have a proper debate'. The Scottish question transcended the result of the election itself, he said: he wanted to 'speak for Scotland'. But a fall-back position was also prepared, in words he would be asked about *ad nauseam* for the next few months: 'After the election, we will take stock.'

Among businessmen and Conservative politicians especially, the real meat of the argument about Home Rule and independence concerned the public-expenditure position and the large flows of money from London to Scotland. This was also influential in Major's decision to stick with outright Unionism and probably influenced many voters too. In 1990–91 each Scot got £3,196 of identifiable public spending, compared with £2,586 for each English citizen: any Home Rule reform might well involve an equalization of that share, with unpleasant effects for Scottish public spending. But those figures represent only *easily identifiable* spending, 70 per cent of the total, and tell nothing about the rest. And they hide some significant trends. Scotland's total share of public spending in

Britain is historic and based on factors like the higher numbers of Scots who attend university, the requirement for transport across an emptier country and so on. In modern times it has always been higher, and it has not been reassessed on the basis of Scottish needs since the 1970s – a sharp contrast to the way Northern Irish spending is worked out every year. Increases in Scottish spending have been allocated automatically by the so-called Barnett formula – Scotland gets ten eighty-fifths of the extra money agreed by English departments. But because *total* Scottish spending is historically higher, this means a slightly smaller *per capita* increase for each Scottish citizen. So Scottish spending and English spending on each citizen will eventually, in theory, meet. No one can say when, since that will depend on the extra cash spending agreed each year by English departments; the higher inflation is, the faster that convergence will happen. What it suggests, though, is that if the Home Rule argument bubbles up in another five years' time, the public-spending issue will be a less serious one.

This effect of the Barnett formula, which might have taken the sting out of English complaints about higher Scottish spending, was masked by another trend in the 1970s and 1980s: the decline of the Scottish population. As Scots headed south, so *per capita* spending in Scotland stayed up. It had to, of course – you can't suddenly spend less on roads because a hundred motorists have left home, or close hospitals or schools. The formula also helps to explain why services sometimes suffer more in Scotland despite the higher spending; the annual increases are lower, in proportion to the spending on each citizen, than in England. So it is harder for the Scottish Office to fund the same improvements.

The real question, then, is what would happen to this higher public expenditure under either Home Rule or independence? Scotland has a smaller middle class and a narrower tax base than England (a penny on the basic income-tax rate would raise only £150 million in Scotland). And it has higher spending on easily identified items of the public budget. So it seems perfectly clear that Scotland would lose out if it raised its own taxes and spent them accordingly. If a self-governed Scotland pursued pro-business, low-tax policies, it might boom and counteract this quite quickly. But a lot would depend on the policies pursued by any Edinburgh administration.

The Home Rulers and Nationalists counter the gloom-mongering by arguing that the 30 per cent of spending that cannot easily be identified goes mostly to England. It is spent on things like tax relief for mortgages and on what one Scottish newspaper habitually calls 'the real subsidy junkies' of the south of England – the defence contractors, Canary Wharf and so on. Who is right? Scottish Office and Treasury Officials say there are so many assumptions put into the analysis (and they regard the SNP ones as 'heroic') that it is impossible to produce a clear breakdown of a full Scottish budget.

Impossible? It is only a question of will. At the time of the last Nationalist upsurge, in the late 1960s, the Treasury did just that, producing a Scottish budget for 1967–8 that showed that the country would be in the red. That, however, was before the oil started flowing; during the 1970s and 1980s the Treasury refused all requests for a repeat performance. As Jim Sillars put it:

The potential embarrassment of each drop of the magic oil was dealt with by the simple, crooked device of removing oil revenues from any purely Scottish statistics . . . The fish caught and landed from Scottish waters are allowed to remain in Scotland's accounts, but the oil over which those fish swim – well, that is different!

Nationalist propaganda, naturally: but the Treasury was using its 1960s Scottish budget as Unionist propaganda. Sadly, to date there has been no official analysis of the SNP's challenge about the direction of the 30 per cent of general expenditure and the impact of oil revenues (and how much of them would be Scotland's raises another debate about geography lines and international law). If the SNP were right about the seabed boundary and about oil prices, the £3.8 billion in petroleum-tax revenue would keep the Scottish economy going. But an analysis for the securities firm Bell, Lawrie, White concluded that an independent Scotland with two-thirds of the oil revenues would still be running a budget deficit of around £6 billion.

The Cruellest Month?

What does this short account of Scotland's over-excited spring of 1992 reveal about the election result that followed and surprised every honest observer? First, it is clear that the bubble that burst was a bubble largely of the political and media classes' own making. From the *Scottish Sun* to the *Scotsman*'s Usher Hall debate, the press had been heavily implicated in pushing the 'story'. The saturation coverage of Nationalism and Home Rulery showed up in opinion polls, which then became news themselves and kept the thing moving. Once the tartan-bedecked bandwagon seemed to be rolling, it was in nobody's interest to ask how many people were really aboard. Certainly not in the Nationalists'. Labour and the Liberal Democrats were nervous about being left behind, so they promoted their Home Rulery just as patriotically – with pipers and tough talk about an entrenched Scottish Parliament. And the Conservatives? If they shrugged their shoulders and pooh-poohed what seemed to be happening, they risked losing the Union by default. So Mr Major stoked the thing up with some stark and quotable language too. Political journalists, this one included, had an interest in highlighting the implications of a strong anti-Tory swing rather than in question-ing, and questioning again, whether it would actually happen.

What burst was the bubble blown by the political classes. It had little to do with the nerve or otherwise of the Scottish people. A fortnight after the election Jim Sillars declared in a television inter-view:

There is a serious question in my mind about the character and ability of the Scottish people to face up to the responsibility that goes with independ-ence . . . From January on, we were telling the world we were heading for independence. It wasn't just the SNP saying it, it was the people of Scotland themselves, puffing up their chests and saying, 'We are going to do it.'

But (said the author of that interesting book *Scotland: The Case for Optimism*) they had 'bottled out' and shown themselves, like the patriotic song-roarers at football games, mere 'ninety-minute patri-ots'. Sillars' outburst deserves recording as a rare expression from a politician of the deepest fears of the Scottish psyche: 'Awwrrgh! We're rubbish!' All the more important, in the context of the election, to point out what nonsense it was, and is. The Scottish people hadn't been 'puffing out their chests'. Politicians like Sillars had been, and their puffing had excited the journalists. It is a bit hard to blame the Broons, of 15 Wallace Place, for that.

They behaved in a way that anyone who had not been spending the spring of 1992 concentrating on events like the Usher Hall debate or the SNP poster campaigns might have expected them to. The majority of the Scottish electorate (52 per cent) voted for Home Rule inside the Union; just over a fifth voted Nationalist; and just over a quarter voted for the status quo. The vast majority of seats, fifty-eight out of seventy-two, went to the parties that backed Home Rule, something immediately ruled out by the Prime Minister. By any normal measurement, whether it be share of the vote (25 per cent) or number of MPs (eleven out of seventy-two), the Scottish Conservatives did badly. There was a small but clear swing to them that was not matched anywhere else in Britain but can be explained partly by the huge anti-Tory Scottish swings of the Thatcher years. But it was only when compared with the hype of politicians and journalists, working hand in hand, that the Tory performance seemed so stunningly good. To the extent that the Conservatives really did do well (which we shall come to shortly) they profited from the excitement of Nationalists and Home Rulers. This scared more Tory Unionists into turning out. April 1992 was not Scotland's independence election, as Salmond had promised. Nor was it the final dismissal of Home Rule, as Major and Lang claimed afterwards. It did, though, hurt the Home Rule movement most. Those who live by the hype shall die by the hype.

Hype, though, is not the whole story. The Scottish Conservative share of the vote, 25.6 per cent, was higher than the 24 per cent it received in the disastrous year of 1987 (though lower than in 1983, when the party managed 28.4 per cent). This, of course, must have reflected many non-constitutional factors, such as the relative popularity of John Major in Scotland compared with Margaret Thatcher and the fear of higher taxation under Labour. It was no longer safe for middle-class Unionists to use a general election vote in Scotland as an anti-London protest vote. Still, it is interesting that some of the key regions where the Conservative vote improved most – Tayside (up 2.1 per cent), Grampian (up 3.4 per cent), Dumfries and Galloway (up 1.4 per cent) – were 'vote no' regions in the 1979 devolution referendum. It may be that the fear of domination by the Edinburgh–Glasgow central belt, which mattered then in the further-flung parts of Scotland, matters still. The fit is not perfect –

the Central region voted for devolution in 1979 but also saw a rise in the Tory vote in 1992. But politicians of all parties reported afterwards that they had noticed a distinct group of voters who said they were turning out this time 'to save the Union', just as Major had asked them to. In many such constituencies, particularly in the north-east, there are significant numbers of English voters.

Another source of much post-electoral head-scratching has been tactical voting. Did Scots, and the Opposition parties, throw away the opportunity for change by failing to vote with sufficient anti-Tory guile, constituency by constituency? The Campaign for a Scottish Assembly and others had tried hard to maximize the anti-Tory vote, yet on the ground the parties refused to play ball. In Stirling, where Michael Forsyth was fighting off a strong Labour challenge, the SNP worked particularly hard. In Galloway and Upper Nithsdale, Ian Lang's seat, which was being heavily targeted by the SNP, Labour had lost its candidate only a few weeks before the election but selected a new one and fought against both Lang and the Nationalists. The situation there was clouded when SNP dissidents, who supported tactical voting, tried to persuade the Labour candidate to stand down just three weeks before polling day – and the story leaked. Had tactical voting worked perfectly, most Conservative seats would have been lost (in Ian Lang's seat, for instance, 5,766 people voted for a Labour candidate who had no chance, and the Scottish Secretary's majority was 2,468). Perhaps, in such circumstances, Mr Major would have been forced to concede a devolved parliament or a referendum. But several points need to be borne in mind. First and most important, voters cannot be parcelled up and handed about. Many Labour voters are bitterly anti-Nationalist; many Nationalist and Liberal Democrat voters loathe the idea of a Labour government. Second, Scots have been voting tactically, in a four-party system, for ages; there were probably relatively few potential tactical voters waiting to be converted.

The failure of tactical voting is not the whole story. In all but the most important seats, both the turn-out and the Tory vote rose, typically by 1,500–2,000. In Stirling, where the Tory majority was 703, the extra 1,583 votes Michael Forsyth squeezed out, compared with his 1987 performance, were clearly vital. In Ayr (majority 85, extra Tory vote, 1,230) the same story applied. The fact that Forsyth was able to count on about 3,000 postal votes, and anecdotes from Ayr about voters who had bought their council houses or shares in privatized industries being phoned up late on polling-day and cajoled into voting Tory, show how hard the Scottish Conservatives worked in the seats where it really mattered. John Major and Ian Lang, once they had decided to fight the election on an unequivocal defence of the Union, led their party with courage, humour and panache during the campaign; it would be absurdly churlish of Nationalists and Home Rulers not to acknowledge that the Tory Unionists kept their nerve and scored some real successes. Even so, having chosen to fight the election in Scotland on their defence of an unchanged Union, the Conservatives lost – and overwhelmingly.

John Major's New Scotland . . .

What kind of Scotland might have been created by independence or Home Rule in 1992 is now an unknowable and irrelevant speculation. That Scotland, like the assembly-ruled Scotland of 1979, has sunk into might-have-been. The real Scotland, meanwhile, continues to alter. The contemporary battle for Scotland is one between opposing visions of its identity in the later 1990s: on the one hand, the assertive, left-liberal, semi-independent northern European state that most Home Rulers dream of; on the other, continued inclusion in Greater Albion, the Conservative-ruled 'country at ease with itself' that Mr Major, recessions permitting, is trying to build.

For the time being, Mr Major will have his chance. As Ian Lang said in June 1992 – with, perhaps, excessive optimism – 'We are entering a new era, an era in which constitutional issues will be less prominent in political debate.' Patches of Scotland are already moving the Tories' way. The Grampian region in the north-east, where Labour MPs found oilmen and executives complaining bitterly about the prospect of higher taxation during the election campaign, produced twice as many Conservative as Labour voters. Certainly, it sustains Nationalist, Liberal Democrat and Labour MPs too, but it is materially nearer to the Conservative contentment culture than most of the rest of Scotland. Labour and Nationalist bravado about preventing Scotland being affected by Thatcherism was exposed as hollow in the 1980s. Scotland may be changed as dramatically, or more so, in the 1990s. The applications from hospitals for trust status outside the health board structure after the 1992 election were surely an early sign of this.

Scotland is already one of the better-doing parts of the United Kingdom. Its income per head in 1989 was similar to that of the English Midlands, below the south and south-west of England but higher than Yorkshire, the north of England, Wales or Northern Ireland (the poorest part of the UK by far). It lags a long way behind only one region, the English south-east, which is itself the only part of the UK that really belongs to the central-west European region of fast economic development. Scotland suffered less obviously from the recession of the early 1990s than did parts of the south; its (lower) house prices have been less deflated; unemployment is bad (9.4 per cent of the work force in summer 1992) but had dipped below the British average, for the first time since the 1920s, and was actually less bad than in London. Scotland's old industries, where so much of the macho national character was forged, have now mostly gone, leaving thistle-strewn waste-ground and rusting sheds protected by razor wire. In their place have come gentler ones: electronics, whisky and salmon farming matter more, these days, than coalmining or steelmaking. Nearly seven in ten Scots in work are employed in the service sector – in shops, schools, tourism. Scottish universities have become a magnet for English students and staff, to the point where some, like St Andrews, Stirling and Edinburgh, no longer feel quite Scottish to the Scots who teach there. In 1990, for the first time since 1932, the population of Scotland actually rose slightly, by 13,500.

These are some of the things on which Conservative hopes for reversing the century-old Home Rule movement are based. They are not, of course, the only things. The Conservatives still have a weak base on which to build in Scotland and are no nearer solving their old dilemma of how to appear patriotic and anti-Home Rule at the same time. The country they administer is sullen rather than converted. While some Conservative remedies have been eagerly swallowed, others have been spat back. The hostility of teachers and parents to primary-school testing, resulting in a rare retreat by ministers, was one example. Nor is Scotland a land of contentment.

After Ravenscraig dies much of Lanarkshire is going to be a gloomy place. Glasgow, Edinburgh and Dundee contain some of the grimmest, dampest, most crime- and drug-ridden housing in the European Community. Whole Hebridean communities can be bought and sold by foreign, anonymous landlords. According to Shelter (Scotland), homelessness had risen tenfold in the decade to 1991–2, to 34,600. Scottish health is a national disgrace.

But, looking five years on and assuming that the world economy will start growing again at a reasonable rate, it is hard to see Scotland doing other than to become more prosperous. Major's strategy for Scotland is not based merely on sitting back in his Downing Street drawing-room and waiting for prosperity. His removal of Michael Forsyth from the Scottish ministerial team and the arrival of Lord (Peter) Fraser of Carmyllie, the former Lord Advocate, in his place was a clear sign that Major wanted a more soothing tone in the Scottish Office. He was ready to talk about anything short of substantive change. A wide range of ideas, from modest but useful reforms to shameless gimmicks, was circulating around Whitehall by the summer of 1992. As Mr Major attempts to spread the Conservative settlement in England, he intends to contain the problems of Scotland, hoping that soft words, warm smiles and acts of appeasement, such as his modest Westminster reforms, will quell the political turbulence and lead, in time, to a steady Tory revival. And he may be vindicated.

Indeed, the first period of political opposition after the election was marked more by internal faction-fighting in the Opposition parties than by a ground swell of mass protest. Disillusioned MPs reported that there was little anger in their constituencies, only a morose acquiescence. The Liberal Democrats pondered the fact that their well-meant work in the Convention might have contributed to a poor electoral performance. They talked instead of returning to lower-profile politics – a potentially dangerous idea for a party already seen more as a collection of individual constituency MPs than as a national movement. Jagged and painful divisions opened up again between those Labour MPs who wanted to put the party's British strategy first and the hard-line Labour Home Rulers who were again demanding a devolved Scottish Labour Party and a campaign of disobedience and protest in Scotland. At a two-day meeting in Dundee in mid-June Labour's Scottish executive voted to keep quasi-Nationalism, or indeed any form of protest, at arm's length. Alex Salmond managed to persuade a divided SNP to back the idea of cross-party cooperation to mount a multi-option referendum on Scotland's future. But the Labour leadership rejected this too, and Nationalist hardliners told Salmond he should be 'putting the boot into Labour' instead. Nationalist extremists plagued Labour men with obscene and bitter phone calls; and Labour scorned everybody but Labour. Vision was out of fashion; party sectarianism oozed back into the daylight; and boldness seemed discredited as mere ranting vanity. Many of the amateur politicians noted the cynicism of the professionals and turned back to their golf handicaps and rosebeds. Scotland seemed, yet again, to have confirmed the judgement of the poet Edwin Muir in the 1930s:

> This is a difficult land. Here things miscarry
> Whether we care or do not care enough . . .

Yet again the Scottish political world had slithered from delusion to disillusion – it had accomplished its familiar water-slide into cold porridge.

. . . And Its Uneasiness with Itself

The aftermath of an election is a bad time for predictions and conclusions: it would be a foolish observer who used the despair of politicians, only months after their defeat, as a pointer for years ahead. Not that all the evidence pointed one way. The 1992 election also produced an outbreak of new Home Rule groups. People with little political experience expressed dismay and upped and outed, determined to 'do something'. There may have been fewer of them than there were of the burned-out veterans who stumbled back to their gardens. But the mere fact of a new cycle of protest should make us cautious about writing off Home Rule politics in Scotland. At the time of writing, the new groups offer promises rather than accomplishments. Common Cause is a smallish collection of thinkers, politicians and writers. Democracy for Scotland is really a grand name for a vigil outside the would-be parliament in Edinburgh. The most substantial of the 'civil politics' groups, Scotland

United, has brought Labour politicians, trade-union leaders and SNP-supporting pop stars together on the same platform. It is slowly turning itself into a national organization but will make life harder for its high-profile Labour supporters as it does so. And its first post-election rallies attracted only around 5,000 people, with enough Nationalist support to cause the Labour leadership to distance itself.

In the political mainstream too the Home Rule movement remained eloquent, numerous and self-confident. John Smith, the devolution minister of old, then Labour leader, said of the Scottish situation shortly before his election that it 'cannot last; it is intrinsically unstable'. Among his close allies Robin Cook reaffirmed his membership of the Home Rule pressure group Scottish Labour Action, and Donald Dewar, who moved to the social-security portfolio, argued that it would be wrong to allow the Constitutional Convention to die. In England constitutional reform became a prime cause for the non-Tory parties and for the civil politicians in groups such as Charter 88. Scottish Home Rule was accepted as an integral part of this agenda of the politically optimistic, alongside a written constitution, a Bill of Rights, voting reform and so on. In Scotland, though the future role of the Constitutional Convention was a matter of debate, a wide swathe of opinion was in favour of retaining it as a national voice and a vehicle for protest. Despite the legal and financial complexities, some local and national politicians were working away at plans for a Scottish referendum. Civil disobedience was again being discussed by other groups.

The old question remained, however: was all this activity in any way representative of the Scottish people? Scotland carried on much as usual. St Andrew's House remained unstormed. Ian Lang amused the Commons a few weeks after the election when, asked how many people had written complaining about the lack of a Scottish parliament, he revealed that a grand total of eighteen such letters had been received. (Perhaps the most astounding thing is that there were eighteen Scots so naïve as to think writing Mr Lang a letter when all else had failed would do the trick. Bully for native shrewdness.) The more serious answer to the old question was that the Scottish people had delivered their verdict in the proper way, through the ballot box. What more were they expected to do? March on London with billhooks? This was a politicians' problem, a failure of politics, as it had been all along. The people had voted for Home Rule time and time again. They had been promised it by Asquith, Ramsay MacDonald, Winston Churchill, Alec Douglas-Home, Edward Heath, Harold Wilson, Margaret Thatcher, Jim Callaghan, Neil Kinnock. Again and again the politicians had dangled it and (for varying reasons) failed to deliver it. If there was a mood of weary suspicion among Scottish voters on this subject, then there was no one to blame but the politicians. Apathy had been hard-earned: a lot of broken promises went into that omelette. For politicians to turn round and blame the level-headed Scottish people for letting *them* down would have been . . . what? Plain, old-fashioned cheek?

The point was well made during the same Asquithian Parliament that is briefly described on the first page of the introduction to this book. The debate on the Scottish Home Rule Bill that nearly became law in 1914 had some uncanny echoes with modern times. There had been a campaign backed by the vast majority of Scottish MPs but opposed by a small Conservative–Unionist minority (nine of the seventy-two then, eleven of the seventy-two now). It was the demand of the Scottish political establishment – then that meant the Royal Convention of Scottish Burghs, with its 404 representatives from the cities and small towns, rather than the Scottish Constitutional Convention. Then too there was also a younger and more aggressive brand of Home Rule agitation – not Scotland United or the SNP but the Young Scots Society, whose excited partisans proclaimed 'the unquenchable and indefinable spirit of nationalism'. And then, as now, the Unionists argued that true Scots were deeply uninterested. George Younger, Unionist MP for Ayr (great-grandfather of the current George Younger), commented: 'I do not find any strongly expressed sentiment in favour of this change in Scotland.' But the Liberal MP for Ross and Cromarty who introduced the 1914 Bill, J. I. Macpherson, argued that Scotland's biggest party had won 80 per cent of the seats on a Home Rule policy. It had fought for this 'by every means in its power, by platform, press and pamphlet'. A political demand 'is none the less sincere, none the less ardent', he told the Commons, 'if it is quietly expressed'.

Macpherson's law is a good one. It is offensive to suggest that the demand for Scottish self-government, or anything else, deserves notice only when the petitioners start pelting the police. Why should they so demean themselves? They expect their politicians to get on with business and work these things out. A Scottish parliament has been the desire of a majority of these people for most of the time between Macpherson's day and our own. There have been nineteen parliamentary Bills on the issue, varying in detail, prescription and coherence. An impressive array of British political leaders has promised it at one time or another. But in power the Conservative leaders have changed their tune, while the Labour ones have been unable to deliver. Today's various Home Rule groups, and the protests of Home Rule MPs, and the evidence of opinion pollsters and ballot boxes are all useful as symptoms of a continuing and persistent national complaint. But this is clearly a politician-made problem, and it deserves a proper political diagnosis and remedy. Today John Major argues that a second parliament in Britain would undermine the 'whole delicate balance' of the (unbalanced, centralized) British constitution. Humph. As we have seen, the constitution is as fluid as water when the Prime Minister of the day finds it convenient to go with the flow and congeals to icy rigidity the moment the political heat is turned off. From diaphanous nothing to Westminster marble in the twinkling of an Aye.

So if British domestic politics is left to itself, nothing much may happen. In Scotland movements surge and retreat; parties form, split and die; marches march; conventions convene; and grand covenants are gathered in. But because of the parliamentary arithmetic, Home Rule comes on to the Westminster agenda only when some outside force propels it there and gives Scottish Home Rulers their chance. That outside force has been Ireland, war, North Sea oil. But Europe may be the next propellant. The political shape and constitutional structure of the continent is unfixed and controversial in a way it has not been for a generation. Questions about sovereignty, devolution, Home Rule and federalism are being asked by many more peoples than the Scots. It is possible that the proposed European Union will now dissolve into a lightly policed free-trade area and that the old nation-states, including Britain, will revive. But the record of Anglo–Saxon scepticism has so far been a poor one: usually London predicts that 'they' won't do it, and usually, even if after a pause, 'they' do. Unless the Community collapses, desire for freer trade, environmental protection and a common defence will continue to pull power to the centre. For the peripheral states and the smaller regions and peoples it will not much matter whether 'the centre' means national leaders meeting privately in the Council of Ministers, or the Commission or, indeed, Strasbourg's parliament. It will seem far away, out of reach, just as the people of Edinburgh complained in 1707 that the old Scottish parliament had moved out of their reach when it joined the English one and moved 400 miles south.

In June 1992, when the Danish voters refused in a referendum to ratify the Maastricht treaty of the previous November, they were blowing a raspberry on behalf of the smaller European peoples. If European union continues, it will be sustainable only where accompanied by clear and substantial retained powers for the countries and regions. Mostly this will be power retained. In some cases it may require power being passed back. Subsidiarity, so important to Mr Major, means that power should be exercised at the lowest possible level. This doctrine, and the general cultural and political arguments used by English Conservatives against European union, contradict the fluent assumptions of the same people when they discuss the British constitution. Mr Major himself told the Commons in May 1992 that subsidiarity meant 'We cannot be forced into policies we do not approve of.' Scottish MPs quickly reminded him that it rather depended on whom he meant by 'we' – what is sauce for the goose is sauce for the haggis. If, despite a long war of attrition by English Conservatives, the Commons finds itself looking after English education, planning, the regeneration of English cities and a few other less elevated matters, then the prospect of a Scottish parliament doing similar local things will seem uncontentious, even plain common-sensible.

Such a parliament in Edinburgh would also, of course, be incompatible with the desires of hard-left Scottish socialists or xenophobic nationalists. The logic of economic integration and freer trade has been embraced by hundreds of millions of people as the best available route out of conflict and poverty. There would be no place in such a Europe for an anti-English Scotland, levying high taxes and subsidizing inefficient shipyards. Europe may also help blur the frontier between Home Rule and nationalism. If overriding economic and even defence powers are handed to a European centre, then the debate about those powers that remain will concern merely levels of local government – important though that is. The SNP's 'independence in Europe' is not very different from the vision of the more European Labourites and the outright federalists of the Liberal Democrats – not so different, at any rate, as to justify perpetual mutual hatred. If mutual hatred persists, there will be nothing to blame but the nastiness of individual Scottish politicians.

So waves lap Westminster's foundations even yet. It is important to remember that the grand gothic palace is built on a mudbank. In practical terms, Westminster's claim to absolute power across every inch of Britain depends on a residual British nationalism buttressed by a constitutional system that is centralized and concentrated to a remarkable degree. None of it is any more logical or forward-looking than the darkest, least forgiving strain of Scottish nationalism. Imperial mumbo-jumbo, political mysticism and ancestor-worship are the forces that still persuade London politicians to regard the pretensions of a modest high school, built in the Greek classical manner on an Edinburgh hillside, with the irritation that Plantagenet monarchs felt when confronted by Edinburgh Castle. Because I cannot take the central political arguments against Scottish Home Rule seriously, I remain of the view that it will one day come about. It is possible that John Major, a decent and clever Conservative, will be able to suspend the battle for Scotland with an armistice on Unionist terms. But my guess is that he will not be able to bring about permanent political peace. To do that would require an unpredicted and irreversible shift in Scottish feeling – a shrugging off of history and a retreat from real politics altogether. Yet that offers no real way out either. The prize of a wealthy, happy Scotland, contented with its position, is a glittering one, but it is unlikely to mean a depoliticized, purely material Scotland – a sated Scotland. A Scotland genuinely at ease with itself would be an argumentative, grown-up Scotland with a lively parliament as well as a strong economy – a conscience and a tongue, as well as limbs and a body. And when it does speak, its voice will be sharp and fresh. And its views will perhaps surprise us.

Selected Reading

Much of the best source reading is contained in Labour and Scottish
National Party documents, including Labour's conference records,
Scottish Council statements and pamphlets and the SNP's records
of its National Council meetings. Conservative and Labour parliamentarians have been particularly helpful in passing over their
collections of documents; so has the SNP in Edinburgh. Pamphlets
produced by the Scottish Covenant Association, the (Tory) Thistle
Group, the Scottish Home Rule Association, the Saltire Society,
Scots Independent, the Scottish Liberals, the Labour Campaign for a
Scottish Assembly, the Scottish Secretariat, the Church of Scotland
and the Scottish Constitutional Convention have all been useful. I
am also grateful to a number of politicians and private individuals
for the loan of letters, notes and diaries. No journalist is going to
deny that colleagues are essential: without the high-quality political
coverage of Ewen MacAskill, Peter Jones *et al.* at the *Scotsman*, the
Herald team in Glasgow, Iain MacWhirter of the BBC and *Scotland
on Sunday*, and the other Scottish papers, this kind of book would be
much harder to write.

The books I have used (in no particular order) include the following.

Scottish Politics Generally

Patronage and Principle, Michael Fry, Aberdeen University Press,
    1987. (This is the best single book on Scottish politics, and
    is particularly absorbing on nineteenth-century Scotland.)
No Gods and Precious Few Heroes: Scotland 1914–1980, Christopher
    Hervie, Edward Arnold, 1981. (A good basic history but above
    all distinguished by its splendid title.)
A History of the Scottish People, 1560–1830, T. C. Smout, Collins,
    1967. (Famous.)
A Century of the Scottish People: 1830–1950, T. C. Smout,

Collins, 1986. (Famous, despite the curious arithmetic of its title.)

The Scottish Government Yearbook: 1979–1992, various eds., Unit for the Study of Government in Scotland, Edinburgh University. (An essential annual handbook and guide to the past year.)

A New History of Scotland, 2 vols., George S. Pryde and William Croft Dickinson, Nelson, 1961.

A Political History of Scotland: 1832–1924, I. G. C. Hutchinson, John Donald, 1986.

Scotland Revisited, ed. Jenny Wormald, *History Today*/Collins and Brown, 1991.

Court, Kirk and Community, Jenny Wormald, Edward Arnold, 1981. (Wormald is said to be a brilliant whisky-drinker at Oxford; she certainly writes well.)

A Claim of Right for Scotland, ed. Owen Dudley Edwards, Polygon, 1989.

Scottish Identity: A Christian Vision, William Storrar, Handsel Press, 1990.

Scotland 2000, ed. Kenneth Cargill, BBC Scotland, 1987.

Historical and Fiction

Scotland and the Union, David Daiches, John Murray, 1977.
A Search for Scotland, R. F. Mackenzie, Fontana, 1989.
The Scots, Ian Finlayson, Constable, 1987.
A Scots Quair, Lewis Grassic Gibbon, Penguin, 1986.
Scottish Journey, Edwin Muir, Mainstream, 1981.
The Monarch of the Glen, Compton Mackenzie, Chatto and Windus, 1941.
Compton Mackenzie: A Life, Andro Linklater, Chatto and Windus, 1987.
Magnus Merriman, Eric Linklater, Jonathan Cape, 1934.
The Awakening of George Darroch, Robert Jenkins, Penguin, 1987.
Surviving the Shipwreck, William McIlvanney, Mainstream, 1991.
The Kirk and its Worthies, Nicholas Dickson, T. N. Foulis, 1914.
The King's Jaunt, John Prebble, Collins, 1988.
Neil M. Gunn: A Highland Life, F. R. Hart and J. B. Pick, Polygon, 1981.

Hugh MacDiarmid: Complete poems 1920–1976, eds. Michael Grieve and W. R. Aitken, Martin Brian and O'Keefe, 1978.

The Letters of Hugh MacDiarmid, ed. Alan Bold, Hamish Hamilton, 1984.

MacDiarmid, Alan Bold, John Murray, 1988.

On the Labour Party

J. Keir Hardie, William Stewart, ILP publications, 1921.

John Maclean, Nan Milton, Pluto Press, 1973.

Maxton, Gordon Brown, Mainstream, 1986.

John P. Mackintosh on Scotland, ed. Henry Drucker, Longman, 1982.

Forward! Labour Politics in Scotland 1888–1988, eds. Donnachie, Harvie and Wood, Polygon, 1989.

Labour and Scottish Nationalism, Michael Keating and David Bleiman, Macmillan, 1979.

Labour and Scottish Home Rule, Parts One and Two, Robert McLean, Scottish Labour Action, 1989.

Political Thoughts and Polemics, Bernard Crick, Edinburgh University Press, 1981.

The Red Paper on Scotland, ed. Gordon Brown, EUSPB, 1975. In addition, the Benn, Castle and Crossman diaries are interesting in parts.

The Tories and Nationalism

Patronage and Principle, Michael Fry, Aberdeen University Press, 1987.

Conservatives and the Union, James Mitchell, Edinburgh, 1990.

Memory Hold-the-Door, John Buchan, Hodder and Stoughton, 1940.

Bob Boothby, Robert Rhodes James, Hodder and Stoughton, 1991.

Nationalism

The Growth of Nationalism in Scotland, Keith Webb, Molendinar Press, 1977.

The National Movement in Scotland, Jack Brand, Routledge and Kegan Paul, 1978.

SELECTED READING

Scottish Nationalism, H. J. Hanham, Faber and Faber, 1969.

Scotland: The Case for Optimism, Jim Sillars, Polygon, 1986.

Scotland, Douglas Young, Cassell, 1971.

Towards Independence, Paul H. Scott, Polygon, 1991.

Nationalism in the Nineties, ed. Tom Gallagher, Polygon, 1991.

The Flag in the Wind, John MacCormick, Gollancz, 1955.

Scotland Lives, William Wolfe, Edinburgh, 1977.

The Referendum Experience: Scotland 1979, eds. Bochel, Denver, Macartney, Aberdeen University Press, 1981.

Index

Thatcher, Margaret 5, 168, 169–
71, 186, 206, 230
and devolution 154–5, 160,
169, 237
at General Assembly 33, 168
as Opposition leader 154–5,
162–3
and poll tax 177, 178, 179
Thistle Group 124–5
Toothill, Sir John 114
Treaty of Union *see* Act of
Union
Trevor-Roper, Hugh (*later* Lord
Dacre) 15, 156
Turnbull, Ronald 23
Tweedsmuir, Lady 206

Union of 1707 *see* Act of Union
Unionists 108–9, 110–13
see also Conservative Party
universities 47–8, 233
Kirk and 24, 43
see also Glasgow University
Upper Clyde Shipbuilders'
work-in 133–4
Usher Hall debate (1992) 219–
21, 229

violence 150–51, 166, 179, 188

Waldegrave, William 177
Wallace, William 12, 13
Watchdog group 144–6
Watt, Donald 13
Webb, Keith 166
Welsh, Andrew 185
West Lothian by-election (1962)
115–16, 117

'West Lothian question' 158
Westminster MPs, number of
20, 136, 157–8, 222
Wheatley, John 53
White, John 40–41
Williams, Shirley 141–2
Wilson, Alex 119
Wilson, Brian 134, 159, 161
Wilson, Gordon
and Constitutional
Convention 194, 199, 202,
203, 204
and devolution 156, 158, 161
and factions 189–90, 191
and oil 131, 132
Wilson, Harold 106, 107, 120,
121–2, 129–30, 138–41,
142, 152–3, 237
winter of discontent 159, 161
Witherspoon, John 38
Wolfe, Billy 115–16, 119, 132,
133, 135, 187, 188
and devolution 149, 150, 151,
152
Womack, Peter 28
women in politics 198, 206–7
Women's Claim of Right group
207
Wood, Wendy 87–8
Woodburn, Arthur 99–101
World Cup (football)
1974 138–9
1978 15, 161
Wormald, Jenny 16
Wright, Canon Kenyon 32, 198,
206
Wynton, Andrew 11–12
Wyper, Hugh 196

He just wanted a decent book to read ...

Not too much to ask, is it? It was in 1935 when Allen Lane, Managing Director of Bodley Head Publishers, stood on a platform at Exeter railway station looking for something good to read on his journey back to London. His choice was limited to popular magazines and poor-quality paperbacks – the same choice faced every day by the vast majority of readers, few of whom could afford hardbacks. Lane's disappointment and subsequent anger at the range of books generally available led him to found a company – and change the world.

'We believed in the existence in this country of a vast reading public for intelligent books at a low price, and staked everything on it'
Sir Allen Lane, 1902–1970, founder of Penguin Books

The quality paperback had arrived – and not just in bookshops. Lane was adamant that his Penguins should appear in chain stores and tobacconists, and should cost no more than a packet of cigarettes.

Reading habits (and cigarette prices) have changed since 1935, but Penguin still believes in publishing the best books for everybody to enjoy. We still believe that good design costs no more than bad design, and we still believe that quality books published passionately and responsibly make the world a better place.

So wherever you see the little bird – whether it's on a piece of prize-winning literary fiction or a celebrity autobiography, political tour de force or historical masterpiece, a serial-killer thriller, reference book, world classic or a piece of pure escapism – you can bet that it represents the very best that the genre has to offer.

Whatever you like to read – trust Penguin.